# MILITANT
# MEDIA

T0363835

Spector Books  CRA Press

**Edited by Riccardo Badano, Tomas Percival, and Susan Schuppli**

**CASE STUDIES**

**FIELD NOTES**

# SERIES FORWARD

This book series situates you, the reader, at our Roundtable in the Centre for Research Architecture on the third floor of the aptly named Richard Hoggart building at Goldsmiths, University of London. Gathered 'around' this table you will find yourself amongst a group of emergent but also established spatial practitioners and researchers who convene to work together, sharing their projects and insights. These assemblies have produced a space of critical encounter and pedagogical experimentation with the aim of developing new investigative methods and speculative insights aimed at responding to and intervening into the urgent political conditions of our time. Students work collaboratively with their peers as well as with the affected communities in which their research projects are embedded. Staff and guests bring critical ideas and key works into this context.

This Roundtable—which we now seek to re-animate through a series of written reflections, investigative accounts, and documented fieldworks, as well as transcribed conversations and glossaries—is both the spatial form that organises our encounters non-hierarchically and the material surface upon which projects are laid out and ideas debated. As this book series unfolds across its thematic issues we invite you to become a part of this lively environment that has nourished us intellectually and shaped us politically.

Across the series we have sought to foreground the distinctive pedagogy and field of research that distinguishes the Centre for Research Architecture. Since its founding in 2005, the Centre has brought together a diverse group of architects, artists, urbanists, geographers, lawyers, scientists, journalists, and activists to work on expanded notions of space. Projects in the Centre address contemporary struggles and conflicts as they register themselves in the transformation of environments: shifting scales and intensities from the architectural and urban to that of territorial and planetary processes, from the micro-scale of buildings and infrastructure to the macro-scale of borders and global flows. In the Centre, space is analysed as an elastic medium that is constantly reshaped by political and mediatic forces. To address such complex interrelations, our researchers have necessarily developed diverse creative and practical approaches for conducting their fieldwork and developing their conceptual frameworks. The book series explores these spatial entanglements by drawing upon contributions from current as well as former graduate students and staff, many of whom have gone on to establish investigative agencies and teach in programmes directly inspired by our work. It also includes the research of collaborators, friends, and thinkers who have informed and motivated our interventions.

Alongside spatial reformulations, the Centre has also developed specific aesthetic considerations. In conceptualising the books and laying out contributions, we have tried to retain the inventiveness of these methods and practices. Images, audio recordings, videos, maps, and other media take on specific roles within each of the projects presented. In particular, many audio-visual materials become fields of investigation in and of themselves. Alongside their means of production, their modes of circulation and their networks of exchange, such media are treated as sites of research that open areas of investigation and intervention. The quality of a photograph, the metadata of a file, the resolution of a satellite image, the frequency of an audio recording, all become registers of the complex politics of events. To transform this mode of 'investigative aesthetics' into book format, we worked with Ariadna Serrahima from Oficina de disseny, to develop a number of design strategies to help readers identify the different roles that materials play throughout its pages. These highlight the interrogation of media that 'do not speak for themselves' but rather need to be patiently studied and carefully narrated in order to make their specific political claims.

Each book in the thematic series brings together a heterogeneous range of materials and contributions, with a particular attention to collective modes of knowledge production. As stated, our aim is to invite the reader into this ever-evolving pedagogical context. For those of us studying and working in the Centre for Research Architecture, the book series offers another iteration of this generative assembly in which knowledge is co-produced, shared, and mobilised. Publishing is for us, an extension of our Roundtable forums. In this regard, each book is a collection that engages with current spatial processes and research practices and the series is a critical reflection on how these act and are acted upon in the world. Here, we must thank Spector Books for providing the framework and context for this endeavour and for their guidance and expertise on translating these projects into book form.

Riccardo Badano, Tomas Percival, and Susan Schuppli
10 October 2022, London

# REFLECTIONS ON MILITANCY AND MEDIA

*The following text originates from a conversation between Eyal Weizman, Tomas Percival, and Riccardo Badano held in July 2023. We have transcribed and reconfigured this dialogue to serve as the introduction for this volume. In this transformation, we have preserved the spirit of the original discussion while expanding upon some of its reflections to include references to projects emerging out of the Centre for Research Architecture and the Forensic Architecture agency. We hope it captures the collective nature of our pedagogy, practices, and politics.*

What role does *media* play in making claims for truth or justice, and how might this necessitate a new conception of *militancy*? Our work has often been marked by a militancy that moves between critique and intervention, aesthetics and politics. The Centre for Research Architecture's staff, students, and affiliates have individually and collectively confronted the ways that media re-organises political and state violence. This has opened up new areas of investigative potential and even enabled them to make direct interventions.[1]

The second publication in the Centre for Research Architecture series, *Militant Media*, embarks upon an interrogation of this dual condition to examine the various media contexts and media modalities that militate our practices. This sets up several questions for the book's contributors: How does one construct an operative proposition? How does one illicit an argument around what we might call the 'truth'? How can one establish a relationship to 'facts' or 'realism' while maintaining a steadfast commitment to dismantling normative assertions? From within our contemporary conjuncture at Goldsmiths, what kinds of claims around justice can we generate from the standpoint of the arts and humanities? How might we articulate a diagnostic critique of the present while also proposing a future-tense articulation of liberation yet to come?

A diverse array of insights emerge around these questions throughout this book. The history and impact of the 'Gangs Matrix' database are explored in relation to the Black community's struggle against police violence in the UK. So-called 'split-second' judgments within law enforcement are examined in relation to questions of temporality, perception, and the law. We are guided through an exploration of what open-source investigations would look (and feel) like, if conducted through the lens of feminist practice. Platform-based labour and algorithmic governance are examined alongside workers' strategies to resist such computational exploitation. A conversation unfolds around how an artistic practice registers the considerable scale and impact of Israeli incursions over Lebanon's skies. Social media's role in documenting state violence and grassroots protests, particularly within racialised communities, is unpacked in detail.

While some readers might rightly assume that militant media concentrates on aesthetic materials that are disseminated in direct service to human rights campaigns and activist agendas—perhaps conjuring images of propaganda, agitprop, or other manifestations of politically charged media—the force of this book's analysis lies elsewhere. In fact, we understand militant media as an approach to *undertaking* research and as a potent modality for engaging with affected communities. For us, it is a methodology. We propose a conception of militant media as an active, practice-based approach that shapes the

---

1   In articulating the notion of 'making claims,' we draw upon the works of Thomas Keenan and Eyal Weizman, specifically, their proposition that there is no unmediated access to facts or truth. Instead, they assert that claims must be actively constructed, meticulously staged, and rigorously debated, especially when claiming rights or denouncing their violation. See Thomas Keenan, 'Getting the Dead to Tell Me What Happened: Justice, Prosopopoeia, and Forensic Afterlives', *Kronos* 44, no. 1 (2018): 113.: Thomas Keenan and Eyal Weizman, *Mengele's Skull: The Advent of a Forensic Aesthetics* (London: Sternberg Press, 2012).

production of research, guiding how knowledge is composed, the ways that arguments are framed, and the manner in which claims are substantiated. Rather than framing militancy purely in terms of its confrontational nature or as the prioritisation of political struggle over all other activities–including that of knowledge production–in this book, we aim to map some key examples of how practice-led research can question and operate beyond the established authority taken up by investigative organisations and advocacy groups. Each of the contributors takes a different stance and approach towards this proposition.

## AGAINST DISINTERESTEDNESS

Our reflections began with a conversation in which we attempted to conceptualise a notion of *militancy* in contrast to the traditional mission of human rights—a context the Centre has consistently worked within, albeit often from a critical and interrogative vantage point. However, in this volume, we aim to destabilise the taken-for-granted contours of militancy, making instead a dialectical move that positions the diagnostic function of knowledge production—the evidentiary value of materials collected to substantiate claims of state violence, sometimes manifested as a violation of humanitarian law—against the ability to aggregate claims that contribute to communal resistance and emancipatory politics. In doing so, we felt that we needed to briefly examine how the human rights sphere came to understand its role as an arbitrator of universal rights and how the principle of neutrality, disinterestedness, or impartiality has become indispensable for both evidence's admissibility and the act of asserting claims.

Historically, this disinterested conception of human rights results from the bipolar relations of the Cold War period, when human rights were tasked with dealing with two types of geopolitical tensions: the East-West divide, on the one hand, and the tensions between imperial powers and former colonies during and after decolonisation and liberation struggles on the other.[2] These two types of conflicts produced two different conceptions of human rights. Anti-colonial struggles in Southeast Asia and Africa led to a conception of human rights in which radical political transformation could only result from the retreat of white European domination and its replacement with local sovereignty.[3] A decade or two later, the Cold War projected human rights as an anti-totalitarian force standing for the rights of individuals against repressive regimes. However, as war erupted in countries that were nominally decolonised, such as Vietnam, the Western model of human rights founded upon a telos of liberal democracy became complicit with the violence they denounced. In adopting their avowed role as neutral observers operating from a non-partisan position, human rights observers and organisations did not see themselves as imbricated in the conflicts they engaged with.

Claims to legitimacy within this paradigm are grounded in the very universality of the value—the rights of all humans—they stand in defence of. Practitioners refuse militancy as a form of deleterious particularism. Whereas in anti-colonial struggles, human rights were indeed a militant claim, not tied to a demand to be granted by the "international community", but a consequence of the political struggles that led to inde-

2    For more on the history of the transformation of Human Rights Discourse in the aftermath of the Cold War, see Robert Meister, *After Evil: A Politics of Human Rights* (New York: Columbia University Press, 2012).
3    In the aftermath of WWII, anti-colonial struggles in Southeast Asia and Africa, tasked to replace white European domination with forms of local sovereignty, were faced with the choice between Woodrow Wilson's conception of *self-determination* as a legal right–a re-inscription of previously colonial markets into capitalist state economies and legal systems–and the achievement of rights through national liberation struggles. For a detailed analysis of this, see Radha D'Souza, 'Epoch of Imperialism', in *What's Wrong with Rights?: Social Movement, Law and Liberal Imaginations* (London: Pluto Press, 2018).

pendence. In later decades, human rights would come to position itself against militancy and thus fully inscribe itself within the logic of liberalism. Neutrality and objectivity are, by definition, non-militant features. It is against the assumption of the practical necessity of apoliticality that we define our approach.

We advocate for working in solidarity with the affected communities with which, and on behalf of whom, our research is undertaken. We are talking about taking positions, working politically, and inhabiting spaces of endless contradiction. This is an attempt to evolve the position of human rights research once more. The break from human rights has gone in two directions, putting pressure both on "human" and on "rights", the latter asked what the right-bearing subject is: from humans to non-humans and also environments. At the same time, we need to ask what the source of rights is and whether they ensue from a universal or a poly-perspectival position.

If a key feature of non-militancy (and the condition of its emergence) is a form of operationalised *distance,* this spatial diagram could help to provide us with an outline of militancy as its opposite. This is an attempt to mediate between the universality of values and the particularism of situated material, political, and historical conditions. Having defined the aim and historical relevance of this "critical proximity", another task remains unfulfilled in our attempt to recast militancy in relationship to human rights work.[4] How do we understand the spaces opened by the "refusal" of a specific form of neutrality and objectivity in which the non-militant evidence is rooted? In other words, what is to be gained in being militant today?

While it has been argued that the field of human rights is currently undergoing an attempt to reform itself in response to the reinvigorated discourses and practices of and around decolonisation, what we advocate for is a further step that looks to reconnect knowledge and evidence production with liberation and political struggles.[5] For those of us studying and working in the Centre, a pivotal concern arises in the capacity to situate the violation or injustice that is being recorded within a larger history of repression and within an ongoing nexus of struggle.[6] How do we discern the precise coordinates of an incident within the intricate genealogy of expulsions, cleansings, thefts, and destruction of life worlds? Achieving this necessitates subjecting the very modality of research to intense scrutiny, questioning not only how the research is undertaken, but also who the community of research is and what the shared stakes are, if any. Such a pursuit compels us to remain acutely cognisant of the broader socio-political landscapes in which the research is situated, positioning it within the affected communities and in *continuum* with their demands and aspirations.

From our position, militancy ceases to be an obstacle in the production of truth but, instead, becomes the scaffold for assembling a collective claim that can locate the present within broader histories of violence alongside the experiences and desires of affected communities. The blurring of the threshold between research and activism becomes the site where the language of a new form of militant research can take shape; one that recognises liberation as the strongest guarantee for the protection of future rights. Liberation articulated, not according to universal values, but through the claims and traditions of affected communities. Within this framework, human rights can no longer be seen to operate as a kind of *arbiter.*

4   Eyal Weizman and Zachary Manfredi, '"From Figure to Ground": A Conversation with Eyal Weizman on the Politics of the Humanitarian Present', *Qui Parle* 22, no. 1 (1 June 2013): 172.
5   See, for example: Salil Shetty, 'Decolonising Human Rights', *Amnesty International*, 22 May, 2018, https://www.amnesty.org/en/latest/news/2018/05/decolonizing-human-rights-salil-shetty/.
6   Eve Tuck and K. Wayne Yang, 'Decolonization is not a Metaphor', *Decolonisation: Indigeneity, Education & Society* vol. 1, no. 1 (2012): 1-40.

Our conversation also led us to consider how militant methods of knowledge production can construct an argument without relying on conventional forms of authority, such as modes of liberal objectivity and neutrality upon which human rights has traditionally depended. This prompted us to contemplate how claims can be contextualised in relation to particular struggles and what it would entail to formulate concepts of 'militant objectivity'.

In this regard, we began with an example from Forensic Architecture's work in Israel-Palestine. From a conventional human rights perspective, you would be expected to give equal space and relevance to both violations of Israeli rights and Israeli violations of Palestinian rights. You would be required to call things by their official given names: you would call the Israeli army, the IDF, the Israeli Defence Forces. Now, suppose we locate human rights within the tradition of the Palestinian liberation struggle, and understand that Palestine liberation is the only way to assure human and non-human rights in this region. In that case, human rights do not become a value in themselves, but become part of a wider struggle for liberation, and liberation itself then becomes the guarantee of rights. There is much debate within organisations looking at Israeli colonisation/apartheid about how we name the IDF. For example, should it be called the Israeli occupation forces, which is what many Palestinian organisations call it? In this regard, researchers at Forensic Architecture have adopted 'positions' on the Israel-Palestine conflict that are reflected in how they work across the entire spectrum: how the work is produced, who is doing the work, how research is undertaken, by whom, how it is worded, and how it is used. The objective is to provide as much insight into the processes of undertaking and deploying the work as in the specific situations it seeks to address.

Another example is drawn from the seven human rights and civil society groups active in Palestine that have been declared "terrorist organisations" by the Israeli state.[7] If we look at the history of this argument, it is rooted in a form of universalism exercised by the Marxist-Leninist group, the Popular Front for the Liberation of Palestine (PFLP), which aimed to create forms of international solidarity as part of a broad anti-imperial project. The PFLP engaged in acts of militancy to achieve their goals, such as armed attacks, releasing prisoners, and aircraft hijackings. The PFLP share a common understanding and way of describing the Palestinian condition and the situation on the ground from the Palestinian perspective. Here, force operates not only towards the future but also towards a shared historical materialist understanding of conditions: the foundation on which politics can operate. It is a meta-political condition. This is why, for the PFLP, history could become a revolutionary force, in as much as it is mobilised and appealed to as a driver of political and historical change. The Israeli government has falsely claimed that this militant organisation, the PFLP, has now fragmented into seven human rights groups.[8] However, these organisations—Addameer, Al-Haq, Defense for Children International-Palestine, the Union of Agricultural Work Committees, the Bisan Center for Research and Development, Health Work Committee, and the Union of Palestinian Women

7    UN human rights experts "strongly and unequivocally condemned the decision" by the Israeli Minister of Defence to designate Palestinian human rights and civil society groups terrorist organisations: Office of the United Nations High Commissioner for Human Rights, 'UN Experts Condemn Israel's Designation of Palestinian Human Rights Defenders as Terrorist Organisations', *OHCHR*, accessed 28 September, 2023, https://www.ohchr.org/en/press-releases/2021/10/un-experts-condemn-israels-designation-palestinian-human-rights-defenders.
8    Aaron Boxerman, 'Gantz Declares Six Palestinian Rights Groups "Terror Organizations"', *The Times of Israel*, 22 October 2021, https://www.timesofisrael.com/gantz-declares-six-palestinian-human-rights-groups-terrorist-organizations/.

Committees—amongst others, are all part of a communal project to increase the resilience of the Palestinian society.

These groups are obviously not the PFLP. What they do is collect information and produce reports and accounts that have become a material, textural, and situated history of Israeli occupation—a history of expulsion, apartheid, and colonisation. Upon the basis of this research, these organisations also started appealing to international forums—such as the International Criminal Court (ICC), the United Nations (UN), the International Court of Justice (ICJ), and others—in a tactical way, recognising that Palestine's disputed status, in relation to bringing grievances forward to international bodies, is simultaneously at the heart of the violations for which they are seeking redress. Therefore, there are two ways in which the occupation views these groups: on the one hand, it's about the damage that they inflict upon the Israeli government by appealing to international forums, and on the other, it is about international solidarity as a way of building resilience for the communities of refugees and oppressed people. In response, the Israeli government has declared these human rights organisations terrorist groups, and their offices have been continually raided.[9] Consequently, the active engagement of these organisations in this specific political arena has ignited a concerted effort to strip them of their legitimacy. Indeed, their findings, research, and claims have come under intense scrutiny precisely because they have adamantly rejected the supposedly *disinterested* gaze characteristic of the human rights paradigm. This rejection, this embrace of militancy, has been instrumentalised by the Israeli government to cast doubt upon their role as impartial observers within the long-standing liberal framework of human rights, providing the state with a potent mechanism for undermining their credibility within international forums.

Paradoxically, however, it is within this act of de-legitimisation that we unearth the essence of militancy. Far from obscuring the production of truth, militancy, for us, serves as the indispensable framework in which collective claims are being constructed. It operates to situate the present within a broader narrative of historical violence and functions to express the aspirations of communities striving for a liberated future. In effect, militancy becomes the force of a set of counter-histories that unfurl towards a future-oriented liberation rooted in lived experiences, struggles, and the pursuit of justice.

This mode of research and approach we characterise as a form of 'militant objectivity', in that knowledge cannot be produced from a generalist, non-position. Feminist epistemologies, in particular, have been extremely useful in helping us understand how all knowledge is situated knowledge and how all positions offer specific vantage points from which to view the world.[10] It is not possible to create knowledge from a non-place. Moreover, when considering the impact of research, its potential to catalyse specific processes, and its strategic utilisation of different forums, one must understand it in relation to the creation of a commons; one that entails a collective project in which the world is depicted as a collective undertaking, marked by an acute awareness of its material realities. This insight becomes even more potent within a pedagogical research paradigm dedicated to spatial politics.

The juxtaposition between (non-militant) objectivity and militancy is a false opposition. Rather, we tend to see it as a pre-requisite for every good piece of research because militancy comes with clarity; it requires stating our ideas, affiliations, and

9   See Bethan McKernan, 'Israeli Forces Raid Offices of Six Palestinian Human Rights Groups', *The Guardian*, 18 August 2022, https://www.theguardian.com/world/2022/aug/18/israeli-forces-raid-palestinian-human-rights-groups-offices. Even Forensic Architecture's regional office there was broken into as part of those raids.
10  Donna Haraway, 'Situated Knowledges: The Science Question in Feminism and the Privilege of Partial Perspective', *Feminist Studies* 14, no. 3 (1988): 575–99.

aspirations without subterfuge. The "how" knowledge is produced and situated within a specific historical context and community is made transparent and available. As such, it does not try to eschew cross-examination but welcomes it as another opportunity to give voice to both affected communities and researchers. This approach is a militant mode of objectivity, one that can generate and defend robust results precisely because it is grounded in the people who have experience of specific struggles. These experiences inherently contribute to the expertise that informs the research process and help it gain more focus, energy, knowledge, and a wealth of sources intricately woven into the fabric of how it articulates its claims and the architecture of its argument.

## INDETERMINACY AND VERIFICATION

Through our discussion of making situated claims, the question of truth emerged more clearly for us. Researchers and practitioners may face challenges in making and verifying claims when official information is not readily accessible. As such, we began to discuss our interest in the role that contaminated forms of data and evidence play, given that we actively examine the significance of imperfections, errors, and misremembrances within the data mobilised for a research project.

There are different ways that truth tends to get conceptualised: this can range from transcendental and universal certitude to a notion of truth that accepts positionalities and indeterminacies.[11] Complex situations often require us to strive for clarity despite diverse and potentially conflicting sources of information. In such cases, it becomes necessary to navigate a variety of sources that might be low in fidelity, unreliable, or inaudible, where origins and authorship might be uncertain and where accounts inevitably conflict. It is essential to acknowledge that contradictions and indeterminacies are inherent components of any research project. Rather than *veritas,* we are interested in discussing *verification* as a process to characterise this situated, partial truth as a form of 'contaminated knowledge'.[12]

Similarly, traumatised witnesses can say something that is not exactly an empirical description of what has happened, but it is true to their experience of events. For instance, researchers at Forensic Architecture, instead of disregarding the recollection of witnesses and victims of violent crimes as untrustworthy, focus on the gaps and overlaps in the memory of traumatic events. By exploring why individuals may misremember and drawing from trauma studies, we can understand how misremembering is itself a form of registering trauma.[13] When someone introduces tangential or inaccurate information, it becomes important to treat this articulation as valuable data and attempt to discern its origins and underlying positionality.

The same approach applies when indeterminacy is caused by technical or material factors such as low image resolution, lack of focus, faulty film, sensor failure, or incomplete data backups. In fact, additional contaminating factors that this approach would seek to investigate could be the images themselves. Perpetrators often claim that image quality is too raw, grainy, blurry, or shaky to show they violated human rights conclu-

11    For more on this see: Matthew Fuller and Eyal Weizman, 'Introduction', in *Investigative Aesthetics: Conflicts and Commons in the Politics of Truth* (Brooklyn: Verso Books, 2021), 1–30.
12    Eyal Weizman, 'Open Verification', *E-Flux Architecture*, June 2019, https://www.e-flux.com/architecture/becoming-digital/248062/open-verification/.
13    Matthew Fuller and Eyal Weizman, *Investigative Aesthetics: Conflicts and Commons in the Politics of Truth* (Brooklyn: Verso Books, 2021), 83–84.

sively.[14] In times of conflict and political unrest, media is often taken on the fly, in haste, at personal risk, in conditions of precarity, and at peril to life. In light of this, we need to foreground, rather than conceal, the process of assembling conflicting accounts and uncertain sources into claims. Perpetrators, once again, claim that the victims have manipulated the evidence and the videos. Responding to this involves organising research projects in ways that do not dismiss inconsistencies, incoherencies, unruliness, or excesses but rather utilise them as the very foundation upon which a robust claim can be effectively constructed.

While an apparent link may be argued between notions of "post-truth" and the forms of militant objectivity, we are discussing, in that both approaches question statements made by government agencies like the police, intelligence services, and the court, there is a crucial difference.[15] The approach we advocate in relation to the current scepticism towards expertise, is not that of resignation or relativism in the sense of anything goes. Rather, we advocate for that of a more vital and risky form of truth production based on establishing an expanded assemblage of practices, which incorporate aesthetic and scientific sensibilities alongside the inclusion of new as well as traditional institutions. This approach brings together diverse practices and institutions to construct an expansive form of common truths.

The intent of state perpetrators (and what has been called dark epistemology) is to dismantle any possibility of a shared foundation.[16] Without a state or universal principle to guide us, establishing common ground becomes a political project. With each new research project, a new community of praxis is constructed from the meshing of its divergent viewpoints. In this regard, militant objectivity becomes a form of social architecture. Ultimately, the production and dissemination of evidence establishes an unlikely, but fundamental commons, built around a shared perception and understanding of the world. This is the requisite meta-political condition for meaningful political action. Rather than keeping its boundaries open and expanding, these commons thrive on the infusion of fresh perspectives, interpretations, and evidence, perpetually growing through the embrace of divergent viewpoints.[17]

Reality, for us, is a *common* that can only come from the weaving together of various forces. That is not to say these exist in different universes in a relativistic model. It means to recognise "verification" as the points where these multiple perspectives meet; interpolating what a leaf registers, what the community is saying, what the movement of clouds indicates, what a satellite senses, and what images taken from the ground show. This complex field of interacting elements composes what we are trying to address in signalling a shift from disinterested truth to militant objectivity—the process of assembling material, technological, testimonial, human, or non-human perspectives.

14  For example, Israel makes U.S. satellite providers degrade the resolution of available images over the country and its occupied territories, where most of its violations occur, and then often claims that satellite surveys of the destruction it brings about in Gaza are unverifiable. See Dan Williams, 'Israel feels exposed as U.S. drops satellite-imaging cap', *Reuters*, 6 July 2020, https://www.reuters.com/article/uk-israel-usa-satellites-idUKKBN2470VE.

15  See Isabelle Stengers, 'The Cosmopolitical Proposal', in *Making Things Public: Atmospheres of Democracy*, eds. Bruno Latour and Peter Weibel (Cambridge, Massachusetts; Karlsruhe, Germany: MIT Press; ZKM Center for Art and Media in Karlsruhe, 2005), 994–1003.

16  For a discussion of dark epistemology, see Rick Searle, 'How Dark Epistemology Explains the Rise of Donald Trump', *Utopia or Dystopia* (blog), 6 March 2016, https://utopiaordystopia.com/2016/03/06/how-dark-epistemology-explains-the-rise-of-donald-trump/; Eliezer Yudkowsky, "Dark Side Epistemology", *LESSWRONG*, 18 October 2008, https://www.lesswrong.com/posts/XTWkjCJScy2GFAgDt/dark-side-epistemology.

17  Stengers, 'The Cosmopolitical Proposal'.

This approach also necessitates a commons-oriented commitment towards research. Here, the production of 'common sense' can be regarded as a mode of creation, an ongoing cultivation of a research commonality that is integral to the creation of knowledge.[18] When you have a considerable research network, you need to keep each line of analysis and evidence as coherent as possible; what is important is the multi-perspectival weave. This approach is indebted to the work of filmmaker Harun Farocki as a "weaving together of separate media elements, technologies of vision, imagining, automation and detection, into a series of essay films that offered deep critical and investigative interrogation of the intersection of politics and technology" and highlight how such a weaving can describe a mode of practice.[19] It is a kind of cubism to the "nth" degree: you see all perspectives at the exact same moment, the perspective of different people, communities, and other non-human entities, such as trees and rivers and clouds, fostering a rich and multifaceted understanding.

## MEDIA PERSPECTIVES

While debating militancy as a form of situated practice—insofar as our physical and historical location shapes our perspectives and the assertions we put forth—we became curious about how media might also relate to this situatedness, and how media, too, occupies a situated position. Let us take, for instance, the analogue film camera. There is the image distortion produced by the choice of lens, there is perhaps chemical distortion in the film stock because of the temperature at which it was stored, there may be dirt in the housing or contamination in the air itself that distorts the behaviour of sunlight, and there is of course always spatial distortion that results from the positioning of the angle of the camera to the event documented. We need to take into account how none of those media elements are faithful witnesses: they are all situated witnesses. In essence, we do not have a faithful record but a situated record. Obviously, because it's a situated perspective, one cannot assume a mechanical relation between what is experienced and what is communicated.

Media is thus grounded in the various and unique vantage points that shape our perception of the world. It does not function (in our account) as a mode of mere representation but as an expression of the positionality of relations and practices: a vast multiplicity of situated records.

Expanding on a recurrent concept within visual theory, we are said to be inhabiting a "post-photographic" condition.[20] When we consider media within this paradigm, it becomes increasingly challenging to discern an ontological disparity between a photograph and the Earth's surface itself. They are simply different material forms of registration. When one undoes the privileged position of a camera or a satellite as an evidence-producing device, what you have instead are modes of registration without frames that are continuous and situated. Following this thinking, a forest or a landscape could be seen as media that captures and stores information, producing what Jennifer Gabrys

18  Matthew Fuller and Eyal Weizman, *Investigative Aesthetics: Conflicts and Commons in the Politics of Truth* (Brooklyn: Verso Books, 2021), 196.
19  Fuller and Weizman, *Investigative Aesthetics*, 4–5.
20  For the genealogy of the term and an extended explanation of the ways in which digital photography and the proliferation of images on the Internet have produced ontological and epistemological breaks within the field of photography, see: Joan Fontcuberta, 'The Post-Photographic Condition', in *Le Mois de La Photo a Montreal: The Post-Photographic Condition*, ed. Joan Fontcuberta (Montréal: Kerber Verlag, 2015), 10–15.

has called digitised environments.[21] These modes of environmental sensing do not rely upon a singular vantage point from which a photograph or recording was taken; they depend instead on the aesthetic interplay between sensing and making-sense (interpreting), between what can be perceived and what can be known.

Between these modes of registration—and the vast array of possible worlds that connect data points—there is an inherent indeterminacy that can never be fully overcome. Thus, media evidence serves to delineate possibilities, sometimes opening doors while at other times constraining the potential occurrence of events. Consequently, everything that operates between fields always resides in the realm of probability; perpetually oscillating between the hypothetical, the factual, and the counterfactual.
In order to account for this, what is important is not only the findings of a research project, but also how the investigation was conducted, the type of community of practice it engendered, and the manner in which it was articulated. This is the essence of militancy for us. The DNA of such work weaves together a multi-perspectival tapestry, drawing from grounded and situated experiences involving people, objects, and technologies.

As we conclude our reflections, it becomes evident that the disinterested observer we began with, represented by classical human rights discourse, has given way to a multitude of perspectives and situated positions. This shifting paradigm ushers in a new era where engagement with the world becomes intertwined with the very processes of producing about the world. The composition of truth, pieced together from fragments of media, technology, and human and non-human experiences, must establish thresholds of verification to make sense and make sensible the cacophony of divergent narratives. How do we bridge the gaps between memories, experiences, forms of non-human testimonies, and data points while acknowledging that what lies beyond the sensible is as vital as what is captured? It is only through embracing these uncertainties that our work adopts a distinctly political character.

## CONTRIBUTIONS

Each project featured in this volume navigates these conditions in specific ways, exploring diverse facets of political, technological, and epistemological militancy. They provide valuable insights into the evolution of investigative tools and aesthetic methodologies while articulating a distinct perspective within the multi-perspectival present. While each contribution engages with militant media in its own way, we have observed a network of commonalities and interconnections.

Several of these contributions are at the crossroads of technology and race, exploring the intricate relationship between the Black community and media. Kodwo Eshun, in his essay "On the Implications of Black Studies for Counter-Forensics and Counter-Forensics for Black Studies" (developed from his presentation at the monthly Forensic Architecture Forums convened by Samaneh Moafi to bring CRA students and FA researchers together), embarks on an examination of the intricate dynamics of split-second judgments through an analysis of the FA investigation into the police killing of Harith Augustus. Eshun's text examines the link between the short duration of the incident, the shooting, the violence captured on camera, and the *long durée* of systemic and structural racism through the

---

21   Jennifer Gabrys, 'Smart Forests and Data Practices: From the Internet of Trees to Planetary Governance', *Big Data & Society* 7, no. 1 (1 January 2020): 1–10.

lens of Black studies.[22] Similarly, Stafford Scott examines the historical context for the infamous 'Gangs Matrix', a predictive police database. He sheds light on the aftermath of Mark Duggan's tragic death. He delves into how this database emerged to compound further the pre-existing issues of pervasive over-policing of the Black community in the UK.

Through a critical engagement with the constraints inherent in human rights investigations, specific contributions in this context challenge established methodological paradigms. Sophie Dyer and Gabriela Ivens's updated essay, titled "What would a feminist open-source investigation look like?" advocates for an alternative mode of investigative process—from data collection and analysis to labour practices and communities—rooted in feminist principles. Correspondingly, Leila Sibai, a legal investigator and researcher within the context of the Syrian war, offers insights into the role of pedagogies in supporting investigative research practices. Her pedagogical approach is designed to assist students and practitioners in exploring how they might integrate legal strategies and ethical methods into their investigative work. It also highlights the ethical considerations surrounding witness vulnerability and the well-being of affected communities.

Exploring the continuum of colonial violence and resistance into the present, Simon Barber, Arama Rata, Waireti Roestenburg, and Huriana Kopeke-Te Aho speak to the history of Māori dispossession and struggle. Barber's text unpacks the British colonial occupation, navigating the clashes between the traditional concepts of authority and property imposed by the British Crown and the expansive notions that derive from Māori's ancestral connectedness to the land.

Other interventions within this book address the intricate and often contentious relationship between media, aesthetics, and legal frameworks. They explore how media forms can either participate in or explicitly challenge the notions of accountability and justice set forth by legal forums. In "Revisiting the Disobedient Gaze", Lorenzo Pezzani and Charles Heller critically reflect on the impact of militant research on shaping migration politics. The authors contextualise their research within a broader "ecology of knowledges" rooted within border struggles, emphasising its aesthetic dimensions and direct influence on the border regime's operations in the Mediterranean. Similarly, Helene Kazan's contribution delves into feminist, decolonial, and critical legal theory in relation to witnessing and visual evidence. Her essay investigates testimonies that question the legalistic gaze as the sole bearer of evidentiary value, focusing on accounts often disregarded within the framework of the law.

Other projects aim at countering the myriad ways digital culture has become entwined with contemporary spatial governance. In "Digital Autonomia", Júlia Nueno Guitart investigates platform-based labour and mechanisms of algorithmic governance, contemplating the transformation of work into the aggregation of data points. This project is grounded in practical activism and the development of a software app aimed at restructuring labour relations within platform capitalism. Ariel Caine and Faiz Abu-Rmeleh's article delves into the role of sensor technologies in the Silwan neighbourhood of Jerusalem. It sheds light on the transformation of Silwan due to the 'City of David' cultural heritage project, which has included extensive surveillance networks. The district, from its underground spaces to the sky above, are saturated with sensory apparatuses, which form a dense network of computational media essential for constant civil, cultural, and military occupation processes.

22  Fred Moten, 'Black Topological Existence', in *Arthur Jafa: A Series of Utterly Improbable, Yet Extraordinary Renditions*, by Arthur Jafa, ed. Amira Gad and Joseph Constable (London: Serpentine Galleries, 2018).

Reflecting on the role of media in contemporary warfare, Anna Engelhardt's project explores the challenges posed by synthetic images in relationship to evidentiary regimes. The essay departs from an examination of simulations in different war scenarios. Engelhardt's text asks how simulations and synthetic imagery can be repurposed to produce new modes of investigative practice. Ghalya Saadawi and Lawrence Abu Hamdan expand upon the interplay between creative practice, political intervention, slow violence, and collective witnessing; unpacking Abu Hamdan's most recent work, *Air Pressure* (2022) and the accompanying digital repository *AirPressure.info*, a catalogue of the 22,111 aerial incursions of Israel's warplanes in Lebanese air space.

A central theme within this volume is media's role in documenting state violence, especially against racialised communities. These projects scrutinise the potentials and limitations of media as a tool for both witnessing acts of violence and amplifying protests as well as advancing new forms of resistance or refusal. Gwendolyn Wallace investigates the use of TikTok to document police officers' violent interactions with African-American students. She underscores how Black adolescents often face criminalisation within the education system due to the interplay of race, age, and surveillance in shaping school discipline. Continuing this thematic strand, Sanjana Varghese's "Waiting for Tear Gas Again" delves into the role of social media, mobilisations, and protest. Her essay unveils how grassroots reporters have harnessed Facebook's "live-stream" feature as a tool to cover mass protests following the killing of George Floyd.

The book concludes with a collective pedagogical contribution from the 2022-23 Master's students. "Burning an Illusion" delves into the tragic events of 17 January 1981, when a fire claimed the lives of thirteen young Black individuals in New Cross, London. Despite multiple investigations, no one has been charged in connection with the fire. In the autumn of 2022, the MA Research Architecture course embarked on a collaborative study of the New Cross Massacre. Their goal was not to provide a definitive account of the fire's causes but to reveal the shortcomings in the investigations conducted by the police. They aimed to connect these failures to a broader history of state violence and neglect toward Black communities in the UK, essentially investigating the investigation itself.

## Works Cited

Boxerman, Aaron. 'Gantz Declares Six Palestinian Rights Groups "Terror Organizations"'. *The Times of Israel*, 22 October 2021. https://www.timesofisrael.com/gantz-declares-six-palestinian-human-rights-groups-terrorist-organizations/.

D'Souza, Radha. *What's Wrong with Rights?: Social Movement, Law and Liberal Imaginations*. London: Pluto Press. 2018.

Fontcuberta, Joan. 'The Post-Photographic Condition'. In *Le Mois de La Photo a Montreal: The Post-Photographic Condition*, edited by Joan Fontcuberta, 10–15. Montréal: Kerber Verlag, 2015.

Fuller, Matthew, and Eyal Weizman. *Investigative Aesthetics: Conflicts and Commons in the Politics of Truth*. Brooklyn: Verso Books, 2021.

Gabrys, Jennifer. 'Smart Forests and Data Practices: From the Internet of Trees to Planetary Governance'. *Big Data & Society* 7, no. 1 (1 January 2020): 1–10.

Haraway, Donna. 'Situated Knowledges: The Science Question in Feminism and the Privilege of Partial Perspective'. *Feminist Studies* 14, no. 3 (1988): 575–99.

Keenan, Thomas. 'Getting the Dead to Tell Me What Happened: Justice, Prosopopoeia, and Forensic Afterlives'. *Kronos* 44, no. 1 (2018): 102–22.

Keenan, Thomas, and Eyal Weizman. *Mengele's Skull: The Advent of a Forensic Aesthetics*. Londonn: Sternberg Press, 2012.

McKernan, Bethan. 'Israeli Forces Raid Offices of Six Palestinian Human Rights Groups'. *The Guardian*, 18 August 2022. https://www.theguardian.com/world/2022/aug/18/israeli-forces-raid-palestinian-human-rights-groups-offices.

Meister, Robert. *After Evil: A Politics of Human Rights*. New York: Columbia University Press, 2012.

Moten, Fred. 'Black Topological Existence'. In *Arthur Jafa: A Series of Utterly Improbable, Yet Extraordinary Renditions*, by Arthur Jafa, edited by Amira Gad and Joseph Constable. London: Serpentine Galleries, 2018.

Office of the United Nations High Commissioner for Human Rights. 'UN Experts Condemn Israel's Designation of Palestinian Human Rights Defenders as Terrorist Organisations'. *OHCHR*. Accessed 28 September 2023. https://www.ohchr.org/en/press-releases/2021/10/un-experts-condemn-israels-designation-palestinian-human-rights-defenders.

Searle, Rick. 'How Dark Epistemology Explains the Rise of Donald Trump'. *Utopia or Dystopia* (blog), 6 March 2016. https://utopiaordystopia.com/2016/03/06/how-dark-epistemology-explains-the-rise-of-donald-trump/.

Shetty, Salil. 'Decolonising Human Rights'. Amnesty International, 22 May 2018. https://www.amnesty.org/en/latest/news/2018/05/decolonizing-human-rights-salil-shetty/.

Stengers, Isabelle. 'The Cosmopolitical Proposal'. In *Making Things Public: Atmospheres of Democracy*, edited by Bruno Latour and Peter Weibel, 994–1003. Cambridge, Massachusetts; Karlsruhe, Germany: MIT Press; ZKM Center for Art and Media, 2005.

Tuck, Eve, and K. Wayne Yang, 'Decolonization is not a Metaphor'. *Decolonisation: Indigeneity, Education & Society* Vol. 1, No. 1 (2012): 1-40.

Weizman, Eyal. 'Open Verification'. *E-Flux Architecture*, June 2019. https://www.e-flux.com/architecture/becoming-digital/248062/open-verification/.

Weizman, Eyal, and Zachary Manfredi. '"From Figure to Ground": A Conversation with Eyal Weizman on the Politics of the Humanitarian Present'. *Qui Parle* 22, no. 1 (1 June 2013): 167–92.

Yudkowsky, Eliezer. 'Dark Side Epistemology'. *LESSWRONG*, 28 September 2008. https://www.lesswrong.com/posts/XTWkjCJScy2GFAgDt/dark-side-epistemology.

Williams, Dan. 'Israel feels exposed as U.S. drops satellite-imaging cap,' Reuters, 6 July 2020. https://www.reuters.com/article/uk-israel-usa-satellites-idUKKBN2470VE.15.

# CASE STUDIES

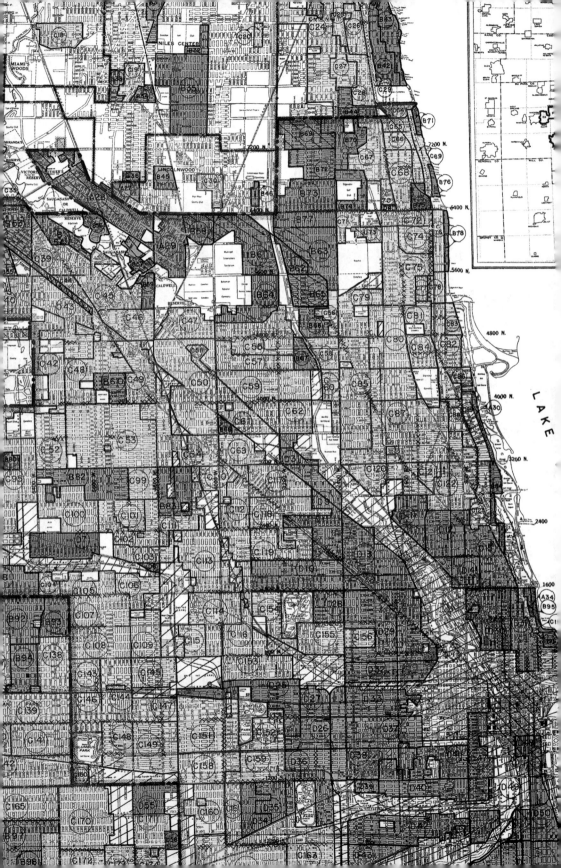

# ON THE IMPLICATIONS OF BLACK STUDIES FOR COUNTER-FORENSICS AND COUNTER-FORENSICS FOR BLACK STUDIES: NOTES ON 'SIX DURATIONS OF A SPLIT-SECOND: THE KILLING OF HARITH AUGUSTUS'

## Kodwo Eshun

*'Ghetto' is a harsh term, carrying overtones of poverty and suffering, of exclusion and subordination. In Midwest Metropolis it is used by civic leaders when they want to shock complacency into action. Most of the ordinary people in the Black Belt refer to their community as 'the South Side', but everybody is also familiar with another name for the area—Bronzeville.*
St. Clair Drake and Horace R. Cayton[1]

*The question of race is always a question of its repetition as hierarchy, segregation, and normativity. To ignore this configuration of repetition is to discount how race has always had a policing function.*
Barnor Hesse[2]

*And how we finally went into Sunday dinner,*
*That is to say, went across the front room floor*
*to the ink-spotted table in the southwest corner*
*To Sunday dinner, which was always*
*chicken and noodles*
*Or chicken and rice*
*And salad and rye bread and tea*
*And chocolate chip cookies-*
Gwendolyn Brooks[3]

*What if we consider blackness to be or to instantiate the pre-history of the post-cinematic?*
Fred Moten[4]

These notes constitute a series of observations on the six videos that constitute the investigation of the police killing of Harith Augustus at 5:30 pm on Saturday 14th July 2018 in the South Shore neighbourhood of Chicago published by Forensic Architecture (FA) under the title *Six Durations of*

1   St. Clair Drake and Horace R. Cayton, *Black Metropolis: A Study of Negro Life in a Northern City*, (Chicago: The University of Chicago Press: 2015), 383.
2   Barnor Hesse, 'White Sovereignty ( ... ), Black Life Politics: 'The N****r They Couldn't Kill', *The South Atlantic Quarterly* 116, no. 3 (1 July, 2017): 586.
3   Gwendolyn Brooks, 'when you have forgotten Sunday: the love story, from A Street in Bronzeville', in *The Essential Gwendolyn Brooks:* (American Poets Project #19) ed. Elizabeth Alexander (New York City: The Library of America, 2005), 8.
4   Fred Moten, 'Black Topological Existence', in *A Series of Utterly Improbable yet Extraordinary Renditions*, eds. Amira Gad and Joseph Constable, (London: Serpentine Gallery, 2018), 20.

*a Split Second: The Killing of Harith Augustus* on 18 September 2019. We
could begin by redescribing the investigation, in its entirety, as an interscalar
vehicle, defined, initially, by Margarida Mendes and popularised subsequently
by Gabrielle Hecht as a "means of connecting stories and scales usually kept
apart" that is not characterised by its "essence but its deployment and uptake,
its potential to make political claims, craft social relationships, or simply open
our imaginations".[5] What the term interscalar vehicle does is draw attention
to the form of the content of this specific forensic investigation as it extends
from the analyses of the police shooting at the scale of milliseconds, seconds
and minutes to the analyses of urban deprivation at the scale of hours, days
and years. Instead of taking this extension for granted, what I want to do is
to pay attention to its implications because its interscalarity is critical for
the distinctiveness of this specific project. The computational modelling of
timelines across milliseconds, seconds, minutes, hours, days and decades
enable investigation to move below and above the threshold of the split-second
decision understood as the temporal state of exception analysed by Matthew
Fuller and Eyal Weizman.[6] That attentiveness enables us to ask the question
of the ways in which this particular killing by this policeman of this civilian
exerted a pressure upon counter-forensics until it has no choice but to expand
its investigation beyond the incident of shooting. What we see and watch is
forensics widening the scope of its investigation beyond the parameters of the
case study that has provided investigative aesthetics with the coherence of its
inquiry and the reason for its existence.

        To read this forensic investigation as it expands its analysis across the
duration of its videos is to attend to the ways in which the diffusion of its object
simultaneously creates the diffusion of its mode of analysis. What is happening
is that the expansion of the scale of investigation begins, gradually, to reconfig-
ure the ways in which counter-forensics can be said to account for its project.
The vocabulary developed and elaborated by the researchers that constitute
Forensic Architecture for explaining and affirming its computational methods—the vocabulary that most critics tend to adopt or scrutinise or reject in
their encounters with forensic investigation—is gradually becoming the object
of and subject to a process of renarration not intended or determined by any
specific person but is emerging in and through a dispersive field of inadvertent
interdisciplinary disarticulation. That means that this process of renarration is
dismissable, if not ignorable. We know the purpose of forensic investigation and
the objective of this specific project. The certainty of that knowledge renders
that inadvertent disarticulation beside the point. Nothing more than an unin-
tended side-effect of the investigation. I think it is worth asking what happens
when those are drawn out of the realm of the ignorable and the unintentional
and into articulation. Without that enunciation, it is difficult to ask what happens
when the methodological novelty of forensics encounters the historical obduracy

5    See Margarida Mendes, *Sensorial Ecologies: Sonic Literacy and Restorative Listening in
     Watery Worlds*, PhD in Research Architecture, Centre for Research Architecture, Goldsmiths
     University of London, 2022. See also Gabrielle Hecht, 'Interscalar Vehicles for an African
     Anthropocene: On Waste, Temporality and Violence', *Cultural Anthropology* 33,
     no. 1 (2018), 115.
6    Matthew Fuller and Eyal Weizman, *Investigative Aesthetics: Conflicts and Commons
     in the Politics of Truth*, (New York and London: Verso, 2021), 101.

of racial violence and the implacable urgency of urban segregation dramatizes the computational agency of the forensic. It becomes difficult to think the racial ordering of knowledge, the computational structuring of the racial and the racial organisation of the computational in their discrepant articulation.

In so far as *Six Durations of a Split Second: The Killing of Harith Augustus* could be said to encroach upon what Reece Auguiste calls the "epistemological terrain"[7] of policing, violence and race in the United States that have, historically been dominated by the disciplines of urban sociology and black studies, it becomes possible for us to approach counter-forensics from the perspectives of those disciplines. Those disciplines begin to impinge upon the understanding of counter-forensics hitherto monopolised by its own vocabulary. By situating the police killing of Harith Augustus within its enquiry into the ghettoization of the South Side of Chicago, forensic investigation supervenes upon urban sociology's claim to produce knowledge of what it called the 'ghetto'; such claims, in turn, had been contested and shared by the analyses of the co-constitutive violence of racialisation, segregation and urbanisation undertaken by black studies throughout the twentieth century. Even though counter-forensics, in 2019, had nothing to say to black studies any more than the latter had actually acknowledged the existence of the former in 2019, the forensic encounter with the slow crime of ghettoization created the context, then and the occasion, now, for us to pose questions to forensics from the perspectives of black studies and to ask questions of black studies from the perspective of forensics. To require each discipline to question their own constitution enables us to estrange the capacity of black studies and the capability of forensics to produce the objects of knowledge that constituted its authority. It offers the occasion to open the question of how and where the real object ends and where and how the object of research begins.

What heightens the stakes of such questioning beyond that of the limits of the disciplinary or the epistemological is the ongoing tension between black studies and urban sociology, each of which produces competing claims about blackness, policing, race, whiteness, violence and ghettoisation in the United States.[8] It is a matter of contestation between fields that stake their claim to authority in and through the ways they produce knowledge of and over black social life and death in Chicago. The computational novelty of counter-forensics suggests its capacity to displace or suspend the history of that competition and that contestation. Such a displacement, however, entails acknowledging the inheritance of contestation and competition. That requires us to reckon, initially, with the role played by the black inhabitants of the South Side of Chicago in the making of the discipline of urban sociology and with the methods

---

7   Reece Auguiste formulated the notion of the epistemological terrain at the Cultural Identities conference on national identity constituted through the institution of cinema at the Commonwealth Institute in London in March 1986 as follows: "Our presence in independent cinema, as it is currently structured and mediated by the institutional and the political is, I believe, engaged in a struggle for its epistemological terrain through modes of visual articulation and narrative concerns which do not desire to emulate or mimic other cinemas." See Reece Auguiste, 'Black Cinema, Poetics and New World Aesthetics', *Undercut: The Magazine for the London Filmmakers' Co-op,* Issue 17: Cultural Identities, Spring 1988, 33.

8   The intervention into the questions of blackness, policing, race, whiteness, violence, and ghettoisation in the US announced by the FA investigation into the shooting of Harith Augustus has been developed and elaborated in the UK since 2018. See Forensic Architecture # 1: *The Police Shooting of Mark Duggan,* (London: Cabinet Books, 2021).

subsequently fashioned by black studies for dismantling the hegemony of the sociological regulation over the imagination of the world of Bronzeville within the Midwest Metropolis of America's second, now third, largest city: Chicago.

Understanding the role played by the black inhabitants of the South Side of Chicago in the making of the discipline of urban sociology requires revisiting the sociological imagination of the so-called Chicago school. The West and South Sides of Chicago, argues Dhanveer Singh Brar, treated as a laboratory for constructing a general theory of ghettoization exemplified by the concentration of black inhabitation. What emerged in Robert Park, Ernest Burgess and Roderick McKenzie's 1925 *The City: Suggestions for the Study of Human Nature in the Urban Environment* and E. Franklin Frazier's 1932 *The Negro Family in Chicago* was the treatment of the South and West of Chicago as a template for producing knowledge of what it called "the ghetto".[9] The ethnographic field work undertaken throughout the South and West of Chicago by the Department of Sociology at the University of Chicago in the 1920s and 1930s reinforced the popular logic of white racialization that rendered the blacks that inhabited the Black Belt responsible for the 'blight' of ghettoisation. White Chicago widely understood the blackness of the inhabitants to stand in for or to do the work of the 'perceived' blackness of their environment. To characterise the relation between inhabitants and their lived environment in terms of osmosis in this way was to racialise the environment and environmentalise racialization. The research undertaken by the Chicago school enshrined these commonly held logics of conflation that justified the formal and informal practices of ghettoization through its recourse to moral vocabularies of responsibilisation.

Those that lived in squalor were and are judged as a part of 'squalor' rather than as sufferers of squalid conditions.[10] In *Squalor*, Daniel Renwick and Robbie Shilliam track the moralizing discourses that underpinned the political history of urban deprivation from the mid-nineteenth century to the present in Britain. Renwick and Shilliam rework Stuart Hall's claim that "race is the modality in which class is lived" to argue that race can be understood as the modality in which squalor is apprehended.[11] Renwick and Shilliam demonstrate that strategies such as slum clearance, new town building, social housing provision and buying incentives aimed at alleviating squalor in the 'colony areas' of Handsworth, Chapeltown, Toxteth, Moss Side, St. Pauls, Brixton and Tottenham have all rested on a fatal flaw in which those who live in squalor have been judged to be part of the dysgenic environment themselves. Understanding the methods fashioned by black studies for dismantling the sociological regulation of the imagination of black urban life requires us to return to the monumental study of black life undertaken by sociologists St. Clair Drake and Horace R. Cayton and published in 1946. From within the Chicago school, Drake and Cayton's *Black Metropolis: A Study of Negro Life in a Northern City* can be read as a counter-sociology that moved against the recourse to osmotic descriptions of racialization as ghettoisation by maintaining a produc-

---

9   Dhanveer Singh Brar, *Teklife/ Ghettoville/ Eski: The Sonic Ecologies of Black Music in the Early 21st Century*, (London: Goldsmiths Press, 2021), 62.
10  Daniel Renwick and Robbie Shilliam, *Squalor*, (Newcastle upon Tyne: Agenda Publishing, 2022), 2.
11  Renwick and Shilliam, *Squalor*, 17-18.

tive tension between the analysis of the 'cordon sanitaire' designed to 'protect' white Chicago from the supposedly antipathetic effects of the Black Belt and the analysis of the sociality of inhabitation engendered within it. When historian Adam Green uses the term 'cordon sanitaire' for the sixth video in *Six Durations of a Split Second: The Killing of Harith Augustus*, this alludes to Cayton and Drake's analysis of the restriction of the free movement of the black population and the expansion of territory in South Chicago.[12]

*Black Metropolis*, argues Brar, breaks with the interpretive conflation of the Chicago school by opening up an analytic hesitation between the external imposition and the internal inhabitation that engenders its own forms of black sociality. By maintaining a degree of differentiation between the structural basis for the existence of the urban zone described as a 'ghetto' and the black social life generated within what are deemed to be its confines, what counts as the urban and what counts as blackness is rendered troublesome for social scientific evidence. What Drake and Cayton do, then, is to exacerbate an analytic instability that problematizes the capacity of urban sociology to regulate black social life in the name of its evidentiary certitude. The instability of methodology entails an analytic hesitation as to the object of research that suspends the moralising recourse to osmosis that exemplifies the common sense of racism adopted the object of the Chicago school. Instead of using the South Side of Chicago as a laboratory for reinforcing the disciplinary coherence of sociology, *Black Metropolis* methodologically heightens the surplus knowledges generated within Bronzeville that precede and surpass sociological capture. The disjuncture between external constraint and internal capabilities, according to Brar, is never settled in *Black Metropolis*; instead, it becomes engrained into its analysis as a kind of 'hesitant sociology' that keeps the distinctions between real objects and the object of knowledge in flux.

When Drake and Cayton state that most of "the ordinary people in the Black Belt refer to their community as 'the South Side', but everybody is also familiar with another name for the area—Bronzeville" and go onto observe that "Bronzeville's people have never let poverty, disease, and discrimination 'get them down'. The vigor with which they enjoy life seems to belie the gloomy observations of the statisticians and civic leaders who have the facts about the Black Ghetto".[13] The very name of Bronzeville signals an analytic attunement in Black Metropolis towards the practice of aesthetic sociality theorised by Laura Harris and elaborated by Gwendolyn Brooks in *A Street in Bronzeville* in 1945.[14] What is noticeable is the appearance of 'axes of feelings',

---

12   Forensic Architecture and the Invisible Institute, 'The Killing of Harith Augustus', 18 September, 2019, https://forensic-architecture.org/investigation/the-killing-of-harith-augustus, accessed 15 December 2023.

13   Drake and Cayton, *Black Metropolis: A Study of Negro Life in a Northern City,* 386.

14   See Laura Harris, 'What Happened to the Motley Crew: C.L.R. James, Helio Oiticica and the Aesthetic Sociality of Blackness', *Social Text* 112, vol. 30, no. 3 (Fall 2012), 49- 75. See also Laura Harris, *Experiments in Exile: C.L.R. James, Helio Oiticica and the Aesthetic Sociality of Blackness*, (New York: Fordham University Press, 2018),1- 61. See Gwendolyn Brooks, kitchenette building, of De Witt Williams on his way to Lincoln Cemetery, the vacant lot, The Sundays of Satin-Legs Smith from *A Street in Bronzeville*, 1945, and A Bronzeville Mother Loiters in Mississippi. Meanwhile a Mississippi Mother Burns Bacon, Bronzeville Woman in a Red Hat and Bessie of Bronzeville Visits Mary and Norman at a Beach-house in New Buffalo from *The Bean Eaters*, 1960, in *The Essential Gwendolyn Brooks* ed. Elizabeth Alexander, *Selected Poems*, (American Poets Project: The Library of America, 2005),1, 9, 10,61, 75, 78.

to use the terminology of Drake and Cayton, throughout the poems of *A Street in Bronzeville*. In her first volume, and throughout her career, Gwendolyn Brooks is preoccupied with the rendering sociographies of the singular lives of black dying and black living that exceed, elude and overwhelm the exemplary form of the case study conceded to the imagination of the forms of black duress by the Chicago school. The analytic reorientation pioneered by Drake, Cayton and Brooks in the 1940s suggests immanent methods for transforming black studies' relation to itself. Methods for breaking with its historical reliance upon the ethnographic and evidentiary authority of urban sociology. Methods for disarticulating sociology's regulatory hold over the external imagination of the world of Bronzeville. Methods for attuning analysis to the scale of black worlds within the segregated world of the Midwest Metropolis.

Undertaking such a break requires the development and elaboration of a disciplinary consciousness that proceeds from a methodological critique. In *The Crisis of the Negro Intellectual: A Post-Date*, her call for black studies to undertake the "transformation of African American studies into an 'object of knowledge' rather than a more or less elaborate repertory of performative gestures and utterances,"[15] Hortense Spillers presses black studies to respond to a "new set of demands" to disarticulate its real object" which can be designated as "black people" from "its object of knowledge" which can be referred to as "blackness" in order to attend to what Alexander Weheliye calls the "productive powers" possessed by black studies in the construction of its object. According to Weheliye:

*Instead of assuming that black studies reflects an already existent series of real objects, we need to draw attention to the complex ways this field of inquiry contributes to, or articulates, the creation of objects of knowledge such as the black community, black culture, and, indeed, black studies. Continuing to identify blackness as one of black studies' primary objects of knowledge with black people as real subjects (just as the human and Man appear as synonymous in western modernity) rather than an articulated object of knowledge accepts too easily that race is a given natural and/or cultural phenomenon and not an assemblage of forces that must continuously articulate nonwhite subjects as not-quite-human.*[16]

Weheliye discerns a "general problem with studies of black diasporic life' that identify or conflate 'blackness' as an object of knowledge with the real object of 'black people".[17] To interrupt that conflation requires black studies to break with its presupposition that it "reflects an already existent series of real objects" that it calls black people. [18] What contemporary black studies needs is to recover and upgrade the analytic hesitation developed by Drake and Clayton for *Black Metropolis* in its account of black social life enjoyed in Bronzeville as the Black Belt. To bring that analytic caesura to bear upon

15  Hortense J. Spillers, 'The Crisis of the Negro Intellectual: A Post-Date', in *Black, White and in Colour, Essays on American Literature and Culture*, (Chicago and London: The University of Chicago and London, 2003), 464.
16  Alexander G. Weheliye, *Habeas Viscus: Racializing Assemblages, Biopolitics, and Black Feminist Theories of the Human*, (Durham and London: Duke University Press, 2014), 18-19.
17  Brar, *The Sonic Ecologies of Black Music in the Early 21ˢᵗ Century*, 62.
18  Weheliye, *Racializing Assemblages, Biopolitics, and Black Feminist Theories of the Human*, 18.

the ways in which social science conflates the distinctions between lived experience and knowledge production is to interrupt sociology's capacity to produce a limited account of black social life. Thinking through the analyses developed by Drake and Cayton together with the methods posed by Brooks and the arguments proposed by Brar, Renwick and Shilliam, Spillers and Weheliye and brings the relation between forensics and black studies into focus and renders it available for thought. Forensics supports the reimagination of black studies. To model is to analyse. The model is a parametrical object of knowledge production that distances or abstracts itself from its real object of analysis so as to enable its investigation. The model heightens the distinction between 'blackness' as an object of knowledge' and the real object of 'black people' by defining the parameters of the former without claiming to exhaust the parameters of the latter.

What I am suggesting, then, is that the formal content of post-optical or post-cinematic modelling—its evidentiary ontology, its parametrical reductionism, its propositional abstraction, its existent virtuality, its perspectival conditionality—offers black studies the analytic possibility for delinking from sociology's regulation of Bronzeville in relation to the Black Belt. What is modelled in *Six Durations of a Split Second: The Killing of Harith Augustus* is an environment defined by and reduced to the parameters of the racializing assemblages, to use Wehilye's term, that police the South Side of Chicago. That which claims to regulate life and death in the South Side is being modelled according to conditional and probabilistic parameters that are ante and anti-regulatory. What is being modelled is the probable, the actual, the conditional and the fatal by means of the evidentiary and the verifiable. To multiply the earshot and the sightlines of police officers and civilians enables the camera to navigate and to analyse the probable perspectives from which the shooting could be heard and its effects could be seen. If 3-dimensional space positions virtual cameras that model perspectives virtually present at the time and the space of the scene of the shooting without having been recorded by any microphone on any camera then what is at stake is the actualisation of the possibilities virtually present at the shooting in the form of computational agencies designed to act upon the configuration of the world within which the shooting occurred.

The images in a forensic investigation do not function according to an epistemology of exposure that renders the invisible visible or makes tangible a hidden truth. As Mahan Moalemi argues, drawing upon Tung Hui Hu, most computational processes remain:

*unrepresentable especially when the scale of operation is increasingly enlarged. Their symbolism does not amount to a representation of the world as much as it introduces new entities by acting on the world, by bringing about a process or realising a function…Computational aesthetics, in this regard, highlights the contours of experience by subjecting it to a certain techno-ontological operation whose status looms within discontinuities and inconsistencies that emerge across the different scales of being and being human.*[19]

19   Mahan Moalemi, 'The Geopolitical Ontology of the Post-optical Image: Notes on The Otolith Group's Sovereign Sisters', in *The Otolith Group: Xenogenesis*, eds. The Otolith Group and Megs Morley (Dublin and Berlin: Irish Museum of Modern Art and Archive Books, 2021), 337.

In thinking through the works of Arthur Jafa, Fred Moten posed the question of blackness in relation to the post-cinematic: "What if we consider blackness to be or to instantiate the pre-history of the post-cinematic?" allows us to think of blackness as that which problematises the cinematic. In its incapacity to be captured by technological practices of sensitometry or cinematography, blackness, as an object of production differentiated from the real object of black people, poses a problem, historically, for industrial cinema. In so far as blackness eludes registration by whatever we think of as cinema, we could say that the problematisiation of cinema posed by blackness inaugurates that which came, or comes before or after cinema. Blackness can be understood, then, as that which announces what Moten calls "antecinematic instantiation."[20] If post-cinematic modelling, as analysed by Moalemi, operates through introducing new entities or agencies that act upon the world that it animates, what happens when the real object of the police shooting of a black civilian is figured as a computational entity? When the external parameters that produce ghettoization begin to act upon that world? What if the modelling of the makes evident the difficulty of holding the real object of the black person distinct and apart from the object of knowledge of blackness?

Thinking the 'antecinematic' of Moten together with the 'post-cinematic' of Moalemi, provides a perspective from which to hear the logics of the Chicago school sociology embedded and engrained in the statement issued by Superintendent Eddie Johnson of the Chicago Police Department on 15th July 2018 that declares "the decision to use lethal force is made in a split second and is based on the safety of the officer and the surrounding community."[21] In Chicago, as in Brixton, the police created the criminals it believed existed; Johnson's statement allows the police to present themselves as what Renwick and Shilliam call the "vanguard of moral behaviour".[22] To return to the script voiced by Trina Reynolds-Tyler of the Invisible Institute is to attend to the vocabulary developed by FA for counter-investigation. The "durational concept of the split second is often invoked as a legal defence when the police are investigated for the use of lethal force. But this supposedly indivisible temporality is treated as a black box that tends to isolate the instant from its context." To reverse-engineer the process by which the instant of decision is isolated from its context entails grasping the mechanism by which cognition is insulated from inspection so as to render opaque or black box the temporal structure of judgement. It is to reconstitute the process through which the law protected the capacity of the police to interpret their own decisions in order to shield their judgements from external interrogation. The police distanced themselves from the panic they generated. They misattributed the threat that emerged from and was generated by their own lethal force to the victim, who they claimed as its cause.

20   Fred Moten, 'Black Topological Existence' in *A Series of Utterly Improbable yet Extraordinary Renditions*, eds. Amira Gad and Joseph Constable, (London: Serpentine Gallery, 2018), 20. See also John Akomfrah and The Otolith Group, 'John Akomfrah and the Otolith Group Discuss Post-cinematic Blackness', *Frieze,* Issue 214, 23 September, 2020, https://www.frieze.com/article/blackness-post-cinema-john-akomfrah-otolith-group, accessed 3 December 2023.
21   Jamie Kalven and Eyal Weizman, 'HOW CHICAGO POLICE CREATED A FALSE NARRATIVE AFTER OFFICERS KILLED HARITH AUGUSTUS', *The Intercept*, 19 September, 2019, https://theintercept.com/2019/09/19/harith-augustus-shooting-chicago-police/, accessed 15 December 2023.
22   Renwick and Shilliam, *Squalor,* 85.

Neurologist Tiago Branco analysed the temporality of the instinctive decisions of Halley's shooting of Augustus in the following terms: "The question is was the shooter reacting to any particular event that led him to press the trigger—that you might call the split second decision, if you want—though I think the term/ time is actually a bit misleading because it comes on the back of this escalation essentially escalation... which in this model of decision making would be you are already pretty close to your threshold and then you just need a little something else to take you over the threshold."[23] Did Branco say that "I think the time is actually a bit misleading because it comes on the back of this escalation". Or did he say that "I think the term is actually a bit misleading because it comes on the back of this escalation?" This discrepancy indicates the way in which analytic attention is required to shift scale between the split-second and the mutual excitation generated by the officers Megan Fleming, Danny Tan, and Halley. The three officers "corner Augustus in the street outside the store thereby causing the situation to escalate and the threat levels to rise."

Halley's decision to shoot emerged from this escalation which generated its own threat that gathered its own momentum that encircled Augustus within the spirals that come 'on the back of this escalation'. The panicked reaction of Augustus provided the three police officers with the 'circular reinforcement' in the words of Drake and Cayton. The police attributed the threat they brought with them to Augustus even as they amplified it. What is the relation between the circular reinforcement of amplification spirals and the capacity for the misattribution of causation? Between the capacity for escalation and the adjudication of the moral thresholds across which threat and panic travel? Between defending what is surrounded from that which surrounds it?[24] How should we understand the 'surrounding community' appealed to by Johnson?

In the sixth and final video of *The Killing of Harith Augustus*, Reynolds-Tyler differentiates between the understandings of the police shooting of the Chicago Police Department or CPD and those of members of the South Shore community. The CPD locate the killing of Harith Augustus within the frame of the split-second decision. Members of the South Shore community, by contrast, situate the killing within an ongoing history of police terror whose effects include the pain of exhaustion that afflicts activist Velma Henry in Toni Cade Bambara's 1980 *The Salt Eaters*. A fatigue with the duration of the repetition of each police murder whose incidence entails a structure that does not resolve itself into a formalizable pattern. A weariness voiced by activist Will Calloway when he states that "We are so tired. We're tired of community violence, and we're tired of police violence".[25] What Calloway and Reynolds-Tyler and Henry attest to is a weariness that requires the attunement of counter-forensics. To expand its investigation across the six durations to

23   Forensic Architecture and the Invisible Institute, 'The Killing of Harith Augustus', 18 September, 2019, https://forensic-architecture.org/investigation/the-killing-of-harith-augustus, accessed 15 December 2023.

24   On the image of a surrounded fort, the life that surrounds it, the surround that antagonizes the laager in its midst and the self-defence of the surround, see Stefano Harney & Fred Moten, *The Undercommons: Fugitive Planning and Black Study*, (London: Minor Compositions, 2013), 17.

25   Forensic Architecture and the Invisible Institute, 'The Killing of Harith Augustus', 18 September, 2019, https://forensic-architecture.org/investigation/the-killing-of-harith-augustus, accessed 15 December 2023.

account for the decelerated, diffused, dispersed duress from which emerges the split second of shooting entails adjusting the focus of investigation towards the accretion and the permeation of the environmental in its regulation of the racial. It entails an investigation capable not only of accounting for the racialising operations of the police but also registering what Barnor Hesse calls the policing operations of race.

It is not so much a matter of investigating tiredness as a mode of slow violence as much as a matter of registering tiredness as a feeling that structures the affordance of counter-forensics. That requires allowing the temporal novelty of post-cinematic investigation to be transformed by the intractability of police killing by expanding the scale of investigation across the twentieth century from those split-seconds in 2018 in which Halley shot Augustus to the so-called race riots of July and August 1919 that took "at least thirty eight lives, resulted in over five hundred injuries, destroyed $250,000 worth of property and left over a thousand persons homeless".[26] According to Cayton and Drake, the riots of 1919 began:

*on a hot July day in 1919 as the result of an altercation at a bathing beach. A colored boy swam across the imaginary line which was supposed to separate Negroes from whites at the Twenty-ninth Street beach. He was stoned by a group of white boys. During the ensuing argument between groups of Negroes and white bathers, the boy was drowned. Colored bathers were enraged. Rumor swept the beach, 'White people have killed a Negro.' The resulting fight, which involved the beach police and the white and colored crowd, set off six days of rioting.*[27]

Moving from Reynolds-Tyler's account of Halley's murder to the testimony of the white riots offered by Timuel Black who was born in the Red Summer of 1919 enables the dimension of the intergenerational to emerge from the imagination of scale mobilized by the interscalarity of investigation. What is invaluable in the recollections offered by Timuel Black for is the insight gained into the way in which the self-defence of black community imperilled by white threat is inseparable from the formation of black community which is in turn indivisible from the aesthetic sociality of the formation of black life:

*When the riot occurred that motivated the concentration of blacks into the same neighbourhood for self-protection because the blacks had come in such large numbers during that period of time—they were four times by 1920 what they had been in 1910.*

What Timuel Black theorises here, at this point, is the way in which the struggle for black community entails the theory, the practice and the project of what Fred Moten calls the 'generative sociopoesis' of black inhabitation in the face of white death. Which emerges from and engenders surplus knowledges that exceeds the policing of race and the interpretive regulation of the 'race riot'. What Timuel Black allows us to understand are the conditions under which

---

26  Drake and Cayton, *Black Metropolis: A Study of Negro Life in a Northern City*, 65.
27  Drake and Cayton, *Black Metropolis: A Study of Negro Life in a Northern City*, 66.

the black working middle and upper classes of the South Side of Chicago make themselves. The ways in which the women, men, and children of the South Side Shore were present at the scene of their own making. In parallel with the Red Summer in the US, communities of Black seamen in the port cities of Britain fought against whites throughout Britain's own 'Red Summer'. In contrast to the US, however, by 1919, observes Barnor Hesse, there were a number of race riots in the port cities of Liverpool, Cardiff, Hull, Manchester, and London:

*A twentieth century logic of racist violence and 'institutionalized racism' was inaugurated on the pattern of groups of local whites repeatedly attacking Black residences, motivated by perceived grievances around economic competition in employment, sexual competition over white women, and in effect regional contestation over the urban meaning to be assigned to the colonial demarcation of an increasingly racialized Britishness.*[28]

What is striking here is the way in which the event of the race riot is understood by Hesse through the analysis of the racial economies of grievance that opens out onto the economic geographies of racialisation. Disputes fought at the level of the regional over the meaning of the urban are contested through struggles as to where the boundaries of the colonial are to be drawn within the escalating racialisation of Britishness. Struggles over the meanings of the regional entail struggles at the level of the urban that cannot be understood outside of the escalating colonial geographies of racialisation that expand throughout all levels of Britishness. The intervention into the questions of blackness, policing, race, whiteness, violence, ghettoisation, and exhaustion in America undertaken by FA investigation into the police shooting of Harith Augustus in Chicago in 2019 has been developed and elaborated in the investigations undertaken from 2018 to 2023 in the UK that render preliminary the preceding analysis.

The investigation conducted into The Grenfell Tower Fire in March 2018 and the subsequent investigation into the killing of Mark Duggan in June 2020, the collaboration with Stafford Scott of Tottenham Rights and curators Kamara Scott and Rianna Jade Parker for the exhibition *War Inna Babylon: The Community's Struggle for Truth and Rights* at the Institute of Contemporary Arts, London from July to September 2021, the CRA Guest Professorship of Stafford Scott of Tottenham Rights and Kamara Scott for 2022-2023 during which Scott and Scott facilitated the investigation entitled *Burning an Illusion* into the police investigation of the New Cross Fire undertaken by the 2022-23 MA Students for their Live Project constitutes a substantive intervention that requires its own analysis. An analysis that accounts for the implications of black studies for counter-forensics for and counter-forensics for black studies as theorised in its black British distinctiveness by Barnor Hesse in 2000. What differentiated its differential investment in the national formation from white or Asian Britishness, argued Hesse, were its transruptive politics of Black (un)

28  Barnor Hesse, 'Diasporicity: Black Britain's Post-Colonial Formations', in *Un/Settled Multiculturalisms: Diasporas, Entanglement, 'Transruptions'*, ed. Barnor Hesse, (London and New York: Zed Books, 2000), 102.

settlement articulated to each other through its discontinuous historicization, its disparate regionalisation, its recurrent politicisation and its dialogic differentiation. How, and in what ways does counter-forensics bear upon Hesse's analysis of the transruptive politics of Black (un)settlement? That is the question that informs current and ongoing research.

## Works cited

Akomfrah, John and The Otolith Group. 'John Akomfrah and the Otolith Group Discuss Post-cinematic Blackness'. *Frieze,* Issue 214, 23 September, 2020. https://www.frieze.com/article/blackness-post-cinema-john-akomfrah-otolith-group, accessed 3 December 2023.

Auguiste, Reece. 'Black Cinema, Poetics and New World Aesthetics', *Undercut: The Magazine for the London Filmmakers' Co-op,* Issue 17: Cultural Identities, Spring 1988, 33.

Brar, Dhanveer Singh. *Teklife/ Ghettoville/ Eski: The Sonic Ecologies of Black Music in the Early 21st Century,* London: Goldsmiths Press, 2021.

Brooks, Gwendolyn. 'when you have forgotten Sunday: the love story, from A Street in Bronzeville', in *The Essential Gwendolyn Brooks:* (American Poets Project #19) ed. Elizabeth Alexander. New York City: The Library of America, 2005.

––– 'kitchenette building, of De Witt Williams on his way to Lincoln Cemetery, the vacant lot, The Sundays of Satin-Legs Smith' from *A Street in Bronzeville,* 1945.

––– 'A Bronzeville Mother Loiters in Mississippi. Meanwhile a Mississippi Mother Burns Bacon, Bronzeville Woman in a Red Hat and Bessie of Bronzeville Visits Mary and Norman at a Beach-house in New Buffalo' from *The Bean Eaters,* 1960.

Drake, St. Clair and Horace R. Cayton. *Black Metropolis: A Study of Negro Life in a Northern City.* Chicago: The University of Chicago Press: 2015.

Forensic Architecture # 1: *The Police Shooting of Mark Duggan,* London: Cabinet Books, 2021.

Forensic Architecture and the Invisible Institute. 'The Killing of Harith Augustus', 18 September, 2019. https://forensic-architecture.org/investigation/the-killing-of-harith-augustus, accessed 15 December 2023.

Fuller, Matthew, and Eyal Weizman. *Investigative Aesthetics: Conflicts and Commons in the Politics of Truth.* New York and London: Verso, 2021.

Harney, Stefano & Fred Moten. *The Undercommons: Fugitive Planning and Black Study.* London: Minor Compositions, 2013.

Harris, Laura. 'What Happened to the Motley Crew: C.L.R. James, Helio Oiticica and the Aesthetic Sociality of Blackness', *Social Text* 112, vol. 30, no. 3 (Fall 2012), 49-75.

Hesse, Barnor. 'Diasporicity: Black Britain's Post-Colonial Formations', in *Un/Settled Multiculturalisms: Diasporas, Entanglement, 'Transruptions',* ed. Barnor Hesse. London and New York: Zed Books, 2000.

––– *Experiments in Exile: C.L.R. James, Helio Oiticica and the Aesthetic Sociality of Blackness,* New York: Fordham University Press, 2018.

Hecht, Gabrielle. 'Interscalar Vehicles for an African Anthropocene: On Waste, Temporality and Violence', *Cultural Anthropology* 33, no. 1 (2018).

Hesse, Barnor. 'White Sovereignty ( … ), Black Life Politics: 'The N****r They Couldn't Kill', *The South Atlantic Quarterly* 116, no. 3 (1 July, 2017).

Kalven, Jamie and Eyal Weizman, 'How Chicago Police Created A False Narrative After Officers Killed Harith Augustus'. *The Intercept,* 19 September, 2019. https://theintercept.com/2019/09/19/harith-augustus-shooting-chicago-police/, accessed 15 December 2023.

Mendes, Margarida. *Sensorial Ecologies: Sonic Literacy and Restorative Listening in Watery Worlds,* PhD in Research Architecture, Centre for Research Architecture, Goldsmiths University of London, 2022.

Moalemi, Mahan. 'The Geopolitical Ontology of the Post-optical Image: Notes on The Otolith Group's Sovereign Sisters', in *The Otolith Group: Xenogenesis,* eds. The Otolith Group and Megs Morley. Dublin and Berlin: Irish Museum of Modern Art and Archive Books, 2021.

Moten, Fred. 'Black Topological Existence', in *A Series of Utterly Improbable yet Extraordinary Renditions,* eds. Amira Gad and Joseph Constable. London: Serpentine Gallery, 2018.

Renwick, Daniel and Robbie Shilliam. *Squalor.* Newcastle upon Tyne: Agenda Publishing, 2022.

Spillers, Hortense J.. 'The Crisis of the Negro Intellectual: A Post-Date', in *Black, White and in Colour, Essays on American Literature and Culture.* Chicago and London: The University of Chicago and London, 2003.

Weheliye, Alexander G.. *Habeas Viscus: Racializing Assemblages, Biopolitics, and Black Feminist Theories of the Human.* Durham and London: Duke University Press, 2014.

## Images

Cover Image: Redlining Map of Chicago, Illinois, 1940. Image courtesy of the *Mapping Inequality: Redlining in New Deal America* project at the University of Richmond. https://dsl.richmond.edu/panorama/redlining/data/IL-Chicago#cityData.

Images from pages 26-37: Images captured from Forensic Architecture and the Invisible Institute, 'The Killing of Harith Augustus', 18 September 2019, https://forensic-architecture.org/investigation/the-killing-of-harith-augustus.

# WHAT WOULD A FEMINIST OPEN SOURCE INVESTIGATION LOOK LIKE?

## Sophie Dyer and Gabriela Ivens

### 'FROM LOOKS TO FEELINGS'

When my co-author, Gabriela Ivens, and I describe writing, "What would a feminist open source investigation look like?" we use expressions such as, "it wrote itself", to communicate the ease, force, and urgency with which the words came out of us. For both Gabi and I, the text was written during a period of uncertainty between stable jobs. Cowriting is not therapy but when resonant it can be the collective reprocessing of experiences and reorganising of thoughts in order to keep moving, to arrive somewhere new.

The article did not write itself but it was co-written with a polyphony of voices: feminists who came before us, contemporary mentors, allies, friends. In it, we quote American civil rights advocate Kimberlé Crenshaw's definition of intersectionality as, "an experience, an approach, and a problem".[1] The intersectional feminisms on which our text draws are approaches, practices, and projections. For me, as approaches, they articulate with clarity the harms that I had previously been unable to name, deconstruct or imagine otherwise. This feminist alchemy—turning hurt, anger, and disillusionment into propositions for doing work differently—was a joyful and meaning-making experience. The resulting article exists as an uneven map, a projection of the field of open source research in 2020. Like all maps, its design acts on and transforms the landscape it documents.

An early idea for this text was to rewrite the article completely. However, Gabriela and I concluded that, while new technologies continue to change open source research, the principles we discuss here remain relevant.[2] This is partly because they operate on a different register: that of politics, values, and ethics. Frustratingly, too, these principles remain relevant because the pace of progress at this register is begrudgingly slow. Incumbent ways of working, even in emergent fields, seemingly have deep roots.

If I were to rewrite this article today, I would update its title to, "What would a feminist open source investigation *feel* like?" *Look* is faithful to the inspiration for the paper, "What would a feminist data visualisation look like?" by Catherine D'Ignazio and Laura Klein. However, investigations can too easily look one way while being another. Put differently, their optics can be progressive (equitable, anti-racist, anti-colonial, …) while, to their subjects and workers, they can feel unnecessarily fraught and unfair.[3] A feminist open source investigation would not feel like exhaustion and disappointment. It would be angry, but that anger would be directed outward at the injustices of this world, not inward at the failed structures, procedures and priorities of today's workplaces.

I am writing from limited experience. After its publication, a group of nine women, queer and trans* workers in or adjacent to the field of open source

---

1   Kimberly Crenshaw quoted in Kathryn Norlock, 'Feminist Ethics,' Stanford Encyclopaedia of Philosophy, accessed 9 December 2019, plato.stanford.edu/entries/feminism-ethics/#Inte.
2   There was also the question of labour-time as non-academics, which I do not address here.
3   The roles "investigation subject" and "investigation worker" are not mutually exclusive.

research formed the Feminist Open Source Investigations Group, abbreviated to femOS.[4] This group's formation was unsolicited and temporary. We existed for each other as an informal alliance. We practised what Chicana tejana lesbian-feminist poet and scholar Gloria Anzaldúa calls "alliance work", that is the labour of identifying and shifting our individual and collective positions, and so what is considered possible.[5] We provided mutual support. The femOS met regularly online, and over the course of one year we, "shared our experiences of working on investigations and writing code; we […] discussed and defined our politics".[6] A core lesson in organising that I take with me from this experience, is how temporary alliances, be they cowriting or the formation of a collective, are no less valuable or transformative than those that endure.[7] After all, feminism asks us to accept endings or "quitting" in recognition of our and others' limits, and that all (alliance) work is sustainable only up to a point.

This article remains a pragmatic and feminist offering for how to do open source research otherwise. It was also always a tactical alliance. In addition to its nine provocations—in particular "Care for yourself"—consider the alliances that you are in or may want to form, and how they might provide mutual support, multiply your power, make-meaning.
Sophie Dyer, 2023

## INTRODUCTION

What would an explicitly feminist open source investigation look like? This is not a thought experiment nor an exercise to identify what is feminist and what is not. Rather, it is an action plan by a group of human rights and tech workers seeking to conduct open source investigations differently. Our aim is to apply feminist thought to open source investigations so as to question and reimagine what, in the last five years, have become dominant and default ways of working.

What follows is a response to the essay 'What would feminist data visualization look like?' by US-based data feminist Catherine D'Ignazio,[8] and the academic paper 'Feminist Data Visualization' co-authored by D'Ignazio with the digital humanities scholar, Lauren Klein.[9] Both texts look critically at the growing field of data visualisation and, in particular, at what was being designed, for whom and by whom. They offer a number of tangible ideas to help the reader imagine what a feminist data visualisation could look like. Our contribution is intended to offer the same for open source investigations.

First, what do we mean by 'open source'? After all, its meanings are multiple. In the context of an investigation, open source can refer to both a category

---

4   "trans*: Originally used to include explicitly both transsexual and transgender, or (now usually) to indicate the inclusion of gender identities such as gender-fluid, agender, etc., alongside transsexual and transgender." Oxford English Dictionary, "trans, adj., sense 2", July 2023, doi. org/10.1093/OED/2707920663.
5   Gloria Anzaldúa, 'Bridge, Drawbridge, Sandbar or Island: Lesbians-of-Color Hacienda Alianzas' in *Bridges of Power: Women's Multicultural Alliances*, eds. Lisa Albrecht, Rose M. Brewer, and Rose M. Brewer. (Philadelphia: New Society Publishers, 1990), 219.
6   'Feminist Open Source Group,' last modified January 2020, feministopensource.group.
7   Sasha Engelmann in discussion with the author, June 2023.
8   Catherine D'Ignazio, 'What would feminist data visualization look like?,' *Medium,* last modified 22 January 2017, medium.com/@kanarinka/what-would-feminist-data-visualization-look-like-aa3f8fc7f96c.
9   Catherine D'Ignazio, and Lauren F. Klein, 'Feminist Data Visualization,' Workshop on Visualization for the Digital Humanities (VIS4DH), Baltimore. IEEE., 2016.

of information and a methodology. Open source information is information in the public domain, obtained with overt methods, as opposed to information that is classified, private or obtained via covert means. The authors of the Berkeley Protocol on Digital Open Source Investigations define this information source as "public information that is accessible by observation, request or purchase and that requires neither illegal means nor special status (such as law enforcement status) to acquire".[10] As a methodology, open source is a grouping of techniques used to identify, collect, and analyse this public information.

Open source investigations offer radical, democratising possibilities for human rights fact-finding.[11] The attention they give to social and local media sources can centre the experiences of groups whose voices are too often heavily mediated, marginalised, or excluded in conventional reporting. For example, the non-governmental organisation (NGO) Syrian Archive used imagery posted on social media by 'civilian witnesses' otherwise cut off by conflict to investigate human rights violations in the ongoing Syrian civil war. The group's work informed media coverage of the conflict, aided criminal investigations and preserved over three million user-generated images and videos at risk of erasure.[12]

From data collection to analysis, a wide spectrum of participation has opened up the investigative space to digital volunteers, geographically dispersed activists and, in theory, anyone with an internet connection, desire, and time to contribute. In 2018, Amnesty International used microtasking to involve over 6,000 volunteers in its open source investigation into abuse against women on the social media platform Twitter. The volunteers marked tweets as abusive or not, to generate a labelled dataset of problematic content—a subset of which Amnesty used to train an algorithm to analyse millions of tweets, thus automating the process and building a case of negligence against the tech platform.[13] In the days after Amnesty's findings were published, Twitter's share price dropped by 12 per cent.[14]

Indeed, it is the leveraging of so-called 'user-generated content' to 'verify' and ultimately, to pitch the realities of marginalised groups against

---

10  Human Rights Center at the University of California, Berkeley, School of Law, *Berkeley Protocol on Digital Open Source Investigations* (New York, NY: United Nations and the Human Rights Center at the University of California, Berkeley, School of Law, 2022).

11  UN Human Rights Council, *Report of the Special Rapporteur on extrajudicial, summary or arbitrary executions, Christof Heyns: Use of information and communications technologies to secure the right to life* (Geneva: United Nations Human Rights Council, 2015): 6.

12  A 2018 investigation by Syrian Archive and Knack into the shipment from Europe to Syria of chemicals that can be used to produce chemical weapons resulted in the conviction of three Belgian companies that had violated EU sanctions law as well as an internal audit of the Belgian customs system. In 2019, Syrian Archive alongside TRIAL International and the Open Society Justice Initiative filed criminal complaints with prosecutors in Germany and Belgium to request that they open further investigations into the role of European companies in separate shipments of chemicals to Syria via Switzerland, which at the time had not been subject to EU sanctions. The requests were evidenced by open source information collected by the Syrian Archive. To date, the Syrian Archive has collected 3,578,591 digital records, of which 651,322 it has analysed and 8249 it has verified. Jeff Deutch, email to the authors, 4 March, 2020; 'Reported 2014 Chemical Shipments to Syria Raise Questions over EU Sanctions,' *Open Society Justice Initiative*, published 27 March 2019, justiceinitiative.org/newsroom/reported-2014-chemical-shipments-to-syria-raise-questions-over-eu-sanctions.

13  'Troll Patrol Findings,' *Amnesty Decoders*, Amnesty International, accessed 17 January 2020, decoders.amnesty.org/projects/troll-patrol/findings.

14  Todd Spangler, 'Twitter Stock Tumbles After Analyst Calls It 'Harvey Weinstein of Social Media',' *Variety*, 20 December, 2018, variety.com/2018/digital/news/twitter-stock-harvey-weinstein-social-media-1203094020/.

those touted by powerful corporations, governments, or militaries, which gives open source a revolutionary feel. In a 'post-truth world' where trust in institutions as fact bearers has been significantly eroded, open source methods present an "alternative set of truth practices".[15]

However, with these opportunities come serious ethical challenges. Within the open source investigator's toolbox are methods of surveillance including applications developed for the online tracking and near-real-time monitoring of anyone of interest to an investigation without their knowing. This includes tools developed to uncover barely visible and thus arguably barely public information, or techniques designed to capitalise on the 'mosaic effect'—that is the piecing together of data from different open sources to reveal new information, only indirectly public. "One person's open source investigation could be another person's 'doxxing'", note Rahmen and Ivens in *Digital Witness*.[16]

Representation is also at stake. "Open source research has the potential to profoundly affect not just whose stories get told, but also who gets to tell those stories, and who will listen to them", write Yvonne McDermott, Daragh Murray and Alexa Koenig of the OSR4Rights research group.[17] Representation issues range from an over reliance on whose voices are already heard in a "cacophonous social media environment" to the types of violations reported and the prioritisation by NGOs of violations presumed to be suited to open source investigations.[18] In a conversation with the authors, writer, researcher and former Deputy Director of the Engine Room, Zara Rahman, stresses the consequences of these dynamics: "Essentially, what is shown to the world by an investigation is shaped by the people with the most power, and these people are almost certainly not the people who are represented in the data, or who generated the data".[19] Crucially, for Rahman, representation issues in open source are rooted in power relations or more specifically the asymmetries that define them.

## ESTABLISHING
## NEW WAYS OF WORKING

Despite these ethical dilemmas, open source investigations—perhaps due to their perceived newness or revolutionary promise—have been afforded a lot of space to push the boundaries of what's possible, to make mistakes and to mature slowly. Open source tools, techniques and the communities

---

15  Eyal Weizman, 'Open Verification', *e-flux*, June 2019, e-flux.com/architecture/becoming-digital/248062/open-verification/.

16  "Doxxing is searching for and publishing identifying information about someone, typically with malicious intent to threaten, silence or do real harm"–Zara Rahman, and Gabriela Ivens, 'Ethics in Open Source Investigations' in *Digital Witness: Using Open Source Information for Human Rights Investigation, Documentation, and Accountability*, eds. Sam Dubberley, Alexa Koenig, and Daragh Murray (Oxford: Oxford University Press, 2020), 251.

17  Yvonne McDermott, Daragh Murray, and Alexa Koenig, 'Digital accountability symposium: Whose stories get told, and by whom? Representativeness in open source human rights investigations,' *Opinio Juris*, 19 December 2019, opiniojuris.org/2019/12/19/digital-accountability-symposium-whose-stories-get-told-and-by-whom-representativeness-in-open-source-human-rights-investigations/.

18  McDermott, Murray, and Koenig,'Digital accountability symposium: Whose stories get told, and by whom? Representativeness in open source human rights investigations.'

19  Zara Rahman, email to authors, 6 January 2020.

formed around them have evolved rapidly over the last five years. From a lone sleuth working in their bedroom to an employee operating within a large team for a media outlet or human rights organisation, there are few formalised and accepted guidelines concerning what is legally or morally permissible in the space of an open source investigation. In certain circles, open source investigation is seen as the Wild West—a new, disembodied digital frontier where anything goes, especially in social media research.

Our impressions are not isolated—the need for ethical codes, protocols and other standards is already being discussed. For example, the Human Rights Center at the University of Berkeley, California is spearheading a collaborative effort to develop a Berkeley Protocol on Digital Open Source Investigations alongside other human rights-based approaches introduced by many of the larger NGOs that are working to integrate open source practices with traditional research methods.[20]

Although welcomed, current efforts largely focus on investigations working within human rights, that is, legal frameworks. In our view, if the radical, democratising potential of open source investigations is to centre the experiences of marginalised or underrepresented populations typically underserved or excluded from judicial forms of justice and accountability, it is vital that we give attention to investigations working outside legal systems in the pursuit of non-judicial forms of social justice.

In 'From Human Rights to Feminist Ethics: Radical Empathy in the Archives', Michelle Caswell and Marika Cifor define social justice as:

*[The] ideal vision that every human being is of equal and incalculable value, entitled to shared standards of freedom, equality, and respect. These standards also apply to broader social aggregations such as communities and cultural groups. Violations of these standards must be acknowledged and confronted. It specifically draws attention to inequalities of power and how they manifest in institutional arrangements and systemic inequities that further the interests of some groups at the expense of others in the distribution of material goods, social benefits, rights, protections, and opportunities. Social justice is always a process and can never be fully achieved.*[21]

If social justice beyond legal frameworks is an inherently an open-ended and "incalculable" process, we ask: what can *feminist thought* bring to open source investigations that a human rights-based approach might not?

20  United Nations and Human Rights Center at the University of California, Berkeley, School of Law, *Berkeley Protocol on Digital Open Source Investigations*; Alexa Koenig, 'Harnessing Social Media as Evidence of Grave International Crimes,' *Human Rights Center, Medium*, 23 October 2017, medium.com/humanrightscenter/harnessing-social-media-as-evidence-of-grave-international-crimes-d7f3e86240d; Ashish Kumar Sen, 'Wanted: A code of ethics for open source researchers,' *Atlantic Council*, 20 June 2019, atlanticcouncil.org/blogs/new-atlanticist/wanted-a-code-of-ethics-for-open-source-researchers/.

21  Michelle Caswell, and Marika Cifor, 'From Human Rights To Feminist Ethics: Radical Empathy In The Archives,' *Archivaria* 81, no. 1 (2016): 26. For the original source of the definition see Wendy M. Duff, Andrew Flinn, Karen Emily Suurtamm, and David A. Wallace, 'Social Justice Impact of Archives: A Preliminary Investigation,' *Archival Science* 13 (2013): 317–348.

## OPEN SOURCE INVESTIGATIONS
## ARE ABOUT POWER RELATIONS,
## SO TOO IS FEMINISM

For decades feminist scholars and activists have worked to problematise unequal power relations and to find ways to resist and transform them. Simply put, feminism "is about power—who has it and who doesn't".[22]

By feminist thought, we mean specifically intersectional feminist thought. Intersectional feminism looks beyond gender to ask how race, class, sexuality, religion, ability and much more, determine our total experience of the world. The authors of this paper, for instance, are two white, native English speaking practitioners based in Western Europe, with higher education degrees. All of these factors and our positionality contribute to the reality that our voices are the ones being heard here, and with them our biases, understanding and outlooks.[23]

The term has existed since the late 1980s when it was used by the critical race scholar and lawyer, Kimberlé Crenshaw in a US court case. Crenshaw used the image of a traffic intersection to describe how her client, a Black woman, had experienced workplace discrimination both because she was Black and a woman.[24] In other words, as a Black woman, Crenshaw's client faced a kind of compounded oppression different from that faced by a white woman or a Black man.

For Crenshaw, intersectionality was "an experience, an approach, and a problem". Since, it has developed as a powerful analytic for naming and challenging compounded power and privilege—or as Black feminist Patricia Hill Collins calls it, the "matrix of domination". At the same time, the intersectional feminist movement has often failed to hold space for our Black and Brown sisters, perpetuating instead the logics and limits of white feminism. Though a thorough engagement with the movement's critiques and failures is beyond the scope of this essay, we invite readers to engage further with works by writers Reni Eddo-Lodge,[25] Tamela J. Gordon,[26] Ashlee Christoffersen and Akwugo Emejulu.[27] Keeping these possibilities and limitations in mind, what can open source investigators learn from a long history of intersectional feminist scholarship and activism?

One tool in the intersectional feminist's toolbox is *equity*. "Equity is different than equality", states the manifesto of 'The Global Open Science Hardware (GOSH)' movement. "Equity recognises that everyone does not start from the same position and so treating everyone the same may leave them in the same uneven positions they began in".[28] In other words, calling attention

22  Catherine D'Ignazio, and Lauren F. Klein, 'Introduction' in *Data Feminism,* The MIT Press open access @ PubPub, 6 November, 2018. bookbook.pubpub.org/data-feminism.

23  Linda Alcoff, "Cultural Feminism Versus Post-structuralism: The Identity Crisis In Feminist Theory," *Signs: Journal of Women in Culture and Society* 13, no. 3 (1988): 405–436.

24  Kimberlé Crenshaw, "Demarginalizing the Intersection of Race and Sex: A Black Feminist Critique of Antidiscrimination Doctrine, Feminist Theory and Antiracist Politics," *University of Chicago Legal Forum*, vol. 1, no. 8 (1989): 138–67.

25  Reni Eddo-Lodge, *Why I'm No Longer Talking to White People about Race* (London: Bloomsbury Publishing, 2018).

26  Tamela J. Gordon, 'Why I'm giving up on intersectional feminism,' *Quartz,* 30 April 2018, https://qz.com/quartzy/1265902/why-im-giving-up-on-intersectional-feminism.

27  Ashlee Christofferson, Akwugo Emjulu, "Diversity Within": The Problems with "Intersectional" White Feminism in Practice,' *Social Politics: International Studies in Gender, State & Society* 30, no. 2, (Summer 2023): 630-653.

28  'GOSH Code of Conduct,' GOSH Gathering for Open Science Hardware, accessed 9 December 2019, openhardware.science/gosh-2017/gosh-code-of-conduct/.

to how power is unevenly distributed and then treating everyone involved in an investigation in the same way will not bring about sustainable change. To achieve change in the long term, we must practice equity.

How can we illustrate this approach? In the words of the Newfoundland-based feminist and anti-colonial science lab 'Civic Laboratory for Environmental Action Research (CLEAR)', the application of feminist thought to a professional space "isn't about getting more women, people of colour, and Indigenous people into science—that would be inviting people into a space that is already stacked against them".[29] Instead, the idea is to change how the work is done "so that different world views, values, and ethics are the basis for knowledge production, which also happens to make the field a better place for women, people of colour, Indigenous peoples, queers, and people with disabilities".[30]

The following provocations expand upon these ideas through practical questions and examples. Of the three section headers, the first two are borrowed, with permission, from the original article by D'Ignazio. The provocations are by no means exhaustive. Rather, they are an invitation to be built upon, debated, and remixed.

### INVENT NEW WAYS TO REPRESENT UNCERTAINTY, OUTSIDES, MISSING DATA, AND FLAWED METHODS

Objectivity and presenting the 'whole truth' matter greatly in open source investigations that, understood as *an alternative set of truth practices* or epistemologies, must win trust through demonstrating technical competency and impartiality. Feminist objectivity "is about limited location and situated knowledge", writes the feminist scientist Haraway.[31] In short, all knowledge comes from somewhere and is incomplete in some way, and more specifically, all investigations contain ambiguities, outsides and "missing data".[32] As such, "an argument for situated and embodied knowledges" is "an argument against various forms of unlocatable, and so irresponsible, knowledge claims. Irresponsible means unable to be called into account".[33] The recommendations that follow, question the language of trust and verification that is inherently bound up with claims of objectivity.

### SITUATE YOUR FINDINGS

All research is situated within a community of practice that has its own "axiology (morals, values, and ethics)".[34] It helps to think of investigations as a string of decisions that enact these morals, values, and ethics. Seemingly innocuous, technical decisions such as "acts of tagging, indexing, aggregating and defining of data and data categories are inherently political", write members of

---

29  CLEAR, 'Feminist and Anti-colonial Science', *Civic Laboratory for Environmental Action Research (CLEAR)*, accessed 15 November 2019, civiclaboratory.nl/citizen-science.

30  CLEAR, 'Feminist and Anti-colonial Science'.

31  Donna Haraway, 'Situated Knowledges: The Science Question in Feminism and the Privilege of Partial Perspective,' *Feminist Studies* 14, no. 3 (1988): 583.

32  For more on missing data, see 'The Library of Missing Datasets' project by Nigerian-American artist and researcher Mimi Onuoha, mimionuoha.com.

33  Haraway, 'Situated Knowledges: The Science Question in Feminism and the Privilege of Partial Perspective,' 583.

34  CLEAR, 'Feminist and Anti-colonial Science'.

Syrian Archive.[35] These acts are political because certain values and interests are reproduced and amplified, while others are not.

Is it possible to communicate that an investigation's findings are not the 'whole picture', and for this to strengthen rather than weaken confidence in them? A large part of situating findings is documenting and publishing the decisions made along the way, along with the reasons they were made.

For example, a video report of an investigation into a United States drone strike in Mir Ali, Pakistan by the London-based group Forensic Architecture merges the presentation of the findings with documentation of how they were reached. The investigation used an all source (as opposed to open source) technique developed by the Forensic Architecture called "situated testimony", which employs "3D models of the scenes and environments in which traumatic events occurred, to aid in the process of interviewing".[36]

From behind, the camera captures the investigators, the witness and a 3D modeller, backlit by the computer graphic they are working on. A voiceover tells us that the witness "is hoping to communicate the realities of life under drones, and the experience of surviving a strike in which she also lost her brother in law".[37] We hear the witness' dialogue with the investigators and see her hand-drawn sketch of the building compound. The video is documentation of a positive feedback loop within the investigative process—it seems that the more the witness models, the more she recalls. "Without the plan", she says, referring to the 3D visualisation, "I could not have remembered". The video report successfully situates Forensic Architecture's findings by laying bare the technical (such as 3D modelling and satellite imagery analysis) and subjective (such as memory, interview, and interpretation) processes that combine to generate the high-resolution, 3D reconstruction of the drone strike that is shown at the end of the video. Without this insight, the accuracy and purpose of such a sophisticated visualisation could easily be misread.

### SHOW YOUR WORKINGS

When we understand how facts are made, where their weaknesses lie, and what are the limits of what can be said, we can better construct and defend them.[38]

An investigation's methodology is the counterpart to its findings. A good methodology not only provides a history of actions taken, invites critique and makes the results potentially replicable—importantly, it also engages with the unknowns and problematises the research and its politics. In other words, it helps illuminate the where, why and how of knowledge production. For instance, in a data-driven open source investigation the methodology could engage with: the provenance of the data; the decisions behind the data; the stakeholders represented; the data not included in the investigation and the reasons why; the rationale behind why the findings were presented in a particular way.

35   Jeff Deutch, and Hadi Habal, 'The Syrian Archive: A Methodological Case Study of Open-source Investigation of State Crime Using Video Evidence From Social Media Platforms.' *State Crime J.* 7 (2018): 46–76.
36   'Situated Testimony,' Forensic Architecture, accessed 18 January 2019, forensic-architecture.org/methodology/situated-testimony.
37   'Drone Strike In Mir Ali,' Forensic Architecture, 16 April 2013, forensic-architecture.org/investigation/drone-strike-in-mir-ali.
38   Eyal Weizman, 'Open Verification,' *e-flux*, June 2019, e-flux.com/architecture/becoming-digital/248062/open-verification/.

In doing so, this methodology not only focuses on how certain conclusions were reached but also, vitally, on the fact that the data which supports them connects to real bodies, real systems and real power structures in the wider world.

Digital reconstruction of a US drone strike which hit a home in Mir Ali, North Waziristan, Pakistan, killing five people. One of the surviving witnesses, pictured, worked with Forensic Architecture in Dusseldorf to build a digital model of her former home. 16 April 2013. Source: Forensic Architecture.

A rendered scene from within the digital reconstruction of the witness' home. 16 April 2013. Source: Forensic Architecture.

## DESIGN FOR AMBIGUITY

Open source investigations engage with real-world 'muddy data' and uncertainties. Working with unconventional sources, often at scale, means handling documentation that can vary hugely in medium, format, resolution, and verifiability. Is it possible to design for different kinds of knowledge and the diverse ambiguities they present, throughout the investigative process?

For instance, it is essential to critically reflect on the legitimisation and the practices of verification—the technique of authenticating a source or information. Verification is an essential process in open source investigations but the language that surrounds it is normative, which is to say, something is either verified or not verified. What are the standards that determine if a source or a piece of documentation is verified? Who decides these standards and who implements them? Importantly, for whom—perhaps external to the investigation team—could these decisions have a negative impact on? Experimenting with gradiented verification or finding new ways to include materials that can neither be verified nor disproved by the investigator, is another way to work with, not against, ambiguities. Or, to "stay with the trouble!" as Donna Haraway might say.[39]

For example, the London-based civilian casualty monitor Airwars uses gradiented verification in its assessments of local reports of civilian casualties from US-led Coalition airstrikes in Iraq and Syria. The NGO's verification system, which ranges from "Confirmed" (conceded by a belligerent) and "Fair" (multiple, credible sources) to "Weak" (single source) and "Discounted", allows it to maintain a public record of all allegations. Tens of civilian deaths from incidents initially assessed by the NGO as Weak have been subsequently conceded by the military Coalition. Had Airwars excluded these incidents because they could not be fully verified, the civilian deaths might never have been investigated.[40]

Such an approach recognises that a high occurrence of unverifiable sources or materials can be evidence of the conditions of reporting, methods of data collection or the position of the investigator (as in geographic, temporal, linguistic or cultural) vis-à-vis the subjects of the investigation. Also, it could simply be indicative of the limits of the investigation (as in resources, time, or expertise).

Outwardly, the language of verification matters greatly because of its effect on the integrity and persuasiveness of an investigation's findings. As such, it should be treated with extreme care. For example, in the process of geolocation, a landmark similar to one depicted in a user generated video is identified in satellite imagery. Should the landmark in the video be labelled "the same as" or "consistent with" the visually similar landmark in the satellite imagery? Put differently, how can ambiguity be communicated? Would the phrase "consistent with" make the findings less persuasive or, in fact, could it improve their integrity by increasing their transparency?

The visual language of verification is no less important. Indeed, the 'coloured box culture' of open source verification (in which coloured boxes are drawn around landmarks to show how they recur in different images) is both effective and, arguably, overused. Is there a clearer or more nuanced way to communicate that the images presented do not "speak for themselves" and that they are interpretations which may require extra or expert knowledge to be read?[41]

39  Donna Haraway, *Staying with the Trouble: Making Kin in the Chthulucene*
    (Durham: Duke University Press, 2016), 1.
40  'Civilian Casualties,' Airwars, accessed 28 August 2019, airwars.org/civilian-casualties.
41  Laura Kurgan, *Close Up at a Distance: Mapping, Technology, and Politics*
    (Cambridge, MA: MIT Press, 2013), 25.

### INVENT NEW WAYS TO REFERENCE
### AND ADDRESS THE MATERIAL ECONOMY
### BEHIND THE DATA AND INVESTIGATION

There are deep disparities in power, risk and reward between the actors who populate open source investigations—from lead investigators to junior researchers, to the people represented in the research and to those responsible for communicating the findings. In short, open source investigators risk reproducing the very power asymmetries they seek to unsettle.[42]

Some of these power differentials are visible. They may be evident in the choice of investigative topic, the makeup of the investigative teams, or the choice of digital tools and mechanisms for participation in investigations which too often exclude those unable to digitally contribute. Are the people who generated the data or documentation absent from its final representation? Are they thus less likely to receive attention and funding?

The responsibility to recognise and address the disparity in power lies with more than the investigators and researchers. Funders themselves can incentivise poor practice by overvaluing what is new and innovative while overlooking the less glamorous aspects of investigative work such as the maintenance of tools and databases or the routine upkeep of servers and other hardware. At the same time, NGOs who engage in more traditional human rights work can be pressured by funders to have a digital component to their investigations in order to keep up with what is perceived to be 'state of the art'.[43] McDermott, Murray and Koenig note how "this is deeply concerning, particularly for those organisations that do not have the capacity (in terms of time, money, expertise, and technological capacity) and inclination to engage with the difficult processes of collection and verification of open source evidence".[44]

### PRACTICE EQUITY IN ATTRIBUTION

In not-so-subtle ways, attribution reproduces power relations both internal and external to the investigation team. Giving credit to those who have contributed to an investigation is an important part of referencing and acknowledging the labour that made it possible, particularly since credit is currency when it comes to future employment or funding opportunities.[45] As D'Ignazio and Klein note, "making labor visible" has particular pertinence "in light of the fact that women and other underrepresented groups have been notoriously excluded from sharing in credit for scientific work".[46] The same could be said for the predominantly male fields of journalism and technology in which many

---

42  Rahman, and Ivens, 'Ethics in Open Source Investigations'.
43  McDermott, Murray, and Koenig, 'Digital accountability symposium: Whose stories get told and by whom? Representativeness in open source human rights investigations'.
44  McDermott, Murray, and Koenig, 'Digital accountability symposium: Whose stories get told and by whom? Representativeness in open source human rights investigations'.
45  See CLEAR, 'Feminist and Anti-colonial Science'.
46  D'Ignazio, and Klein, 'Feminist Data Visualization,' 3.

open source investigators work.[47, 48]

Crediting who worked on which part of an investigation, whose data made it possible and whose tools and methodologies were used is a start. However, practicing equity in attribution means questioning not only who contributed but what counts as a contribution. In other words, what is understood and valued as labour, throughout an investigation–or, as the community technologist Rigoberto Lara Guzmán, and the anthropologist Sareeta Amrute, argue in 'How to Cite Like a Badass Tech Feminist Scholar of Color' practicing equity requires "unsettling" entrenched ideas of who during an investigation is a research subject and who is an "expert".[49]

For instance, who developed the tools, systems, and workflows an investigation is reliant on?; who translated the research materials?; which local contacts were the investigation dependent on and who sent essential information?

Since 2016, a US-based group called the Information Maintainers, has worked to acknowledge and better resource the unglamorous task of caring for information, and importantly, caring for the carers.[50] For the Information Maintainers, care could be understood as repair, maintenance, and attention. Perhaps comparably, for CLEAR, care is "a form of political and ethical practice that 'holds things together'".[51] In the context of an open source investigation, care work or holding things together encompasses a diverse range of tasks from tool building, data cleaning and file archiving to updating and fixing code as well as the maintenance of servers and other hardware perhaps long after the investigation findings have been published. Other tasks that count as care work include supporting colleagues and volunteers both informally and formally through training and reviews, organising meetings, sending email reminders, thanking people, listening to concerns voiced and taking them seriously and so on.

Open source investigations into humanitarian crises or conflicts often involve sustained work with graphic or otherwise distressing content. In this context, care work is heightened, and its acknowledgment can feel particularly important because of the emotional labour involved.

47    Roger Smith, 'Gender pay gap in the UK: 2019,' Office for National Statistics, published
      October 29, 2019, ons.gov.uk/employmentandlabourmarket/peopleinwork/earningsandwork-
      inghours/bulletins/genderpaygapintheuk/2019.
48    In the UK in 2019, on average in journalism women earned 11.2 per cent less than men and
      held 40% of jobs; in programming and software development female professionals earned
      6.8% less than male professionals and held only 12 per cent of jobs; in information technology
      female professionals earned 7.1 per cent less than male professionals and held 18 per cent of
      jobs. The same cannot be said for law, another field that open source investigators work in. In
      2019, female legal professionals held over half of all jobs yet earned on average 16.8 per cent
      less than their male peers. Smith, 'Gender pay gap in the UK: 2019,'.
49    Rigoberto Lara Guzmán, and Sareeta Amrute, 'How to Cite Like a Badass Tech Feminist
      Scholar of Color,' *Data & Society: Points, Medium*, 22 August 2019, points.datasociety.net/
      how-to-cite-like-a-badass-tech-feminist-scholar-of-color-ebc839a3619c.
50    The Information Maintainers, Devon Olson, Jessica Meyerson, Mark Parsons, Juliana Castro,
      Monique Lassere, Dawn Wright, Hillel Arnold, et al., "Information Maintenance as a Practice
      of Care: An Invitation to Reflect and Share," *Zenodo*, 17 June 2019.
51    Maria Puig de La Bellacasa,'Matters of Care in Technoscience: Assembling Neglected
      Things,' *Social Studies of Science* 41, no. 1 (2011): 85–106; Max Liboiron, Justine Ammendo-
      lia, Katharine Winsor, Alex Zahara, Hillary Bradshaw, Jessica Melvin, and Charles Mather et al.
      'Equity In Author Order: A Feminist Laboratory's Approach,' *Catalyst: Feminism, Theory, Tech-
      noscience* 3, no. 2 (2017): 1–17; Aryn Martin, Natasha Myers, and Ana Viseu, 'The Politics of
      Care In Technoscience,' *Social Studies of Science* 45, no. 5 (2015): 625–641.

In this vein, CLEAR published the paper 'Equity in Author Order Protocol' which lays out a number of standards transferable to open source investigations. The protocol covers principles such as agreeing by consensus-based decision making as a way to (re)distribute power, considering care work as a form of labour and, when all seems equal, considering the "different social markers associated with oppression and privilege for different groups of people".[52] In the context of open source investigations, it could be helpful to ask the following questions adapted from CLEAR's guidelines:

— Who needs the capital of attribution more?
— Consider the immediate and long-term impact of attribution.
— Which unsung or underfunded groups do you want
   to promote or highlight?
— Is this a unique opportunity for particular people to be recognised?
— Who is being paid, underpaid, or unpaid for this work?[53]

## FIND NEW WAYS OF LOOKING AFTER OURSELVES AND OTHERS

A critical feminist ethics of care focuses on the moral challenge of listening attentively to all of those whose needs exist, intertwined, in a given time and place. While we cannot respond to all of the needs of everyone, the task is to judge with care by considering who will be harmed or isolated by our actions or policies in a given, particular context.[54]

There has been a clear shift in the language around open source investigations away from the Hippocratic Oath copy-and-paste principle of "do no harm" towards a more realistic principle of harm reduction.[55] The shift, echoed in related fields such as digital security, acknowledges that the potentially harmful impacts of open source investigations are continually evolving in ways that are unknowable.[56] As such, the obligation to mitigate against harm must also evolve. Such an approach is recognition that using novel investigatory techniques and tools makes possible harms harder to predict.

## CARE FOR YOURSELF

In the words of African-American lesbian poet, librarian, and activist Audre Lorde, "caring for myself is not self-indulgence, it is self-preservation, and that is an act of political warfare".[57] Open source investigative techniques are often used in moments of violent conflict or crisis. Investigators will analyse events at a granular level: poring over the documentation—watching, reading, hearing the violence—indirectly experiencing them. This can lead to vicarious trauma, a response to the accumulation of exposure to the pain experienced by others.

---

52  CLEAR, 'Equity in Author Order,' Civic Laboratory for Environmental Action Research (CLEAR), 23 May 2016, civiclaboratory.nl/2016/05/23/equity-in-author-order.
53  Max Liboiron, Justine Ammendolia, Katharine Winsor, Alex Zahara, Hillary Bradshaw, Jessica Melvin, Charles Mather, et al., 'Equity In Author Order: A Feminist Laboratory's Approach,' *Catalyst: Feminism, Theory, Technoscience* 3, no. 2 (2017).
54  Fiona Robinson, 'A Feminist Practical Ethics of Care,' in *The Oxford Handbook of International Political Theory*, eds. Chris Brown, and Robyn Eckersley (Oxford: Oxford University Press 2018), 7.
55  One of the leaders of the discussion around 'harm reduction' has been Alexa Koenig at the Human Rights Center at the University of Berkeley, California.
56  The Engine Room, 'Ties That Bind: Organisational Security for Civil Society,' The Engine Room, published March 07, 2019, theengineroom.org/civil-society-digital-security-new-research/.
57  Audre Lorde, *A Burst of Light: And Other Essays* (Mineola: Dover Publications, 2017), 130.

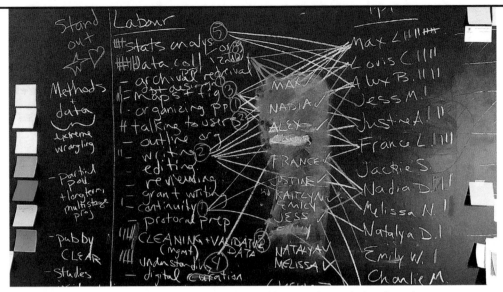

Traces of the Civic Laboratory for Environmental Action Research's approach to equity in author order.
Image courtesy of CLEAR. Creative Commons Attribution-ShareAlike 4.0 International.

Both personal strategies and institutional shifts in approaches can have profound reductions in developing vicarious trauma. First Draft News and Eyewitness Media Hub have published a series of guides on reducing vicarious trauma when working with distressing material.[58] Importantly, by caring for yourself you are not only looking after yourself but also creating space for others to care for themselves.

Talking about care or psychosocial resilience in open source investigations can be met with resistance. Alexa Koenig, the Executive Director of the Human Rights Center at the University of Berkeley, California, for example, counters this in resiliency and professional training through including care within a holistic security framework. "I explain that security in open source activities is tripartite—physical, digital and psychosocial", writes Alexa, "and that they are like overlapping Venn diagrams. When one is affected, the other two usually are as well".[59]

### LET EMPATHY INFORM DECISIONS

Radical empathy is... a learned process of direct and deep connection between the self and another that emphasises human commonality through "thinking and feeling into the minds of others".[60]

Those generating data may have very little control of how it is used in an investigation. In this section, we question the ethics of representation and of consent, or more often a lack of consent. Who decides how a video is used and shared? These decisions are rarely made by the person who is in the video or the person who made the video. Nevertheless, it is the person represented or the person carrying out on the ground work whose safety is potentially affected, possibly without their awareness or ability to consent.

---

58  See Sam Dubberley, Elizabeth Griffin, and Haluk Mert Bal, 'Making Secondary Trauma a Primary Issue: A Study of Eyewitness Media and Vicarious Trauma on the Digital Frontline,' Eyewitness Media Hub, accessed 17 January 2019, eyewitnessmediahub.com/research/vicarious-trauma
59  Alexa Koenig, email to the authors, 29 December 2019.
60  Caswell and Cifor, 'From Human Rights To Feminist Ethics: Radical Empathy In The Archives,' 30.

The questions below, adapted from Caswell and Cifor's article, are intended as a guide to applying radical empathy to decision making in open source investigations. As Caswell and Cifor explain, it is not only the record creator but the subject of the record, the user of the record or the wider community that might have conflicting wishes. In order to address this, "in a feminist approach, each one of these parties is considered empathetically and in relation to each other and to dominant power structures before archival decisions are made".[61]

— What are the desires and needs of the record creators?
  Would they want this material to be used in this way?
  Would they want this material to be preserved indefinitely?
— When highlighting a record or data set: what are the consequences
  for those not being highlighted or represented? Who might be
  silenced by an investigation?
— When publishing an investigation what are the personal consequences
  or affective experiences of those featured in the reporting? For example,
  in an investigation into destruction of houses, what will the impact be on
  those who might be finding out their house is destroyed through the published investigation? Building this into an investigation can be as simple as
  giving those affected the time and space to be heard, both in the research
  process and presentation of the findings. Indeed, at the core of procedural
  justice literature is the idea that most people just want to be heard, and
  fairly so, even when decisions are made contrary to their wishes.[62]

### "PRIORITISE THOSE PROXIMATE!"

"Prioritise those proximate!" urges D'Ignazio over a Skype call during the research for this article.[63] How can the needs, well-being and safety of those most proximate to the violence being investigated be prioritised at every stage of an open source investigation?

*Whose privacy is a concern?*
Will the investigation dramatically increase or alter the visibility of people featured in the investigation or otherwise proximate to it and how? It is different to propel into scrutiny—even positively—a tweet from an account with under 50 followers, compared to one with over 1000 followers. It is reasonable to suspect that an account holder with over 1000 followers will have less privacy expectations than that of an account holder with 50 followers. If included in an investigation's findings, how can the Tweets be handled differently? Another approach increasingly taken by news outlets is to embed tweets into online articles rather than saving and uploading the content, thus providing the authors of the tweet with the option to delete it or change the privacy settings.

*Who can access the published report?*
Publish in the language(s) of the sources, people and places featured in an investigation. This is critical for names that require transliteration between languages such as Arabic and English as one name can be transliterated in mul-

61   Caswell and Cifor, 'From Human Rights To Feminist Ethics: Radical Empathy In The Archives,' 34.
62   Alexa Koenig, email to the authors, 29 December 2019.
63   Catherine D'Ignazio, email to the authors, 03 September 2019.

tiple ways, making it hard to trace. Resources are often scarce by the end of an investigation, so budget from the beginning for professional translation and the skill sets needed to produce materials in multiple languages. How accessible is the report, really? In 2019 half of the world's population did not use the internet, and women, disabled and Indigenous people were overrepresented in this group. Consider alternative ways to circulate findings offline, such as posting physical copies to individuals or communities affected by the events documented in an investigation or, if appropriate, organising in-person meetings or organising a local event. For example, when Forensic Architecture was invited to conduct an investigation into the police killing of Mark Duggan, a young black man whose death was a catalyst for the 2011 London riots, the group chose to present their findings at a community event held in Duggan's local borough of Tottenham before publishing details online. Investigative protocols from other specialisms are transferable. The Argentine Forensic Anthropology Team (*Equipo Argentino de Antropología Forense*) has developed a notification protocol designed to prioritise the needs, well-being and safety of the family members of the disappeared or missing people, who the group have identified the remains of.[64]

**Forensic Architecture** ✓
@ForensicArchi

Our investigation of the 2011 police killing of Mark Duggan, undertaken on behalf the the family's legal team, will be first presented to the community in North London (open time all).
eventbrite.co.uk/e/mark-duggan-... @EventbriteUK

Mark Duggan - The Truth The Whole Truth & Nothing But The Truth
The Killing of Mark Duggan - The TRUTH the Whole TRUTH & Nothing But The
TRUTH The MPS recently agreed to settle a claim brought by Mark's family ...
🔗 eventbrite.co.uk

"Where there is no justice, there is just us!" Stafford Scott, event organiser and campaigner. An invitation, tweeted by Forensic Architecture, to the community event for the investigation into the police killing of Mark Duggan. Screenshot dated 24 November 2019, reproduced here with permission from Forensic Architecture.

64   The Argentine Forensic Anthropology Team notification protocol includes "the compilation, data verification, and review of all case materials prior to scheduling a notification; the completion of an integrated, multidisciplinary identification report in the family's language; risk assessment of the family receiving a notification, be it health related or threat from other persons; conducting the notification in person with the family; providing psychological and medical support; and explaining the repatriation process, among others." Carmen E. Osorno Solís, Mercedes Doretti, and Karla Hernandez, 'A144 Identification Notifications and Their Applicability to Families of Missing Migrants,' 2016.

*Who might need different care in an investigative team?*
Trauma is an intersectional issue. More considerate, thoughtful, and sustainable ways of working might be necessary for those in the team who may have already experienced trauma themselves, generationally or have a personal connection to the subject of an investigation. For example, through the Digital Verification Corps set up by Amnesty in 2016, the NGO has worked with six universities and their students on open source investigations, often on the verification of graphic or distressing user-generated content. The diverse backgrounds of the student investigators' have been critical to the project's success. Mindful of the special circumstances and that the students manage other commitments and pressures alongside the work, Amnesty has paid particular attention to the psychosocial aspects of investigations and worked to train the groups and their coordinators to prevent and identify vicarious stress and trauma in themselves and each other.[65]

## IN LIEU OF A CONCLUSION

These provocations are a sample of how intersectional feminist thought and activism can aid open source investigators in reimagining ways of working. The article is an invitation to share experiences, reflections and ideas. As D'Ignazio and Klein note, feminism is one approach that intersects with and is informed by other social justice movements—including Queer, anti-racism, anti-ableism, Indigenous and anticolonial—and their specific bodies of knowledge.

## Acknowledgements

The original article was a response to 'What would feminist data visualization look like?' by Catherine D'Ignazio, which became the book "Data Feminism" co-authored with Lauren F. Klein. Some of the structure of D'Ignazio's paper has been retained. This article also draws on ideas discussed in the writing of 'Ethics in Open Source Investigations' co-authored by Zara Rahman with Ivens for *Digital Witness*. We thank our reviewers for their generosity (in alphabetical order): Leenah Bassouni, Rebecca Echevarria, Alexa Koenig, Martyna Marciniak, and Zara Rahman. We are grateful to Piper Haywood for her copy editing. We owe a debt of gratitude to former members of the Feminist Open Source Investigations Group: thank you for community reviewing the article in 2020 and its preface in 2023. In particular, Toby Chai whose words open this chapter. We are thankful to Matthew Battles, Jeff Deutch, and Robert Trafford for their insights during the research process.

65   See the blog run by the Evidence Lab at Amnesty International, citizenevidence.org.

## Works Cited

Airwars. 'Civilian Casualties.' Accessed 28 August 2019. airwars.org/civilian-casualties.

Alcoff, Linda. 'Cultural Feminism Versus Post-structuralism: The Identity Crisis In Feminist Theory,' *Signs: Journal of Women in Culture and Society* 13, no. 3 (1988): 405–436.

Amnesty International. 'Troll Patrol Findings.' *Amnesty Decoders.* Accessed 17 January 2020. decoders. amnesty.org/projects/troll-patrol/findings.

Amnesty International. Citizen Evidence. Accessed 9 December 2019. citizenevidence.org.

Anzaldúa, Gloria. 'Bridge, Drawbridge, Sandbar or Island: Lesbians-of-Color Hacienda Alianzas.' In *Bridges of Power: Women's Multicultural Alliances,* edited by Lisa Albrecht, Rose M. Brewer, and Rose M. Brewer. 216–231. Philadelphia : New Society Publishers, 1990.

Argentine Forensic Anthropology Team. 'A144 Identification Notifications and Their Applicability to Families of Missing Migrants'. Accessed 9 December 2019. theforensicbordercoalition.files.wordpress. com/2016/10/aafs-2017-abstract-osorno.pdf.

Caswell, Michelle and Marika Cifor. 'From Human Rights To Feminist Ethics: Radical Empathy In The Archives,' *Archivaria* 81, no. 1 (2016): 26.

Christofferson, Ashlee, and Akwugo Emjulu. "Diversity Within': The Problems with 'Intersectional' White Feminism in Practice,' *Social Politics: International Studies in Gender, State & Society* 30, no. 2 (Summer 2023): 630-653.

Civic Laboratory for Environmental Action Research (CLEAR). 'Equity in Author Order.' 23 May 2016. civiclaboratory.nl/2016/05/23/equity-in-author-order.

––– 'Feminist and Anti-colonial Science.'Accessed 15 November 2019. civiclaboratory.nl/citizen-science.

Collins, Patricia Hill. *Black Feminist Thought: Knowledge, Consciousness, And The Politics of Empowerment.* London: Routledge, 2022.

Crenshaw, Kimberlé. 'Demarginalizing the Intersection of Race and Sex: A Black Feminist Critique of Antidiscrimination Doctrine, Feminist Theory and Antiracist Politics,' *University of Chicago Legal Forum* 1, no. 8 (1989): 138–67.

D'Ignazio, Catherine, and Lauren F. Klein. 'Feminist Data Visualization.' Workshop on Visualization for the Digital Humanities (VIS4DH), Baltimore. IEEE., 2016.

D'Ignazio, Catherine. 'What would feminist data visualization look like?,' *Medium.* Last modified 22 January 2017. medium.com/@kanarinka/what-would-feminist-data-visualization-look-like-aa3f8fc7f96c.

D'Ignazio, Catherine, and Lauren F. Klein. *Data Feminism.* The MIT Press open access @ PubPub. 6 November 2018. bookbook.pubpub.org/data-feminism.

de La Bellacasa, Maria Puig. 'Matters of care in technoscience: Assembling neglected things.' *Social studies of science* 41, no. 1 (2011): 85-106.

Deutch, Jeff, and Hadi Habal. 'The Syrian Archive: A Methodological Case Study of Open-source Investigation of State Crime Using Video Evidence From Social Media Platforms.' *State Crime J.* 7 (2018): 46–76.

Duff, Wendy M., Andrew Flinn, Karen Emily Suurtamm, and David A. Wallace. 'Social Justice Impact of Archives: A Preliminary Investigation.' *Archival Science* 13 (2013): 317–348.

Dubberley, Sam, Elizabeth Griffin, and Haluk Mert Bal. 'Making secondary trauma a primary issue: A study of eyewitness media and vicarious trauma on the digital frontline.' *Eyewitness Media Hub* (2015): 1-69.

Eddo-Lodge, Reni. *Why I'm no longer talking to white people about race.* London: Bloomsbury Publishing, 2020.

Feminist Open Source Group. Last modified January 2020, feministopensource.group.

Forensic Architecture. 'Drone Strike In Mir Ali.' Investigation. 16 April 2013. forensic-architecture.org/ investigation/drone-strike-in-mir-ali.

Forensic Architecture. 'Situated Testimony.' Accessed 18 January 2019. forensic-architecture.org/methodology/ situated-testimony.

Gathering for Open Science Hardware (GOSH). 'GOSH Code of Conduct.' Accessed 9 December 2019. openhardware.science/gosh-2017/gosh-code-of-conduct/.

Gordon, Tamela J. 'Why I'm Giving Up On Intersectional Feminism.' *Quartz.* 30 April 2018. qz.com/ quartzy/1265902/why-im-giving-up-on-intersectional-feminism.

Guzmán, Rigoberto Lara, and Sareeta Amrute. 'How to Cite Like a Badass Tech Feminist Scholar of Color.' *Data & Society: Points, Medium.* 22 August 2019. points.datasociety.net/how-to-cite-like-a-badass-tech-feminist-scholar-of-color-ebc839a3619c.

Heyns, Christof. *Report of the Special Rapporteur on extrajudicial, summary or arbitrary executions, Christof Heyns: Use of information and communications technologies to secure the right to life.* Geneva: United Nations Human Rights Council, 2015.

Haraway, Donna. 'Situated Knowledges: The Science Question in Feminism and the Privilege of Partial Perspective,' *Feminist Studies* 14, no. 3 (1988): 583

Haraway, Donna. *Staying with the Trouble: Making Kin in the Chthulucene.* Durham: Duke University Press, 2016.

Human Rights Center at the University of California, Berkeley, School of Law. *Berkeley Protocol on Digital Open Source Investigations.* New York, NY: United Nations and the Human Rights Center at the University of California, Berkeley, School of Law, 2022.

Koenig, Alexa. 'Harnessing Social Media as Evidence of Grave International Crimes.' *Human Rights Center, Medium.* 23 October 2017. medium.com/ humanrightscenter/harnessing-social-media-as-evidence-of-grave-international-crimes-d7f3e86240d.

Kurgan, Laura. *Close Up at a Distance: Mapping, Technology, and Politics.* Cambridge, Massachusetts: MIT Press, 2013.

Liboiron, Max, Justine Ammendolia, Katharine Winsor, Alex Zahara, Hillary Bradshaw, Jessica Melvin, and Charles Mather et al. 'Equity In Author Order: A Feminist Laboratory's Approach,' *Catalyst: Feminism, Theory, Technoscience* 3, no. 2 (2017): 1–17.

Lorde, Audre. *A Burst of Light: And Other Essays.* Mineola: Dover Publications, 2017.

Martin, Aryn, Natasha Myers, and Ana Viseu. 'The Politics of Care In Technoscience.' *Social Studies of Science* 45, no. 5 (2015): 625–641.

McDermott, Yvonne, Daragh Murray, and Alexa Koenig. 'Digital accountability symposium: Whose stories get told, and by whom? Representativeness in open source human rights investigations.' *Opinio Juris*. 19 December 2019. opiniojuris.org/2019/12/19/digital-accountability-symposium-whose-stories-get-told-and-by-whom-representativeness-in-open-source-human-rights-investigations/.

Norlock, Kathryn. 'Feminist Ethics.' Stanford Encyclopaedia of Philosophy. Accessed 9 December 2019. plato.stanford.edu/entries/feminism-ethics/#Inte.

Onuoha, Mimi. "The Library of Missing Datasets." Accessed 9 December 2019. mimionuoha.com.

Open Society Justice Initiative. 'Reported 2014 Chemical Shipments to Syria Raise Questions over EU Sanctions.' 27 March 2019. justiceinitiative.org/newsroom/reported-2014-chemical-shipments-to-syria-raise-questions-over-eu-sanctions.

Oxford English Dictionary, 'trans., adj., sense 2', Accessed July 2023, doi.org/10.1093/OED/2707920663.

Rahman, Zara, and Gabriela Ivens. 'Ethics in Open Source Investigations.' In *Digital Witness: Using Open Source Information for Human Rights Investigation, Documentation, and Accountability*, edited by Sam Dubberley, Alexa Koenig, and Daragh Murray, 251–270. Oxford: Oxford University Press, 2020.

Robinson, Fiona. 'A Feminist Practical Ethics of Care.' In *The Oxford Handbook of International Political Theory*, edited by Chris Brown, and Robyn Eckersley. Oxford: Oxford University Press 2018.

Sen, Ashish Kumar. 'Wanted: A code of ethics for open source researchers.' *Atlantic Council*. 20 June 2019. atlanticcouncil.org/blogs/new-atlanticist/wanted-a-code-of-ethics-for-open-source-researchers/

Smith, Roger. 'Gender pay gap in the UK: 2019.' Office for National Statistics. 29 October 2019. ons.gov.uk/employmentandlabourmarket/peopleinwork/earningsandworkinghours/bulletins/genderpaygapintheuk/2019.

Spangler, Todd. 'Twitter Stock Tumbles After Analyst Calls It 'Harvey Weinstein of Social Media'.' *Variety*. 20 December 2018. variety.com/2018/digital/news/twitter-stock-harvey-weinstein-social-media-1203094020/.

Stanford Encyclopaedia of Philosophy. 'Feminist Ethics.' Accessed 09 December 2019. plato.stanford.edu/entries/feminism-ethics/#Inte.

Syrian Archive. Accessed 17 January 2020, https://syrianarch ive.org/en.

The Engine Room. 'Ties That Bind: Organisational Security for Civil Society.' 7 March 2019, theengineroom.org/civil-society-digital-security-new-research/.

The Information Maintainers, Devon Olson, Jessica Meyerson, Mark Parsons, Juliana Castro, Monique Lassere, Dawn Wright, Hillel Arnold, et al. 'Information Maintenance as a Practice of Care: An Invitation to Reflect and Share.' *Zenodo*. 17 June 2019.

Weizman, Eyal. 'Open Verification.' *e-flux*. June 2019. e-flux.com/architecture/becoming-digital/248062/open-verification/.

## Cover Image

Mimi Ọnụọha, The Library of Missing Datasets, 2016 Steel filing cabinet, folders. Courtesy the artist & Bitforms Gallery. Photo: Brandon Schulman.

The *Library of Missing Datasets* is an ongoing physical repository of things that have been excluded in a society where so much is collected. The installation consists of a filing cabinet with empty folders. Each folder is titled with the name of a missing dataset, taken from a master list that the artist has been collecting since 2015. A separate aspect of the piece involves the artist working with groups who are missing crucial datasets.

# POETIC TESTIMONY
## Helene Kazan

### VISIBILITY BEYOND
### THE LIMITS OF VIOLENCE

Whilst carrying out research at the Arab Image Foundation in Beirut in 2017, following the careful accumulation of information across a spectrum of archives, I was able to identify and uncover an archival photograph. This photograph constituted evidence of the sexual subjugation of an anonymous woman by Australian soldiers occupying Lebanon whilst fighting for the Allied forces in 1941. In the photograph, the woman stands naked, legs apart; both hands are raised, covering her face. An Australian officer smiles proudly into the eye of the camera, whilst a second takes the shaming photograph. Uncovered following in-depth research into this deeply violent colonial/neo-colonial period—often framed in Western historical accounts as "The Secret War for the Middle East"—there was both an uncanniness and deep shock in the encounter of the image.[1] As the captured vibrations of this violence were felt through time and space. Under what conditions can a war remain secret? The only possibility for describing warfare as *secret* comes from a condition where the people affected by its violence are not recognised, or seen as valuable enough by the telling of their own history. War is surely not secret to those who are experiencing it. In this way, a feminist decolonial archival practice may serve as part of important methods of liberating archival evidence and collections that detail violent activities undertaken by colonial powers.[2]

In the encounter, it was impossible not to observe an analogy between this archival image and the images leaked of captives held and tortured in Abu Ghraib by U.S. occupying soldiers in 2004. It resonated still further with other depictions of such violence taking place against native, indigenous women and women of colour, across different but related contexts during this period.[3] States of exception and governance makes the intimate and domestic nature of the depicted violence nearly invisible, and further difficult to trace or criminalise.[4] Whilst it is not clear in the image if consent was asked or given by the woman, this does not matter; what is revealed in the archive image is the inherent uneven power construct. An intersectional relation of gender and

---

1   Basil Aboul-Enein and Youssef Aboul-Enein, *The Secret War for the Middle East: The Influence of Axis and Allied Intelligence Operations During World War II*, (Annapolis: Naval Institute Press, 2013).

2   I write in detail about what forms a decolonial archive practice in 'Decolonizing Archives and Law's Frame of Accountability', *Special Dossier on Documentary World-Making* 'In the Presence of Others', World Records Volume 4, 2020. It is not possible to cover this also in detail in the scope of this article, as I focus on the use of feminist methods in this writing. However, it is important to recognise that these methods do go hand in hand in the work.

3   I will go into much more detail about this, in particular regarding work in Saidiya V. Hartman, *Wayward Lives Beautiful Experiments: Intimate Histories of Social Upheaval*, (New York: W.W. Norton & Company, 2019).

4   The relationship points to how the intimate and domestic nature of the violence helps make it invisible, referring to how international laws of war are not victim or subject focused. This is discussed in more detail later in the writing. This also highlights how the architecture of the domestic space itself operates and is conducive to such violence, which I've written about in 'The Architecture of Slow, Structural, and Spectacular Violence and the Poetic Testimony of War,' *The Australian Feminist Law Journal* 44, no.1 (2018): 119-136.

race is being exploited by the entitled authority of the male occupying soldiers. The very act of these soldiers taking this kind of photograph of this woman is a form of torture.[5]

In analysing leaked images from Abu Ghraib in 2004, theorist Susan Sontag connects them to a colonial history of mistreated subjects:

*Considered in this light, the photographs are us. That is, they are representative of the fundamental corruptions of any foreign occupation together with the Bush administration's distinctive policies. The Belgians in the Congo, the French in Algeria, practiced torture and sexual humiliation on despised recalcitrant natives.*[6]

The colonial history of this corruption pointed to by Sontag is also evident in the image of the female subject and the two Australian soldiers.[7] Particularly affecting is the gloating soldier standing proudly next to the ashamed woman with her hands covering her eyes and face. Sontag further argues that "the horror of what is shown in the photographs cannot be separated from the horror that the photographs were taken—with the perpetrators posing, gloating, over their helpless captives".[8] Moving across this historical context, the archive image taken in 1941 reveals a long complex history of such a visual culture of colonial abuse. The photographs were no doubt produced by and for the soldiers as keepsakes of the violence they'd perpetrated in each case.[9] In this way the horror of these images can be seen as threefold: first, that they image the institutionally abusive processes of ethnographic photography (and so reveal something of its nature); second, that they are keepsakes of abusive conducted as a group with the anticipation of no consequences; third, that they are a method of engaging in a long colonial practice of sexual violence as warfare in a virtual, deniable way.

In *Wayward Lives, Beautiful Experiments,* scholar Saidiya Hartman engages the intimate lives and social upheaval of the first generation of Black women born after abolition in America. The book describes her own encounter with another image of sexual violence, one being perpetrated against an anonymous Black female child. It's clear in her writing that Hartman shares a similar level of shock and disgust in the uncovering of such a document. Hartman is also then compelled to find the best way to bring the young girl's story back to light. Though clearly captured in different contexts and situations, affecting different people, there is a resonance in what is taking place in these images of violence from an era which Hartmann describes as being

---

5   It is important to add that contemporary state law also appears to be structurally incapable of dealing with certain kinds of violence, such as the described intimate sexual, domestic, gender based and racial violence. Observations of this can currently be seen both in the UK and US as investigations continue on account of such deadly conduct being perpetrated by police forces operating both states.

6   Susan Sontag, 'Regarding The Torture Of Others,' *The New York Times*, 23 May 2004, https://www.nytimes.com/2004/05/23/magazine/regarding-the-torture-of-others.html.

7   Across the testimonies I collected, it came up time and again that the Australians (fighting with the Allied forces) were very cruel in their treatment of people. One interviewee stated that they were so well known for this that the interviewee would run and hide whenever they saw them coming.

8   Sontag, 'Regarding The Torture Of Others.'

9   Sontag, 'Regarding The Torture Of Others.'

"characterized by imperial wars".[10] This resonance is a mode of violence made invisible in its intimate nature, and in taking place at the scale of the body, and within the context of the domestic space. The material captured in the archival images, however, allows a trace of the intimate violent events. From light reflecting off the skin into the eye of the camera, a drawing and noticing of the violence has taken place. That gives this material the potential to travel: to be reconstructed again as evidence and even testimony of the violence that took place for these women and for those that came before and after. The Black and Brown female bodies in these images are an evidential cross-section of interlocking scales of violence. They demonstrate its effects as a complex of legal, political, capitalist systems; systems that even with the capture of the archival photograph, normalise, or by least not criminalising this violence, therefore render it invisible.

In *Unpayable Debt*, scholar and artist Denise Ferreira da Silva connects another narrative of racialised violence against women, which "displaces as well as exposes coloniality as the mode of governance that defines the figure of the captive, which is characterised by authorised total violence".[11] As the archival image makes the intimate moment of violence visible, the broader conditions of the state of exception renders it impossible to observe. As Hartman further describes:

*The odalisque is a forensic image that details the violence to which the black female body can be subjected. It is a durational image of intimate violence. So much time accumulates on her small figure, the girl might well be centuries old, bearing the weight of slavery and empire, embodying the transit of commodity, suturing the identity of the slave and prostitute. [...] The photograph fabricates her consent to be seen. How does she consent to coercion?*[12]

The archival image in each case becomes a forensic object, not just in what it depicts, but in its materiality. The layers of material draw forth this event across time, as non-linear, and as traceably full of noise. Artist and scholar Susan Schuppli describes this as the process of becoming a 'material witness'; investigating the evidentiary role of the materiality of the image itself as a witness of the violent events.[13] However, there is a beckoning forth for these materials, these forensic objects, not just as a witness but even further. Can the reflection, the captured material vibrations of light on the skin of these female subjects, possibly carry agency from these women: a form of testimony of the violent event?

Indeed, Hartman asks "Was it possible to annotate the image? To make my words into a shield that might protect her, a barricade to deflect the gaze and cloak what had been exposed?".[14] In discovering the archival image, I asked myself very similar questions. Would it be possible to utilise an inter-

10 Saidiya V. Hartman, *Wayward Lives Beautiful Experiments: Intimate Histories of Social Upheaval*, (New York: W.W. Norton & Company, 2019), 31.
11 Denise Ferreira da Silva, *Unpayable Debt,* (London: Sternberg Press, 2022), 45.
12 Hartman, *Wayward Lives*, 26.
13 Susan Schuppli, *Material Witness: Media, Forensics, Evidence* (Cambridge, Massachusetts: MIT Press, 2020). This argument also connects to a feminist new materialist theoretical and practice-based framework.
14 Hartman, *Wayward Lives*, 25.

disciplinary approach with the revolutionary potential of feminist and decolonial methods to accomplish these aims. To harness all the stated potency
of the archival document: allowing the material vibrations to speak, to give a
testimony that won't stay silent, as a form of resistance against these acts of
normalised violence. Towards this, Denise Ferreira da Silva argues that a "fundamentally poethical—namely, political (ethical), practical, poetical" methodological response is needed.[15] As will be explained in the following section, I
join various such attempts to engage poethical, feminist, critical legal theory
and methods, producing the formation of what I've come to frame as poetic
testimony.[16] Collectively our aims argue for the necessity of a further expanded,
holistic and reparative re-engagement of testimony and justice in the law.

## POETIC TESTIMONY AND FEMINIST METHODS
## IN INTERNATIONAL LAW

International laws on war are not victim or subject focused. This allows little
room for the human experience of international violence to be registered,
let alone connected to the decision-making processes of international legal
justice. This disconnection between the subjects of violence and the official
account of events—kept in place through the international legal framework—devalues the human testimony in favour of more technical and forensic
evidence in the attempt to successfully hold accountable the perpetrators of
international crimes.[17] In giving testimony to the human experience of violence, it is the inaccuracy or uncertainty of detail, the crack or break in the
voice, and the evident display of emotion that often characterises the embodied
experience of trauma.[18] However, in the technical setting of the law, it is exactly these aspects of testimony that can cause its status as evidence to be seen as
fallible, or be exploited to deem it inadmissible. As such, testimony of violence
is predominantly perceived as a subsidiary part of the larger legal mechanism
of evidence collection for identifying the perpetrator of violence and their
level of culpability. This restricted evidentiary quality of giving testimony
can overshadow the importance of the law's capacity to provide a platform for
disclosing and registering the embodied effect of violence—and diminishes
the reparative process that being seen and heard in such spaces of legal justice
potentially entails. When investigating violent traumatic events and conditions,
the expectant rationale of testimony in the law leads to a lack of recognition

---

15  Ferreira da Silva, *Unpayable Debt,* 294.
16  See: Ferreira da Silva, *Unpayable Debt*, 294, and Kazan, Helene, 'The Architecture of Slow,
    Structural, and Spectacular Violence and the Poetic Testimony of War,' *The Australian
    Feminist Law Journal* 44, no. 1 (2018): 119-136.
17  While I am focusing on international law, there is further room for discussion on the
    argument I make in regards to the poetic testimony of violence also in relation to domestic
    law and the law of tort. My arguments around international law have been developed in
    conversation and in the editing process of 'Gender, War, and Technology: Peace and Armed
    Conflict in the Twenty-First Century', eds. Emily Jones, Sara Kendall, and Yoriko Otomo,
    special issue, *Australian Feminist Law Journal* 44, no. 1 (2018). Also, whilst the tribunal is a
    legal setting where testimony can be given on the effects of international violence, the legal
    process under which these take place is also routed in related problematics of who or what
    is seen in the law. For example, no tribunals have taken place in relation to the history of
    warfare in Lebanon, save a special tribunal in 2005 on the assassination of Rafic Hariri, the
    former Lebanese prime minister.
18  Shoshana Felman and Dori Laub, *Testimony: Crises of Witnessing in Literature,
    Psychoanalysis, and History,* (London: Routledge, 1992).

of the wider harm caused under such conditions. A more holistic and reparative approach to justice would, therefore, need to recognise, conceptualise
and make space for something that it currently actively avoids. Drawing on
established feminist methods, poetic testimony approaches this problem as an
argument, which reframes and reconceptualises poetics as part of the bodily
expression and experience of violence. In this section, I will establish how the
long existence of these methods, could be part of a more expanded and inclusive scope of testimony within the context of the law.[19]

A central argument made in critical legal theory is that in order to understand its current failings, a historic turn is necessary in international law.[20]
The proposition is that a crucial study of the colonial and imperial historic
legacies ingrained in the law and its practice must be undertaken, in order to
expose the coloniality of law's authority and in consequence its limited frame
of accountability.[21] By asserting the need to examine the historical processes
responsible for inequalities produced through law's enforcement, such analysis
comes to challenge law's defining principles.[22] Critical legal scholars argue
that colonial biases and hierarchies remain deeply embedded in the institutions of international law. Efforts to ignore or suppress such legacies only serve
to replicate and exacerbate the ongoing effects of colonial systems. Legal theorist Anne Orford explains that, instead of recognising the continuity between
the colonial past of international law and contemporary multilateral legal
systems, proponents of international law argue that further legal frameworks
are needed to educate and advance the peoples of the decolonized world, in
order to end international violence.[23] Orford points out that this legal rhetoric
parallels the early colonial argument of a "duty to civilise" those encountered
in the colonies.[24] In this way, international law demonstrates an internalised
belief system, producing complacency in regard to its known failures;
a process known as the 'reification' of international law. One key failure is that
international laws on war are not victim or subject focused. This can deny
victims the opportunity to give testimony of their lived experience of violent
events and conditions, and the potentially reparative process this represents.
There is, therefore, a clear misgiving in the 'who' that the legal justice system
is actually intended to represent.

---

19  This will be outlined in more detail later in the section.
20  Anne Orford, 'International Law and the Limits of History', in *The Law of International Lawyers: Reading Martti Koskenniemi,* (Cambridge: Cambridge University Press, 2015): 297–320.
21  This movement in international legal scholarship is observed in critical legal theory and is part of, but not limited to, TWAIL (Third World Approaches to International Law) scholarship. The legal scholars I follow in making this argument are R. P. Anand, Luis Eslava, Sundhya Pahuja, B. S. Chimni, Antony Anghie, Ratna Kapure, Vasuki Nesiah, Anne Orford and Rose Parfitt. I also draw on feminist and intersectional critical legal theory from Emily Jones, Gina Heathcote, Sara Kendall, and Yoriko Otomo.
22  The pros and cons of this proposal are covered in detail in Matilda Arvidsson and Miriam Bak McKenna, 'The turn to history in international law and the sources doctrine: Critical approaches and methodological imaginaries,' *Leiden Journal of International Law,* (2019).
23  Anne Orford, 'The Part as Law or History? The Relevance of Imperialism for Modern Internation-al Law', *IILJ Working Paper 2012/2, History and Theory of International Law Series,* (2012): 1.
24  This proposition was made by theorist Oscar Guardiola-Rivera while narrating Columbus' journey to the tropics during his introduction for 'The Devil's Advocate: a Roundtable for Forensic Architecture', at the Centre for Research Architecture, Goldsmiths, University of London, 2013. In retelling this narrative, Guardiola-Rivera was referencing N. Wey Gómez's, *The Tropics of Empire: Why Columbus Sailed South to the Indies,* (Cambridge, Massachusetts: Massachusetts Institute of Technology, 2008).

Feminist philosopher and theorist Judith Butler considers this issue in relation to what she terms as the "grievable value" of a subject, which in turn engenders a position of precarity and forced resilience.[25] This speaks of a distinct problem in international law, which Butler analyses in more detail in her writing on the human shield. A differential eligibility for recognition imposes a position of vulnerability on those in the line of fire. In *Unconditional Life*, legal scholar Yoriko Otomo writes:

*the idea of 'humanness' has, over the course of the twentieth century, become dependent upon a particular vision of the international domain and upon certain relations between humanness and technological intervention.*[26]

Butler and Otomo both point to the ways in which the technical methodologies of international law's framework erase certain subjects from its legal view. The technical methodological framework that operates through the law must, therefore, be held in mind in discourses addressing its asymmetric effective impact. Greater inclusivity must be determined for the subjects that are experiencing, or under threat of, the violence of warfare, and its interlocking scales of effect.

In response, Otomo points to a turn towards *écriture feminine* as a necessary feminist methodological intervention into international law.[27] Inspired by Luce Irigaray's feminist writing on hysteria as a form of protest against patriarchal oppression, Otomo's argument for its place in international law comes in response to an analysis of two important legal cases where the jury is left with no recourse or language for making a decision.[28] Otomo proposes that a feminist methodological intervention could provide a more expansive and inclusive framework for international law's effective capacity. The potential of engaging feminist methods in legal thinking does not, of course, frame only women's concerns. Rather, it reflects a complex of intersectional issues, a broader framework that resists the inherent inequalities bolstered by international law's asymmetric power structures. This is examined in a range of other important work, including that by postcolonial south-Asian scholars, such as Gayatri Chakravorty Spivak's writing on the subaltern, and the work of Black studies scholars and practitioners, such artist and theorist Denise Ferreira da Silva's work on the 'poethetical' referenced above.[29]

Building on this—and on wider intersectional discourse and engaged practice with many of the aforementioned theorists and practitioners work-

---

25  Judith Butler, *Frames of War: When Is Life Grievable?*, (London: Verso, 2010), 138.
26  Yoriko Otomo, *Unconditional Life: The Postwar International Law Settlement*, (Oxford, New York: Oxford University Press, 2016), 1, 11.
27  Yoriko Otomo, *Unconditional Life*. Otomo refers to writing by Luce Irigaray in *Speculum of the Other Woman*, (Ithaca, New York: Cornell University Press, 1985), 47.
28  The two international law cases Otomo looks at are the Nuclear Weapons Advisory Opinion, where the International Court of Justice was called upon to decide on the legality of the 'threat of use' of nuclear weapons; and the EC-Biotech dispute, where the World Trade Organisation's Dispute Settlement Body was called upon to determine the legality of the European Union's moratorium on genetically modified organisms. Otomo, *Unconditional Life*, 3.
29  Ferreira da Silva, *Unpayable Debt*, 294.

ing across a spectrum of contexts[30]—I began developing the framework of poetic testimony: the necessary engagement with radical forms of poetics in expressing and translating the experience of violence. In this, I draw on the etymological root of *poiesis* from the Greek term meaning *to make*. This alludes to processes building on and from an experience, both as a necessary development of its becoming, and as testimony. This proposal sits in noticeable tension with technical forms of evidence making in the law. However, the need and reason for giving testimony does not only reside in the spaces of law. Therefore, the use of both poetic and forensic methods should neither exclude nor lessen the credibility or necessity of one or the other. This is especially the case in conditions where the perpetration and impact of violence is undeniable, yet scale and temporality make direct causation difficult to determine. Or when the corruption rooted in international legal systems doesn't allow for the criminalisation of the violence as often seen in aerial warfare. Rather, attempts should be made to uphold and make use of the strengths and possibilities of multiple evidentiary modes, as a way of engaging the revolutionary potential of such poetic and feminist methods.[31] In *Revolutionary Feminisms*, theorist Brenna Bhandar and poet and activist Rafeef Ziadah call for collective action and radical solidarity, arguing that: "revolutionary transformations in the organisation of the economy, social relations, political structures, and psychic and symbolic worlds, [...] must take place across multiple scales – from intimate relations between individuals to those among individuals, communities and the state".[32] Pushing beyond the limiting scope of small differences across feminist discourse, Bhandar and Ziadah, as well as their discussants in the publication, look to engage revolutionary feminist frameworks across entangled, intergenerational evolutions of language and practical approach, to conceive of the dismantling of violence at multiple scales of effect. This call reflects the necessity of what became clear in the previous section's encounter with images of intimate violence, hidden through a state of exception.

　　To further bridge this gap in the theory and practice of the law, the potential of such methods is explained in effective detail in the recently published book *Feminist Theory and International Law* by legal theorist Emily Jones.[33] Drawing on her work toward a feminist posthuman legal framework, Jones' argues for how this theory as method can allow a transformation of the way both the human and non-human appear and have agency in the space of the law. The framework "refuses to side-line the issue of inequalities between

---

30　Beyond those texts already mentioned, this includes important interdisciplinary discussions on the potential of revolutionary feminist methods took place in exhibition 'Points of Contact', which I curated in Lebanon in April 2018. This encounter came in parallel to engaging in conversation with artists and theorists Marwa Arsanios and Dima Hamadeh, and organised reading and discussions with the collective 98 Weeks in Beirut, Lebanon.

31　In their later work, the investigative agency 'Forensic Architecture' developed what they term as engaging 'situated testimony' in the use of the human testimony of violence: https://forensic-architecture.org/methodology/situated-testimony.

32　Bhandar, Brenna, and Rafeef Ziadah. *Revolutionary Feminisms: Conversations on Collective Action and Radical Thought* (London: Verso, 2020), 1.

33　Emily Jones, *Feminist Theory and International Law: Posthuman Perspectives.* 1st ed., (London: Routledge, 2023), 24.

humans when focusing on the nonhuman".[34] This can be observed as a call
for greater care and sensitivity in the field, in the reflection of wider issues
in posthuman discourse. Too often, posthumanism fails to recognise the
complex inequalities that exist across human and non-human worlds. In the
introduction of the recently published *More Posthuman Glossary*, editors Rossi
Braidotti, Goda Klumbyte, and Emily Jones also highlight their renewed focus
on this foundational relationship between feminist and posthuman theory, as
a way of drawing on "knowledge through lived experience" in order to find
better ways to "adequately account for the complex present".[35]

There is a long, rich and important history of storytelling and poetics
developed under such circumstances in Lebanon and the wider region—recognising the power of such practices is prevalent. In *The Ruin to Come*, Lebanese artist and writer Walid Sadek describes the relationship between the city,
the war-imprinted human body, and a poetics of seeing, which he describes
using the cypher of a "witness who knows too much".[36] Relating the practices
of Lebanese writers and artists to methods of witnessing, and to themes of
poetics, is a way of articulating the tension that occurs in the need for such a
poetics to describe sustained and catastrophic violence.[37] As in this context, international law has consistently failed to place any accountability for its history
of international and state-perpetrated violence.[38] The practices and works that
have evolved from this injustice are an important expression of its lived experience. They bear its marks as evidence and testimony of the violence, which the
international legal sphere has failed to recognise.

In summary, poetic testimony argues for an expanded and holistic
framing of testimony in its interaction and recognition within the space of
the law: what changes might this make; can it make repair possible? In this,
I believe I join a chorus of voices working with similar aims. Collective
strength may be gained through practices of radical solidarity, aimed towards
dismantling the continued colonial impact of an asymmetric lived condition.
My argument is part of a complex, uneasy, evolving, and necessary supra-dis-
ciplinary movement towards developing ways of dissolving the known limits
of the frankly corrupt frameworks of international law. These perceived limits
constitute a continuation of colonial rule, in the present, in the past, and into

---

34   Jones, *Feminist Theory and International Law,* 13. In this, Jones also points to a further
     complication in wider posthuman discourse. Dominant posthuman scholarship is "increasingly
     ignoring its feminist roots despite the fact that feminist theory was one of the precursors of
     the posthuman turn"–Jones, *Feminist Theory and International Law,* 15. Here, Jones
     is pointing to writing by Rosi Braidotti in 'A Theoretical Framework for the Critical
     Posthumanities,' *Theory, Culture & Society* 36, no. 6, (2019).
35   Rosi Braidotti, Emily Jones, & Goda Klumbyte (eds.). *More posthuman glossary,* (New York:
     Bloomsbury Academic, 2022), 3.
36   Walid Sadek, *The Ruin to Come: Essays from a Protracted War,* (Berlin: Motto Books, 2016), 154.
37   The enduring strain between these methodological frameworks has become a recognisable
     and well-established trope in the array of well-known and established practices that have
     emerged through the violence of the civil war in Lebanon, namely, in the works of Joanna
     Hadjithomas and Khalil Joriege, Rabih Mroué, Walid Raad and the Atlas Group, Rania
     Stephan, Walid Sadek, and Akram Zataari. This is as well as the infamous artist and poet Etel
     Adnan. Across these practices, the witnessing of violence engages a complex combination of
     poetic and investigative methodologies.
38   Following the end of the Lebanese Civil War, on 26 August 1991, the Ta-if agreement granted
     amnesty for those accused of perpetrating criminal acts of war. This also removed any legal
     capacity to witness or testify against the crimes committed during the conflict and meant that
     no justice was brought for the people killed and the many disappeared.

the future. The following section gives an account of my own attempts on engaging such revolutionary feminist methods—considered as an example of poetic testimony—in the development of the interdisciplinary multi-media project 'Frame of Accountability'.

## FRAME OF ACCOUNTABILITY:
## IN HER VIEW

From my first, deeply shocking encounter with the archival image of the anonymous woman and the Australian soldiers at the Arab Image Foundation in 2017, it felt important that any further movement of the material needed to be treated with the greatest care. During a fellowship at the Vera List Centre for Art and Politics, I began to conceptualise more concretely the use of intersectional feminist methods across my practice, and in this project specifically. Using feminist methods in order to situate and translate this anonymous woman's testimony of the violent event from the archival document, my defining ethical decision was that the process needed to communicate her experience without sharing and redistributing the image of the violence itself. This was necessary in order to avoid subjecting her to further continuous effects of the violence: shame and exposure. The uncanniness in finding her would allow the captured vibrations of this violence to travel through time and space, channelled through a 'poethetical' framework of thinking. The question arose: could the archival material therefore be used to position her testimony, without reconstituting the violence of the image itself? I envisioned this as a distinct act of care and sensitivity to her experience, and further as a form of resistance against the violence' effects. Drawing on my skillset as an artist and filmmaker, this premise became the driving principle for developing her poetic testimony: the archival document as a filmic translation titled 'In Her View', forming part of the multi-media project 'Frame of Accountability'.

'Frame of Accountability' is the development of this intent. This project investigates 'risk' as a wider lived condition, produced through the co-evolution of capitalist systems and violent conflict. Explored through film, installation, writing and public engagement, the project focuses on the evolved lived condition of risk in Lebanon and Syria, with a view to understanding the wider regional and global consequences.[39] In highlighting the evolving histories of violence perpetrated through colonial mechanisms of governance,[40] the project attempts to re-contextualise the operation of risk.

I argue that decontextualisation is necessary as a precondition for legitimacy in international law: in the development of risk and insurance mechanisms, colonial forces have intentionally distanced causal relationships—engaging violent and inhumane approaches in breaking contextual ties—in order to allow *risk* itself to become an autonomous object: a separate, exchangeable commodity.[41] This process, described as "capitalist transformations of the environment",

39  I outline this concept in detail in Helene Kazan, 'Dismantling Risk' in *More Posthuman Glossary* ed. Rosi Braidotti, Emily Jones, Goda Klumbyte, (London: Bloomsbury, 2023).

40  See: Ian Baucom, *Specters of the Atlantic: Finance Capital, Slavery, and the Philosophy of History* Durham, NC: Duke University Press, 2005), Jonathan Levy, *Freaks of Fortune* (Cambridge, Massachusetts: Harvard University Press, 2012).

41  See: Sarah Keenan, 'From Historical Chains to Derivative Futures: Title Registries as Time Machines', *SSRN,* (June 2018), Stefano Harney and Fred Moten, *The Undercommons: Fugitive Planning & Black Study,* (London, New York: Minor Compositions, 2013).

goes beyond the production of a mere state of precarity—it produces life under known conditions of increasing threat and violence.[42] In consequence, there are many legal mechanisms in place that effectively remove, distance and legitimise the causal factors behind such interlocking scales of violence, developed through a colonial mindset in order to minimise responsibility and accountability.

Any project to dismantle risk—legally, spatially, materially and psychologically—must therefore go beyond the necessary acknowledgement of its colonial foundations, still in operation today. A *methodological imagining* for undoing this inherently asymmetric power structure may only be possible through sensitive readings and understandings of the complex, interconnected human and non-human histories and potential futures visible in its wake.[43] Such methodological imagining is the aim of 'Frame of Accountability'. In response, the work engages the outlined feminist, critical-legal, and artistic theories and methods, in order to explore their revolutionary potentials alongside other practices of radical solidarity.[44] Through this, the work seeks to develop accountability for the perpetration of the depicted violence, and its ongoing effects. This is attempted with the understanding that to be accountable is to be willing to answer the obligation of responsibility for one's own actions, or lack thereof.

The film work is produced in multi-part, non-linear formation. 'Beyond the Sky's Limits' narrates law as a consciousness coming to terms with its own failings: the speculative voice of a feminist, queered, decolonial international law. Unravelling this complex non-human subjectivity, it narrates the drafting of the Rules of Air Warfare in 1923. As a study of the legal archival draft document reveals how these international laws of war become corrupted by the self-interests of the strong states and colonial powers involved in their making: their ambitions fail quickly and critically. The Rules of Air Warfare, drafted exactly 100 years ago, is evidence of both the knowledge of, and the need for, specific forms of restraint. Instead, aerial warfare entered the Second World War period with nearly no limitations, and continues to be controversial because of the lack of concrete restrictions on the extent of the lethal harm.

Another chapter of the film project '(Un)Touching Ground', began through my discovery of the personal archive of General Spears, the first British Minister of Lebanon and Syria who was closely involved in the Allied invasion of Vichy French controlled territory in 1941.[45] The film traces the multiple routes of the military campaign and its human and non-human effects as—under the legal construct of 'military necessity'—two colonial forces fight for control of and access to natural resources across the territory. This environmental violence is depicted via an anti-aerial view of the warfare, an almost claustrophobic visual (un)touching of the ground.[46]

---

42  Anna Lowenhaupt Tsing, *The Mushroom at the End of the World: On the Possibility of Life in Capitalist Ruins,* (Princeton: Princeton University Press, 2015).

43  See: Mark Fisher, *Capitalist Realism: Is There No Alternative?,* (Winchester, United Kingdom: Zero Books, 2009), Donna J. Haraway, *Staying with the Trouble: Making Kin in the Chthulucene,* (Durham: Duke University Press, 2016).

44  Brenna Bhandar, and Rafeef Ziadah, ed. *Revolutionary Feminisms: Conversations on Collective Action and Radical Thought,* (London:Verso, 2020).

45  Basil Aboul-Enein and Youssef Aboul-Enein, *The Secret War for the Middle East: The Influence of Axis and Allied Intelligence Operations During World War II,* (Annapolis: Naval Institute Press, 2013).

46  More writing contextualising and analysing this history can be found in Helene Kazan, 'Poetic Testimony of War,' *The Australian Feminist Law Journal* 44, no. 1 (2018): 119-136.

'In Her View' engages the analysed archival evidence discovered at the Arab Image Foundation in Lebanon, which depicts the sexual exploitation of the anonymous woman by occupying Australian soldiers fighting for the Allied forces in 1941. The film moves through the archival evidence to sense, trace and position her encounter as a formation of poetic testimony. This part of the film points to the lack of legal accountability for violence perpetrated at the scale of the body and the domestic through state perpetrated violence. In line with da Silva's complex proposal, the work harnesses all the potential of the archival document: making the material vibrations themselves speak.

Having taken four years to develop, the project has evolved through long form discussion: discussion amongst the team that worked with me on developing the work, as well as through consultation through public and private events, and screenings with different stakeholders from across the project in Lebanon, Syria, UK, U.S., and beyond. This all represents careful attempts to think through and explore together the problematics of such a disclosure, and to allow the work to take form through a poethetical framework.[47] This method is the evolution of a porous feminist process, which changes and adapts the work according to feedback and consultation taking place at each stage.

Two important components of bringing her testimony forward from the archival document have come through the work in the project developed with Anabel Garcia-Kurland on the human and non-human modelling and animation in the film. Garcia-Kurland describes her process:

In order to depict the environment in which the violence took place, the photograph was used as a forensic tool. Utilising a reverse engineering methodology of a film camera, extracting the image's values of noise, levels, focal length and balance; these data extractions were then utilised to generate 3D models and their violent points of interaction without ever showing the image itself.[48]

As is clear in this statement, it became of integral importance between us to find a method that would clearly communicate the violence without reconstituting it by sharing the depiction itself. This also came into focus in the writing of the narrative in the first person, and the very close proximity of her experience in film as per direction, as a deep discussion on language in all its expressions became crucial. Building on this further, the process developed with Mhamad Safa regarding the music design of the film also held close these poethics. Describing this process, he outlines that "The musical and sonic repertoire morphs along the scenes to alternate between spectacular, slow, yet subtle tonalities to unpack aural manifestations of the law and her experience".[49]

These long discussions on the process between us reveal the tensions that occur in the aim of producing such a work, and in using the methods framed in this writing and through poetic testimony. These have continued throughout the course of the project, along with the development of our friendships, and through being committed to bringing this work into being. In our roles in the project—in writing/directing, modelling and animation and music design and further—we knew it was crucial that we worked to materialise such aims, and in doing so be able to position her testimony in a poethetical

47   More information about the wider project and events can be found: https://www.foa-
     working-archive.com.
48   Author's interview with Anabel Garcia-Kurland in London, 2023.
49   Author's interview with Mhamad Safa in London, 2023.

way. This has been fundamental to our work, in understanding the revolutionary potential of such methods in engaging this archival evidence, and further in our hopes for what it may achieve by entering a more public life.[50]

## CONCLUSION

My analysis in this essay of archival images that depict intimate and sexual violence against women in different contexts, points to a connected intersectional racialised and gendered condition caused through colonialism and empire that disconnects this violence from legal frameworks of accountability. Following a critique therefore on the limiting ways this condition also allows testimony to currently operate in the law, a discussion for poetic testimony and revolutionary feminist methods in the law, specifically international laws of war, necessarily becomes an argument for the provision of agency within the legal framework for the human and non-human subjects affected by international violence. Engaging revolutionary feminist and poetic methods in the law is an assertion of an altered positionality: a law centred around and for the human and non-human subject, along with a proposal for an expanded and more forgiving notion of testimony as the natural expression of the experience of international violence and harm, and all the forms and matter such testimony might take. With all the care and sensitivity these methods align, I have attempted to bring forward and position the poetic testimony of the anonymous woman from the archive image from 1941 in 'Frame of Accountability: In Her View'. Through this combined theoretical and practice-based approach, I argue for a more holistic reparative framework of thinking, regarding the role of testimony and justice in the international legal setting. Completing this writing in October 2023, amidst global outcry against genocidal violence perpetrated by the Israeli state against the people of Gaza, Palestine and further, this has never felt like a more important argument to make.

---

50  For more information about future events of this work will be updated on the project website: schttps://www.foa-working-archive.com.

## Works Cited

Aboul-Enein, Basil and Youssef Aboul-Enein. *The Secret War for the Middle East: The Influence of Axis and Allied Intelligence Operations During World War II.* Annapolis: Naval Institute Press, 2013.

Arvidsson, Matilda and Bak McKenna, Miriam. 'The turn to history in international law and the sources doctrine: Critical approaches and methodological imaginaries'. *Leiden Journal of International Law,* 2019.

Baucom, Ian. *Specters of the Atlantic: Finance Capital, Slavery, and the Philosophy of History.* Durham: Duke University Press, 2005.

Bhandar, Brenna, and Ziadah, Rafeef. *Revolutionary Feminisms: Conversations on Collective Action and Radical Thought.* London: Verso, 2020.

Butler, Judith. *Frames of War: When Is Life Grievable?* Reprint edition. London: Verso, 2010.

———. 'Human Shields', *London Review of International Law* 3, no. 2 (September 2015): 223–43.

Braidotti, Rosi. 'A Theoretical Framework for the Critical Posthumanities,' *Theory, Culture & Society* (2019).

Braidotti, Rosi, Jones, Emily & Klumbyte, Goda (eds.). *More posthuman glossary.* New York: Bloomsbury Academic, 2022.

Felman, Shoshana, and Dori Laub. *Testimony: Crises of Witnessing in Literature, Psychoanalysis, and History.* London: Taylor & Francis, 1992.

Ferreira Da Silva, Denise. 'Toward a Black Feminist Poethics, The Quest(ion) of Blackness Toward the End of the World', *The Black Scholar,* 2014.

———. *Unpayable Debt.* London: Sternberg Press, 2022.

Fisher, Mark. *Capitalist Realism Is There No Alternative?* Winchester, UK: Zero Books, 2009.

Gómez's, N. Wey. The Tropics of Empire: Why Columbus Sailed South to the Indies. Cambridge, Massachusetts: Massachusetts Institute of Technology, 2008.

Haraway, Donna J. Staying with the Trouble: Making Kin in the Chthulucene. Durham: Duke University Press, 2016.

Harney, Stefano, and Moten, Fred. *The Undercommons: Fugitive Planning & Black Study.* London, New York: Minor Compositions, 2013.

Hartman, Saidiya V. *Wayward Lives, Beautiful Experiments: Intimate Histories of Social Upheaval.* 1st ed. New York: W.W. Norton & Company, 2019.

Irigaray, Luce. *Speculum of the Other Woman.* Ithaca, New York: Cornell University Press, 1985.

Jones, Emily. *Feminist Theory and International Law: Posthuman Perspectives (1st ed.).* London: Routledge. 2023.

Jones, Emily, Sara Kendall, and Yoriko Otomo. 'Gender, War, and Technology: Peace and Armed Conflict in the Twenty-First Century,' Australian Feminist Law Journal 44, no. 1, 2018.

Kazan, Helene, 'The Architecture of Slow, Structural, and Spectacular Violence and the Poetic Testimony of War,' *The Australian Feminist Law Journal* 44, no.1, 2018.

———. 'Decolonizing Archives and Law's Frame of Accountability', Special Dossier on Documentary World-Making 'In the Presence of Others', *World Records Volume 4,* 2020.

———. 'Dismantling Risk' in *More Posthuman Glossary* ed. Rosi Braidotti, Emily Jones, Goda Klumbyte. London: Bloomsbury, 2023.

Keenan, Sarah. 'From Historical Chains to Derivative Futures: Title Registries as Time Machines,' *SSRN*, 2018.

Levy, Jonathan. *Freaks of Fortune.* Cambridge, Massachusetts: Harvard University Press, 2012.

Orford, Anne. 'International Law and the Limits of History.' In *The Law of International Lawyers: Reading Martti Koskenniemi.* Cambridge, UK: Cambridge University Press, 2015.

———. 'The Past as Law or History? The Relevance of Imperialism for Modern International Law.' *IILJ Working Paper 2012/2 (History and Theory of International Law Series),* 2012.

———. *International Law and Its Others.* Cambridge, UK: Cambridge University Press, 2006.

Otomo, Yoriko. *Unconditional Life: The Postwar International Law Settlement.* Oxford: Oxford University Press, 2016.

Sadek, Walid. *The Ruin to Come: Essays from a Protracted War.* Berlin: Motto Books. 2016.

Schuppli, Susan. *Material Witness: Media, Forensics, Evidence.* Cambridge, Massachusetts: MIT Press, 2020.

Sontag, Susan. 'Regarding The Torture Of Others,' *The New York Times,* 23 May 2004.

Tsing, Anna Lowenhaupt. *The Mushroom at the End of the World: On the Possibility of Life in Capitalist Ruins.* Princeton: Princeton University Press, 2015.

## Images

Images captured from 'Frame of Accountability' directed by Helene Kazan (2023).

Cover image: From film chapter '(Un)Touching Ground' where documentation and archival images of a history of protest and resistance movements in Lebanon are put through a process of data-moshing. This highlights the mass of people/pixels that make up these movements and a wider active engagement in intersectional concepts of revolution in this context.

Images from pages 65-75: From film chapter 'In Her View', the images on page 65 show the city of Beirut and exterior views of the house where events in the film take place. On page 67, the images draw the viewer from details of city towards the architecture of the house. On page 73, the viewer enters the house and gets closer to the described violence. Finally on page 75 the images depict extracted noise, levels, focal length and balance from the archive image to generate a 3D model of its violent points of interaction, this is without showing the image itself. A technique developed with Anabel Garcia-Kurland on human/non-human modelling.

# THE GANGS MATRIX
## Stafford Scott

I have been involved in the issues surrounding the Gangs Matrix since
I came across a copy of this secretive database in the middle of 2016. The
Gangs Matrix has played a significant role in the UK's continued criminalisation of the Black community. Our roundtable discussion today contributes
to efforts to document these histories as we continuously seek to make our
mark in the ongoing battle within the War Inna Babylon—a topic we frequently address. Consequently, my presentation will try to shed light on the
system's operation through a dissection of the events that led to the development of the Gangs Matrix, as well as recent developments and anticipated
future events.

### THE MURDER OF MARK DUGGAN

Let me start at the very beginning: 4 August 2011, a moment etched in Britain's history, the day Mark Duggan was tragically killed by police officers on
the streets of Tottenham.

At the time, a narrative was disseminated [by authorities] asserting
that a gunman, a notorious gangster, emerged from a minicab and opened
fire on the police. In response, the officers discharged their firearms, resulting in his death.[1] Numerous accounts were circulated during the ensuing
days, yet throughout this time, consideration and sensitivity towards his family was profoundly lacking. Astonishingly, the authorities neglected to inform
his loved ones of his death on the streets.

### THEY UNDERTOOK ACTIONS
### THAT MAY BE UNFAMILIAR TO THE PUBLIC

Among them, when certain family members in Tottenham were finally noti-
fied, including the mother of Mark Duggan's children and his brother, they
went to the location where the incident occurred. In their search for confirmation, they repeatedly approached the police, enquiring if the deceased was
Mark Duggan. Regrettably, the officers repeatedly denied their enquiries.
Eventually, one of the officers pointed to an air ambulance soaring above and
uttered, "Do you see that air ambulance up there?" They were instructed
to follow it. It was approximately 5pm on a Friday in London, and they were
expected to track the air ambulance. Pursuing an ambulance on the ground
would pose a formidable challenge, let alone attempting to follow it in London traffic.

However, they persevered and embarked on this journey, trailing
the ambulance to the hospital. They entered the medical facility on arrival,
indicating they had come for Mark Duggan. The receptionist at the hospital
claimed that no one by that name was there. The family insisted that he had
arrived via the air ambulance, only to be told that the individual in question

---

1 For an investigation into the circumstances surrounding Mark Duggan's death, see: Forensic
  Architecture, 'The Killing Of Mark Duggan', 9 June 2020, https://forensic-architecture.org/
  investigation/the-killing-of-mark-duggan.

was a police officer who had been shot. Imagine what it must be like in the first place, the anguish of chasing an air ambulance, while believing that a loved one had been shot by the police, only to be confronted with the need to return to the scene.

So, several things happened at the scene that were already causing real consternation within our community, including media reports that Mark Duggan had fired upon the police. Everyone who knew Duggan said he wasn't "bad enough or mad enough" to have shot at anyone, much less police officers. However, what is truly significant here is that his parents, Bruno Hall and Pamela Duggan, witnessed these developments from the confines of their home. Pamela watched the events unfold on television in real-time. While we cannot retrace the steps of time, it is crucial to acknowledge the emotional toll inflicted during this period.

Subsequently, on the 6th of August, I was one of those who led a demonstration to Tottenham Police Station. It was mainly young women in attendance, as Simone Wilson, the mother of his children, had organised it. To be honest, I was wary of going to the police station with just young women and their children in case it kicked off. However, I also recognised that the presence of young women and children reduced the likelihood of confrontations. So, we walked to the police station. We did not march; we just walked down there. Some people had some scribbled-on bits of cardboard that they made into placards. But we walked there, and as we walked, we tried to decide what we would do there and decided that we wanted the demonstration to be non-aggressive. We determined that on arrival, only women should enter the police station.

Three women went inside and approached the desk. In response to their enquiries, the officers at the desk said, "We can't talk to you about this", followed by, "We can take a complaint if you want to make a complaint." We planned for the women to enter the station and ask the officer on duty: "Do you know that somebody got killed out there a couple of days ago?" If the officer acknowledged this, the question would be, "Well, why don't you do your job and go and inform the family?" However, the officers refused to engage; they said, "We can't talk to you about it because the Independent Police Complaints Commission (IPCC) is investigating the matter". Subsequently, the women were escorted out of the police station while the shutters were swiftly pulled down on the station. It was as if they were saying, we're closed for business, and we're definitely not talking to you.

Consequently, the young women present reached for their phones and began disseminating messages to others, informing them of their presence at the police station and telling them that they were now being treated with the same dismissive contempt shown to Mark's parents. They were adamant that they were not leaving. It was clear that they intended to close down Tottenham High Road and stop traffic from passing through. They wanted to cause disruption as they did not want the rest of Tottenham to carry on as usual as if nothing's happened. Moreover, it meant that some of the young men, or 'mandem' as they call themselves, started to turn up. Now, the nature of the protest was changing in front of our very eyes. We could see this, and so could the police as they increased the number of officers outside the police station. Still, none sought to speak with the family members who had joined the demo.

## POLICE FAILURES
## TO CONSULT AND ENGAGE

After we had been there for over two hours, a more senior officer appeared. The officer, who I now know to be DCI Adelekan, claimed to be the highest-ranking officer on duty that day. However, we had been made aware of the Gold Command meeting that had taken place in Tottenham police station that morning with officers of a far higher rank in attendance. We told the DCI it was these officers that the family wished to engage with. Then, when the rest of the crowd caught sight of the officer, who happened to be Black, their reaction turned incredibly hostile. The officer himself appeared taken aback by the reaction; you could see him shiver. Normally, you don't see that. But we also saw his white colleagues, comrades, move away from him. They left him there without offering any support. He subsequently entered the police station and stayed out of sight for approximately an hour. Afterwards, Adelekan began calling our phones. I had never spoken to this man before, and suddenly, he was reaching out to me via a friend who handed me his phone. I was puzzled and asked him who he was. He disclosed his name and identified himself as the head of operational policing. He expressed his desire for me to come inside the station to speak with him. I was taken aback and asked him what he was talking about. I emphasised that this situation was not about me but about Mark Duggan's family and that he needed to come out and address the family's concerns. In the end, he eventually emerged and promised to get a senior officer to come and engage with the family.

As mentioned, a Gold Command had been initiated in Tottenham that morning. The police and emergency services use a Gold, Silver, and Bronze (GSB) hierarchy of command in response to major incidents. For example, in the case of a terrorist attack, the police, ambulance, and fire services coordinate their efforts. Under this structure, the Gold Commander serves as the highest-ranking authority, holding ultimate responsibility and accountability for incident management. In such situations, there would also be Silver Command and Bronze Command. The Bronze Command represented the operational command and was the individual we wanted to speak to. They are typically present on-site, overseeing operations. However, the Bronze Command had mysteriously vanished after the morning's Gold Command meeting.

With no one senior available to communicate with, DCI Adelekan promised to bring the Bronze Command to the station to address our concerns. We informed him that we had been waiting outside for approximately four hours, and as the evening approached, we had to consider the families' well-being. It was nearing 8pm in the evening, and we reluctantly agreed to wait one more hour before the families left to go home, feed their children and put them to bed. That was the understanding. DCI Adelekan assured us they would send a police car with sirens and lights activated from Tottenham to Ilford to fetch the senior police officer. Looking back, it should have raised suspicions because there were police stations nearby that could have quickly dispatched an officer. However, we fell for whatever ploy they were executing at that time.

## UPRISINGS AND RIOTS

It seems that they were buying time to bring additional officers to the scene. The designated hour passed without any sign of the Bronze Command appearing. We later discovered that he didn't turn up at all that evening, which is ludicrous given his role as 'operational commander'. At this point, Simone Wilson and other family members decided to leave the location. The frustration of witnessing the families leaving quickly, having been completely ignored, impacted the young individuals present, and fuelled their growing dissatisfaction with the actions of the police.

The situation escalated further when additional officers were brought in. These officers lacked the experience and familiarity with the dynamics of the community and layout of the locality. They seemed oblivious to the history and traditions of the community. In the past, when we gathered at the police station, we would stop traffic, and there was a system in place for managing the flow of vehicles. But these officers didn't know how to handle it. They failed to divert traffic at Bruce Grove, as they traditionally do, allowing it to continue flowing. They stationed officers around the police station but neglected the rest of Tottenham High Road. There was a police car parked on one of the side roads without any officers nearby. When the young people saw the unattended vehicle, they took advantage of the police's inaction and attacked it. The police did nothing to intervene, which only emboldened the young people, and eventually, the situation erupted into chaos.

Stafford Scott addressing the gathering outside Tottenham Police Station in London on 11 January 2014, during a vigil following the jury verdict on 8 January 2014, ruling that Mark Duggan was lawfully killed when he was shot dead by police. Source: Leon Neal/AFP via Getty Images.

It almost feels like we were being set up for this to happen because the sequence of events doesn't make sense, and the police allowed it to unfold without taking appropriate measures.

As a result of the events in Tottenham, a series of uprisings and riots erupted across the country, prompting the return of then-Prime Minister

David Cameron and London Mayor Boris Johnson from their summer vacations. They attempted to shift attention away from the underlying socio-economic issues by denying that the riots were a response to government austerity measures. Instead, they blamed 'urban gangs' for what they perceived as senseless violence.

## CREATION OF THE GANGS NARRATIVE

Following the riots in Tottenham, MP David Lammy and the then Chief Executive of Haringey Council Nick Walkley, initially refused to engage with me claiming that I wasn't a community representative because I hadn't been elected and didn't reside in the borough. However, I challenged them by pointing out that the Chief Executive hadn't been elected and didn't live in the borough either. Eventually, they were forced to recognise my role as a valuable community activist, and discussions began, leading to my involvement in the Operation Shield pilot.

During this time, another activist obtained an embargoed version of the Council's Gangs Matrix database. Patrick Williams, a fellow discussant at our roundtable, has described the Gangs Matrix as follows:

*Responding to the civil unrest that took place in 2011 across London and other cities in the country, the Metropolitan Police Service and former Mayor of London, Boris Johnson, introduced the Gangs Violence Matrix in 2012. The Gangs Matrix is a database, containing the names and personal information of people suspected to be "gang nominals". Underpinning the database is a set of algorithms that use an established scoring criterion to generate an automated violence ranking for individuals. Each person receives a ranking classification of either red, amber or green. Controversial at the time of its inception, the database was created as an intelligence tool that monitors and manages people identified to be involved in criminal activity. It has continued to gain notoriety over the years with critics highlighting its blatant racial disparity. In Amnesty International UK's recent report, Metropolitan Police data from October 2017 shows that there are 3,806 people on the Matrix, of which over three quarters (78%) are black. In contrast, according to other Metropolitan Police data only 27% of people accountable for serious youth violence are black.* [2]

Initially I didn't fully understand its contents, but I found it intriguing, so I obtained a copy. Through local research, we discovered that a significant percentage of those listed on the Haringey Gangs Matrix were neither violent nor actual gang members. In response, I organised a community meeting to inform the public about what I saw as another form of institutionally racist policing.

At this meeting, we highlighted the government's alleged 'war on gangs' and its negative impact on the grassroots Black community. We pointed out that the 2009 Police and Crime Act introduced the first official definition of a gang, primarily to address issues in northern towns where young people facing economic hardship engaged in what the government deemed anti-social behaviour.

2    Patrick Williams, 'Being Matrixed: The (Over)Policing of Gang Suspects in London,' London: Stopwatch, 2018.

The Act emphasised measures like Anti-Social Behaviour Orders (ASBOs) and Super Gang Injunctions to disperse and prevent groups of young people from congregating. However, it acknowledged that wearing hoodies or being in groups didn't necessarily indicate menacing behaviour but could result from fear and other factors.

However, the narrative surrounding gangs shifted after the 2011 summer uprisings, known as the English riots when the government began using the riots to justify their 'war on gangs' and 'gang culture'. However, even a Metropolitan Police review called '4 Days in August' rejected the idea that gangs were responsible for organising the riots in London.[3] Additionally, the Riots Communities and Victims Panel, established by the government to investigate the causes of the riots, found that only a fraction of its recommendations had been implemented, primarily focusing on punitive measures. The government's response to youth violence and gang culture has primarily centred on punitive measures, such as gang injunctions and multi-agency gang prevention programs. These measures, while allegedly aimed at tackling serious youth violence and gang culture, have overlooked addressing the root causes, resulting in increased violence among young people across the country.

This narrative started to take shape in the late 1990s, soon after Tony Blair's Labour Party came to power with the introduction of 'Community Safety Partnerships' as replacements for 'Community Police Consultative Groups' (CPCGs). CPCGs, created after the Scarman inquiry into the 1981 Brixton riots, allowed the community to have a voice in policing matters. However, under Blair's government these partnerships side-lined the community and prioritised so-called 'community safety' from the police's perspective.

This shift led to the creation of multi-agency gang prevention programmes, where various agencies collaborated, excluding the very communities affected. They redefined gangs to include as few as three people, a definition that many found absurd, as gangs typically involve larger memberships and clear structures. This redefinition allowed authorities to justify breaking up groups of young people who came together for reasons other than criminal activity.

Now, let's delve into the redefinition of the term "gang," which they have used as a means to criminalise our community. This shift occurred against the backdrop of the recent riots. As the government grappled with the aftermath and planned its next steps, Theresa May, as Home Secretary, not only created a hostile environment for individuals linked to the Windrush generation but also for those of us whom she couldn't simply deport.

This hostile environment was forged through collaboration between the Home Office, the Department of Work and Pensions (DWP), the Crown Prosecution Service, the Association of Chief Police Officers, and the College of Policing. They formed a government working group to address the aftermath of the riots following the police killing of Duggan. Their response came in November 2011 when they initiated a 'cross-party' effort to address youth and gang violence, resulting in the 'Ending Youth and Gang Violence' report.[4] This

3   Metropolitan Police Service, '4 Days In August: Final Report into the Disorder of August 2011,' London: Metropolitan Police Service, 2012.
4   Home Office, 'Ending Gang and Youth Violence: Cross-Government Report,' https://www.gov.uk/government/publications/ending-gang-and-youth-violence-cross-government-report, London: Home Office, 2011.

report gained significant attention and implementation, outlining actions and principles of good practice for local authorities to tackle street gangs.

At the same time, Theresa May granted new powers to Boris Johnson in London to address the issue, leading to the creation of the Mayor's Office for Policing and Crime (MOPAC). Deputy Mayors Kit Malthouse and Stephen Greenhalgh played central roles in this initiative.

## APPROACHES TO INVENTING AND IDENTIFYING GANGS

Their approach involved reaching out to different regions and requesting reports on their gang issues. In response, the Home Office criticised some areas for their need to improve gang identification and offered additional funding to aid in the identification process. This created a situation where local authorities, facing austerity measures, were incentivised to find and label gangs. Those considered of little value, such as Black children in certain estates, became more valuable when classified as part of a gang. This classification enabled local authorities to access additional financial resources for dealing with them.

Moreover, individuals with purported experience in gangs, referred to as 'practitioners,' were dispatched to all areas labelled as 'priority areas' following the riots. Many of these practitioners came from the DWP, raising questions about their expertise in understanding gangs and identifying gang members – but data revealed that the practitioners at the DWP were identifying hundreds of gang members in 2015.[5]

| Ethnicity | 2014 | 2015 | 2016 | |
|---|---|---|---|---|
| IC1 White – North European | 316 | 341 | 355 | Includes |
| IC2 White – South European | 108 | 114 | 127 | English |
| IC3 Black (SIC) | 2712 | 2890 | 2817 | Includes |
| IC4 Asian (SIC) | 219 | 238 | 229 | Turkish |
| IC5 Chinese, Japanese, SE Asian | 6 | 5 | 6 | |
| IC6 Middle Eastern | 87 | 93 | 92 | |

Source: Information Rights Unit

These so-called 'Gang Specialists' from the DWP might misconstrue the intentions of young people. For instance, a young person might resist going to a certain place, like a college, and claim, "I can't go there." However, these specialists could interpret this as gang involvement, even though it might be a simple excuse to avoid going to college or other training facility. Consequently, young people can be trapped in situations where they are unjustly perceived as members of a violent gang despite any evidence of gang membership or involvement in violence. Their statements may be misinterpreted simply due to their attempts to avoid certain situations.

5   Correspondence between Dr. Patrick Williams and Stafford Smith, November 2023, with reference to a Freedom of Information Act request, information received 18 September 2015. See also: Dr. Patrick Williams and Becky Clarke, 'Dangerous associations: Joint enterprise, gangs and racism", London: Centre for Crime and Justice Studies, 2016, https://www.crime-andjustice.org.uk/publications/dangerous-associations-joint-enterprise-gangs-and-racism.

In January 2012, less than six months after the summer riots, the Mayor's Office for Police and Crime (MOPAC) was established. Mayor Boris Johnson assumed responsibility for the Metropolitan Police Service from the Home Office. However, it's evident that they continued to work in coordination, as shortly after MOPAC's formation, it was announced that Operation Trident would be transformed into the Metropolitan Police's Gangs Command Unit. Before this transformation, Trident had focused on 'Black on Black' gun crime within the MPS. Since its inception in 1998, the unit primarily dealt with crimes committed by members of the Black community, as that was their area of expertise. By rebranding them as the Gang Unit, it became apparent that the Met's primary focus was on so-called Black gangs, to the exclusion of almost all others. This is corroborated by a 2015 Freedom of Information request, where the MPS provided a breakdown of the numbers and ethnicity of gang members across London.

### THE GANGS MATRIX
### AND DISCRIMINATION

This national adoption of the 'Ending Youth and Gang Violence' strategy meant that the local authorities were now treating any interaction among young people as gang-related. The entire public sector had bought into the gang's narrative and were busy trying to identify their local gang members. On the Broadwater Farm estate in Tottenham, immediately after the riots, they implemented special surveillance measures; installing cameras and listening devices on all the landings where they knew young people congregated, hoping to catch confessions about their involvement in the events. It was as if the entire system was coming together with the intent of criminalising young people. Even youth workers were no longer just 'regular' youth workers; they were now referred to as 'gang' youth workers. Any resources allocated to an area now had to be linked to gangs.

Media and especially YouTube videos also played a role. We were surprised to discover that merely appearing in the background of a YouTube video could lead to one's classification as a gang member. This happened to my nephew, who was simply part of a group of friends. There are various ways young people can be labelled as gangsters and included in the Gangs Matrix. For example, when individuals like my nephew Wretch 32, an internationally renowned Rap Artist, want to make a music video, they may gather young people from the estates to participate in the background. But post-riots, simply appearing in a video of certain music genres can lead to the assumption that you're a gangster and can get you put on the Gangs Matrix. Being subjected to frequent stop-and-searches can also result in your inclusion. Recently there has been talk of removing large numbers of young people from the Matrix, as it has become apparent that many are not involved in gangs.[6]

The mentality of Trident, the police unit, seems to be that if you are a victim of violence perpetrated by gangsters, you must also be in a gang. However, the reality is that a significant portion of the violence in these com-

---

6   Towards the end of 2022, approximately 1,200 names were removed from the Gang's Matrix although the disclosure of who these individuals are remains unknown, including to those taken off the database.

munities is not directly related to gangs, turf wars, or territorial disputes. Some young people engage in violence for various reasons, such as jealousy or petty conflicts. Despite this, Trident operates on the belief that involvement in any violence equates to gang membership.

When we examined the Haringey Gangs Matrix, it became clear that many individuals were classified in the lowest category. Yet only 6 per cent were classified as red (the most violent), while most, 65 per cent, fell into the green category. This was surprising because if the police were to be believed, the expectation would have been to see at least 75 per cent classified as red. Furthermore, out of the 100 names on the list, 99 of them happened to be Black youths. The presence of only one Turkish individual associated with the Tottenham Turks, the largest gang in Haringey, raised concerns and provided further evidence that the Met's Gangs Matrix disproportionately targeted Black youths.

## DATA INCONSISTENCIES
## AND COLLECTIVE PUNISHMENT

What also caught our attention was that only 44 per cent of individuals on the list were in custody or subject to any form of judicial restrictions, such as being on probation, wearing an electronic tag, or completing community service. This discrepancy raises questions about why individuals who were supposedly dangerous were not under stricter control if they genuinely posed a threat. This is where the concept of the "pyramid of risk", developed by academics Simon Hallsworth and Tara Young, comes into play.[7] Trident utilises this pyramid, which justifies its focus on middle-risk individuals, as charging the top-tier individuals is seen as more challenging. The "pyramid of risk" justifies gathering people's names and social connections, placing them on the Gangs Matrix. It's not merely a list; being on the Matrix carries significant risks and implications for those listed. This discriminatory targeting sends a troubling message that Black youths are considered criminals. The police's absolute focus on the Black community has reached a point where evidence is no longer necessary and assumptions and stereotypes prevail.

The Runnymede Trust, an independent race equality think tank, highlighted the problematic nature of interpreting benign youth activity or ordinary daily interactions among young people, particularly those from deprived urban neighbourhoods, as deviant or gang-related.[8] The criminalisation of young people based on their associations, such as where they live, which youth club they attend, or which school they attend, has become prevalent. Guilt by association and joint enterprise [a common law doctrine] are used as grounds for prosecution, where individuals can be held responsible for the actions of others, even if they had no direct involvement or intent.

This pattern of criminalisation has even caught the attention of international media, such as *The New York Times*, which has highlighted how Black children in England are being mistreated and how the law is being

---

7    Simon Hallsworth and Tara Young, 'Urban Collectives: Gangs and Other Groups', London: Metropolitan Police Service, 2006.
8    Ian Joseph and Anthony Gunter, 'Gangs revisited: What's a Gang and What's Race Got to Do with It?', (London: Runnymede Trust, 2011), https://assets-global.website-files.com/61488f-992b58e687f1108c7c/617bd64a676d90fd04b82860_GangsRevisited(online)-2011.pdf.

abused to target and imprison them.[9] Instances like the conspiracy to murder case in Manchester, where ten youngsters were put away for a non-event where no violence took place, demonstrate the severe consequences young people face based on flimsy evidence and social media activities. The police often use social media posts to justify placing individuals on the Gangs Matrix, even though social media can be a platform where people act out or express themselves without necessarily reflecting on their real-life actions.

This systemic bias and discriminatory approach not only leads to the overrepresentation of Black people on the Gangs Matrix, but also perpetuates stereotyping and further marginalises these communities. Hundreds of people are in prison, charged with being involved in a 'joint enterprise', but we don't know how many because the statistics are not collected. The ethnicity of those in prison is also unknown due to the lack of data collection.

## COLLECTIVE PUNISHMENT
## AND OPERATION SHIELD

In January 2015, The Home Office sought to clarify and extend the definition of the gang "to make it less prescriptive and more flexible".[10] The changes to the gang definition were accompanied by legislative changes that widened the scope for the use of (super) gang injunctions. There was no longer any mention of geographical territory or gang emblems. Now, the Crown Prosecution Service defines a 'gang' as any group that commits a crime and has one or more characteristics that enable its members to be identified as a group.[11] In the same month, MOPAC announced a budget of 200K had been set aside for a tough new anti-gang initiative entitled Operation Shield. Operation Shield was modelled on the 'Boston Model', which, as the name suggests, had been created in the American state in response to a pandemic of 'Black on Black' gang crime. Most worryingly, new powers are created, including for the first time the use of collective punishment.

London's *Evening Standard* newspaper reported that Operation Shield will enable the Met's Trident unit and local authorities to bring civil or criminal sanctions to "known members" of a gang if one member commits an assault, stabbing, or serious crime.[12] The penalties will range from recall to prison, gang injunctions banning them from parts of the capital or from mixing with their associates, mandatory employment training, or possible eviction from social housing. The offender who commits the crime will be "fast-tracked through the criminal justice system for swift sentencing".[13]

9   Jane Bradley, 'U.K. Doubles Down on a Tactic Disproportionately Targeting Black People' *The New York Times*, 12 November 2022, https://www.nytimes.com/2022/11/12/world/europe/uk-criminal-justice.html; Jane Bradley, 'U.K. Acknowledges Signs of Race Disparity Over Prosecution Tactic,' *The New York Times*, 23 November 2022, https://www.nytimes.com/2022/11/23/world/europe/uk-race-joint-enterprise.html.

10  Home Office, 'Crime and Policing News Update: June 2015', (London: 2015), https://www.gov.uk/government/publications/crime-and-policing-news-update-june-2015/crime-and-policing-news-update-june-2015.

11  "Crown Prosecution Service, 'Gang related offences - Decision making in,' last updated 4 November 2021, https://www.cps.gov.uk/legal-guidance/gang-related-offences-decision-making.

12  Martin Bentham, "Punishment for All Gang Members If One Carries out a Violent Crime", *Evening Standard*, 22 January 2015, https://www.standard.co.uk/news/crime/punishment-for-all-gang-members-if-one-carries-out-a-violent-crime-9994860.html.

13  Bentham, 'Punishment for All Gang Members If One Carries out a Violent Crime'.

In other words, if one member of the gang commits a violent crime, then that person will be sent to prison, and the other gang members will also face a range of civil or criminal proceedings against them.

This clearly unfair practice of 'collective punishment' goes a step further than even the doctrine of joint enterprise would allow, as the other 'gang members' do not have any knowledge of the crime whatsoever. As stated in the heavily redacted Shield Operating Model, "From this point on, police, partners, and community representatives will pay special attention to the entire gang when a single member commits a violent act".[14]

The other official 'partners' in the Operation Shield partnership were Her Majesty's Court Service (HMCS), the Crown Prosecution Service (CPS), the Community Rehabilitation Company (CRC), the National Probation Service (NPS), the Department of Work and Pensions (DWP), Youth Justice Board (YJB), the local Safer Communities Partnership, and the Local Authority's in the target areas.

Yet again, we see governmental departments working in conjunction as part of an "all-out war on gangs and gang culture,"[15]. It should be remembered that they, too, are all working from the misinformation that is contained within the Gang Matrix.

## MISUSE OF POWER
## AND COLLATERAL DAMAGE

This misinformation is then shared as fact and evidence with the rest of the public sector including all the agencies involved in the 'Community Safety Partnerships', the Local Authority, Schools, Social Services, Youth Services, Housing Associations, and even the Driver and Vehicle Licensing Agency (DVLA). What is clear is that when they work with third parties, they do so with the intent of causing harm and distress to their targets. It is called 'Achilles Heel' policing as they are seeking to find their target's 'weak' spot.[16]

An example of how misinformation works to intensify harm is exemplified by their collusion with the DVLA. When we stopped Operation Shield in Haringey, the police expressed dissatisfaction because we wouldn't allow them to proceed. As a result, they decided to target all of the youths on the Haringey GM using the DVLA, the drivers, and the licensing authority to do so. The police informed the DVLA that these young people, whom they called gangsters, smoked excessive amounts of skunk weed, making them unfit to drive. According to the police, these young people should not be on the roads. The DVLA then wrote to these young people, stating that the police had informed them about their unfitness to drive due to their use of skunk weed and/or other drugs.

---

14  The Model was made available through a Freedom of Information Request: London Crime Reduction Board, 'Operation Shield Partnership Agreement and Operating Model', accessed 18 September 2023, https://www.whatdotheyknow.com/request/258657/response/649273/attach/html/2/Operation%20Shield%20Partnership%20Agreement%20and%20Operating%20Model.pdf.html.

15  'PM's speech on the fightback after the riots,' GOV.uk, 15 August 2011, last accessed 9 November, 2023, https://www.gov.uk/government/speeches/pms-speech-on-the-fightback-after-the-riots.

16  Local Government Association, 'Tackling serious and organised crime, a local response', (London: Local Government Association, 2015), https://www.local.gov.uk/sites/default/files/documents/tackling-serious-and-orga-44a.pdf, L.

A video camera films replica cars in a reconstruction of the scene of Mark Duggan's shooting in Tottenham on 2 December 2013. Source: Oli Scarff/Getty Images.

The police officers' statements formed the basis for this correspondence. Many of these young people had already faced challenges, including academic failures and involvement in the criminal justice system. It is remarkable that some of them even managed to take a driving test, considering their difficult circumstances. Unfortunately, they are now stripped of their driving licenses without the need for any actual evidence. They initially requested a urine test, but some individuals used other people's urine, so they now require a blood test. They are forced to complete a questionnaire that asks about the last time they smoked weed, took heroin, or consumed Diazepam. Ultimately, the licenses of many young people were revoked, even if they only had a provisional license. Some of these young people, wanting to drive, will still use a car and consequently get arrested for driving. They then face a civil fine of £1,000 and if they are caught driving again, it will be considered a criminal offence.

### EFFECTS OF OPPRESSIVE POLICING

When young people are consistently treated in this way, oppressive and harmful policing like Operation Shield, brings the entire weight of the system to bear and eventually pushes some of them to a breaking point. They feel cornered by the state and the system. When someone infringes on your personal space or steps on your toes, it can feel like you are being cornered; creating a sense of us against-the-world. This treatment, and the pressures exerted on young people, are well-known triggers. A child who gets bullied in their youth may become a bully as they grow older. When the system acts as a bully, targeting innocent children, it creates a vicious cycle. This is a modern-day iteration of what Stuart Hall and his colleagues outlined in

Policing the Crisis.[17] The Gangs Matrix was created to alienate and to continue the mass criminalisation of young Black men.

## TRAPPED IN THE MATRIX

As a result of our initial investigations and community consultations, we wrote the report, 'The War on Gangs'.[18] We then shared the Haringey Gangs Matrix database with colleagues at Amnesty International, which used our research as part of their extensive examination into the workings of the Matrix, resulting in the landmark human rights report 'Trapped in the Matrix'.[19]

17  Stuart Hall et al., *Policing the Crisis: Mugging, the State, and Law and Order*, (Basingstoke: Palgrave Macmillan, 2013).
18  Stafford Scott, 'The War on Gangs: Or a Racialised War on Working Class Black Youths, State of Nation 2018', London: The Monitoring Group, 2018.
19  Amnesty International, 'Trapped in the Matrix: Secrecy, Stigma, and Bias in the Met's Gangs Database', London: Amnesty International, May 2018.

### Works Cited

Amnesty International. "Trapped in the Matrix: Secrecy, Stigma, and Bias in the Met's Gangs Database." London: Amnesty International. May 2018.

Bentham, Martin. "Punishment for All Gang Members If One Carries out a Violent Crime." Evening Standard, 22 January 2015, https://www.standard.co.uk/news/crime/punishment-for-all-gang-members-if-one-carries-out-a-violent-crime-9994860.html.

Bradley, Jane.'U.K. Acknowledges Signs of Race Disparity Over Prosecution Tactic.' The New York Times, 23 November 2022, https://www.nytimes.com/2022/11/23/world/europe/uk-race-joint-enterprise.html.

———. 'U.K. Doubles Down on a Tactic Disproportionately Targeting Black People.' The New York Times, 12 November 2022,https://www.nytimes.com/2022/11/12/world/europe/uk-criminal-justice.html.

Crown Prosecution Service, 'Gang related offences - Decision making in,' last updated 4 November 2021, https://www.cps.gov.uk/legal-guidance/gang-related-offences-decision-making.

Forensic Architecture. 'The Killing Of Mark Duggan,' 9 June 2020. https://forensic-architecture.org/investigation/the-killing-of-mark-duggan.

Hall, Stuart, Chas Critcher, Tony Jefferson, John Clarke, and Brian Roberts. Policing the Crisis: Mugging, the State, and Law and Order. Basingstoke: Palgrave Macmillan, 2013.

Hallsworth, Simon, and Tara Young. 'Urban Collectives: Gangs and Other Groups,' London: Metropolitan Police Service, 2006.

Home Office. 'Crime and Policing News Update: June 2015.' London, 2015. https://www.gov.uk/government/publications/crime-and-policing-news-update-june-2015/crime-and-policing-news-update-june-2015.

———.'Ending Gang and Youth Violence: Cross-Government Report.' London, 2011. https://www.gov.uk/government/publications/ending-gang-and-youth-violence-cross-government-report.

Joseph, Ian and Anthony Gunter, 'Gangs revisited: What's a Gang and What's Race Got to Do with It?' London: Runnymede Trust, 2011. https://assets-global.website-files.com/61488f992b58e687f1108c7c/617bd64a676d90fd04b82860_GangsRevisited(online)-2011.pdf, accessed 9 November 2023.

London Crime Reduction Board. 'Operation Shield Partnership Agreement and Operating Model,'. Accessed 18 September 2023. https://www.whatdotheyknow.com/request/258657/response/649273/attach/html/2/Operation%20Shield%20Partnership%20Agreement%20and%20Operating%20Model.pdf.html.

Metropolitan Police Service. '4 Days In August: Final Report into the Disorder of August 2011' London: Metropolitan Police Service, 2012.

Scott, Stafford. 'The War on Gangs: Or a Racialised War on Working Class Black Youths.' London: The Monitoring Group, 2018.

Williams, Patrick. 'Being Matrixed: The (Over)Policing of Gang Suspects in London'. London: Stop Watch, 2018.

Williams, Patrick and Becky Clarke, 'Dangerous associations: Joint enterprise, gangs and racism", London: Centre for Crime and Justice Studies, 2016, https://www.crimeandjustice.org.uk/publications/dangerous-associations-joint-enterprise-gangs-and-racism.

### Cover Image

Policemen headed into acrid smoke at Clapham Junction in London on 8 August 2011. Clashes with police continued for a third day in parts of the capital after the killing of Mark Duggan by armed police. Source: Chris Jackson/Getty Images.

# ROUNDTABLE DISCUSSION

*The following text consists of reflections excerpted from a transcript of the Gangs Matrix roundtable, which took place on 17-18 November 2022 at the Centre for Research Architecture. Guests: Stafford Scott, Kamara Scott, Katrina Ffrench, Patrick Williams, Becky Clarke, Ilyas Nagdee, Allan Hogarth.*

**PATRICK WILLIAMS**
**(MANCHESTER METROPOLITAN UNIVERSITY)**

In 2009, I was approached by a colleague to work on an academic project into the 'gangs' problem in Oldham (Greater Manchester). And it was through this piece of work that I really became intrigued and concerned with what was going on.

I was inspired by the work of Claire Alexander, who had written a report called *(Re)thinking 'Gangs'* in 2008. "Given the failure to describe the individually lived realities of gang social life, gang research is essentially an argument over the correct description of a ghost".[1] And there was something really interesting about this characterisation for me because it speaks to that question and challenge of definitions, but also imagery. What is it that we're speaking to (when we talk about 'gangs')? What are the behaviours that we are concerned with? Alexander also highlighted the crucial point that "the harder researchers look, the bigger the gang problem becomes".[2] There's a sense then that academics and social researchers are (re)producing the gang in and of itself. How do we begin to make sense of the academic contribution we're making to the emergence of the 'gang', the 'gang' problem, and the Gangs Matrix?

---

1   Jack Katz and Curtis Jackson-Jacobs, 'The Criminologists' Gang', quoted in Claire E. Alexander, *(Re)Thinking 'Gangs'* (London: Runnymede Trust, 2008), 3.
2   Dick Hobbs, 'Criminal Collaboration: Youth Gangs, Subcultures, Professional Criminals and Organized Crime', quoted in Alexander, *(Re)Thinking 'Gangs'*, 3.

So, I was struck by this notion of the 'gang' as ghost. I was interested in the culture around what we do know about ghosts. Yeah, we're fearful of the ghost, but I'll try to make sense of the ghost. And it was through making these diagrams that I began to see the ghost. It begins to emerge and evolve. It has different forms. It is presented in a range of different ways. But essentially, what we're beginning to see here is a ghost as an embodied (and racialised) subject. So what?

These are charts from a social network analysis developed by academics on the gangs problem in Manchester. The empirical haggling begins to take place when the gang researcher begins to plot. Soon, they're incorrectly plotting where murders are taking place as a resource to empirically demonstrate the reality of the gang. So, the gang becomes this growing problem when it falls into the hands of the police and the state and those criminal justice organisations, the ghost also begins to take on a form which stretches beyond our community's understanding of what is taking place, and certainly moves beyond any community control that we can have over the 'gang' problem. It begins to evolve into something which I believe we no longer have control over; in other words, the ghost is a police product.

**BECKY CLARKE**
**(MANCHESTER METROPOLITAN UNIVERSITY)**

I think we really see the 'gang' take this particular form through policy. Patrick and I had been working in the local area probably for about 15 years in the context of prisons and probation when, in 2011, we were approached by somebody in the council, leading on the implementing Ending Gangs and Youth Violence policy who said: We can't make sense of this issue from what the police are showing us. We're not sure what's going on here. Can we get you access to the data, and will you do this work by looking at how youth violence and gangs are profiled in Manchester?

There was some data in the police system, but we said that we needed data from probation, data from the youth offending teams, as well as data from prisons. We wanted to build a picture of what was being captured in all these data systems to reflect 'gang' flagging, as well as those who, in the same period, were convicted of serious youth violence offences.

We knew from what community members were telling us that this information had consequences, and not just through policing. The prisons were obviously collecting some 'gang' data because it was affecting where prisoners were being placed within the prison system and what level of privileges they were being given in prison because they were being identified as gang members. So, this gang labelling and identification had been happening across the system for quite a while, even if it wasn't called a Gangs Matrix. The juncture of policing practices and ideas of collective punishment have a long history.
I don't know whether people are aware, but the Ending Gangs and Youth Violence policy has much of its basis in what came out of the Centre for Social Justice around that time. They had published 'Dying to Belong'. Then, the Iain Duncan Smith think tank said that gangs were responsible

for the uprisings in 2011, even though the data never supported this conclusion. I always think of policies like black boxes. Once something is put in there, the box is closed, yet everything stems from the basis that what's in that black box is real and true. That this is an 'evidence-based' policy. We hear that term all the time. Our job is often going back to that box and asking, "Wait a minute, what was put in the box?" How can we explore the underlying assumptions? That's what we did when analysing the local data for the problem profile. We didn't necessarily assume that what had been put in that box was wrong, but we needed to be inquisitive and find out exactly what the assumptions around 'gangs' and their relationship to violence and harm were and how they came to be.

**ALLAN HOGARTH**
**(AMNESTY INTERNATIONAL)**

You're not told if you're on the Matrix, and you're not told if you have been taken off. The police have no formal process for letting you know if you're on it or not. And if you ask if you're on the Matrix, they're probably not going to tell you. So, it's a bit like, an Alice in Wonderland experience, where you fall into a rabbit hole, and you're asking yourself, "What's happening?". In fact, the primary indicator that you might be on the Matrix is frequent stops or questioning by the police.

Only a handful of individuals ever have their Matrix status confirmed. One such case is Paul (not his real name), who only became aware of being on the Matrix through his involvement with the council.[3] Paul grew up on an estate in a London borough where the Metropolitan Police has a dedicated gangs taskforce. When he was a teenager, he was involved with gangs, although he questions the loose definition of the term. "I lived in a certain area, had certain friends, went to a certain school. Does that make me in a gang?" Paul had been recruited as a Youth Ambassador for the borough's Gang Prevention Programme and had given workshops to young people in schools in London and other parts of the UK, and advised local authorities, specialised services, government, and the police. Paul only became aware of the Gangs Matrix through his work with the council, when a council official disclosed that he was on the list. The police never told him. He was a pillar of his community and was doing positive good work, contributing and yet he was still on the Matrix and couldn't get off it.

He spent years trying to get them to remove him and was eventually told that he was off, only to discover he was still on it because he had a driving offence from when he was 12. Paul wonders, "Why are you still on to me? Just let me live my life. If I was a white guy from Essex this wouldn't be happening". He is confident that he was only on it because he's a young Black male from a 'problem estate' as he called it, with indirect associations from his network, family, and friends. Paul is just like one of the thousands that we know of that were on that database. This sort of insidious stuff goes on around the database... these

3   For more on Paul's case, see Amnesty International, 'Trapped in the Matrix: Secrecy, Stigma, and Bias in the Met's Gangs Database' (London: Amnesty International, May 2018), 28.

Achilles Heel practices that weaponise vulnerabilities.

With the help of a solicitor, Paul submitted a formal request to receive all the information about him held on the Matrix, including when he was put on it, why, and how he could appeal. The police refused, saying that they were not required to give the information because under the Data Protection Act, it falls under the exemptions for data processing for purposes including the prevention or detection of crime.

**KATRINA FFRENCH
(UNJUST UK)**

Liberty approached UNJUST UK because they had a client named Awate Suleiman, a musician and writer from London. Awate has been subjected to over-policing since he was a child and spent years trying to find out if he was on the Gangs Matrix. At that point, we decided to launch a judicial review claim because it took the Met several years to confirm or deny if he was on the Matrix, which had a severe impact on his life. We wondered if Awate would have standing sufficient to bring the case because it turned out that he wasn't on the Matrix. And so, UNJUST UK joined the case as a claimant to support it as a public interest case.

We were due to go to court this week to argue that the Matrix discriminates against people of colour, particularly Black men, and breaches human rights, data protection requirements and public law principles. We were basically trying to get the Met to admit that they had breached privacy law and that the system was racist. But last Friday, 11 November 2022, we received a settlement from them.

They did not acknowledge that the system was racist; in fact, they wouldn't even recognise institutional racism. So, having them admit it was a discriminatory database was a long shot. But they did acknowledge that they had breached Article 8 of the European Convention on Human Rights, which is the right to private and family life. Additionally, the Met agreed to inform people who ask if they are on the Matrix, and to remove the majority of individuals from the database. This includes removing all people classified as 'green' (those allocated the lowest risk scores). So, all of that is very good. However, we were concerned that some people might have their risk scores adjusted and become marked as 'amber' to keep them on the list.

I think that overall, it's a win. But I'm not going to lie to you; I think the Gangs Matrix, in a sense, is already obsolete. I'm worried about what else is replacing it. We already know to some degree what is happening because there are the Concern Hubs, a new multi-agency diversion which shares data around gang activity piloted in 2019. The language has changed from targeting so-called perpetrators to safeguarding victims. The Concern Hubs claim to be intervening to help young people at risk of becoming involved in violence, drugs, or gang activity. That also means this initiative widens the net of agencies that will be brought in, including health, housing, and education, given that it's framed as a duty of care issue. With this, we are seeing the switch of rhetoric and tactics.

# FIELD NOTES

# MĀORI MAURI MAGIC

S. BARBER, A. RATA, W. ROESTENBURG,
H. KOPEKE-TE AHO

# INTRODUCTION
by Simon Barber (Kāi Tahu)

The texts and images gathered within this collective contribution express a radical tradition that has asserted the inalienable connection of Māori to their land and to the inherent political authority that emerges from it; a set of practices that existed long before the arrival of colonisers in Aotearoa. It consists of a poem by Arama Rata, a narrative penned by Waireti Roestenburg, and illustrations produced by Huriana Kopeke-Te Aho. Together with this introduction, they aim at reconfiguring understandings of politics and aesthetics within the context of Māori radical anti-colonial traditions.

The first text is a poem by Arama Rata that gives voice to an ancestor as they call out from the stone of a wall they were forced to build while imprisoned by the settler state, charged with sedition. The second text is a personal narrative by Waireti Roestenburg in which she teaches us the importance of learning to hold our hurt and our healing in balance. She does this through the "kawakawa", a medicinal plant whose leaves develop potency after they have healed from caterpillar bites. The poem and the stony wall, the teaching and the kawakawa are all forms of media that militate for the righting of injustice; the ending of colonisation and the restoration of the fullness of our connection to our ancestors. They are also mediums for the voices of the ancestors who talk to, into and through us in the present. By "medium" here, I mean it more in the sense of media theory than that of seance. For Marshall McLuhan, it was not, for example, that the car was the messenger of a new age. It was the whole system that produced and supported it: the infrastructure of highways and roads, the extractive industries of fossil fuels, associated cultural practices. In short, the entire world that was given over to automotivity.[1]

Similarly, for Māori, everything in existence is co-constituted by way of a holistic relational web. Time is not linear but co-present with all other time, so the past, the present and the future interpenetrate as "now-time". This, then, is the medium from which the texts in this section instaurate radical temporal conjunctions whereby our ancestors speak to and through us on behalf of generations to come. To address the co-presence of the past, present, and future in visual form, we asked Huriana Kopeke-Te Aho, an artist producing posters and flyers for Māori political struggles, to illustrate the texts.

The authors add their voices to the enduring Māori struggle for the return of land that was stolen as well as for the political authority and autonomy that was illegitimately taken. For Māori, political authority is grounded in an ancestral connection that stretches back to ngā Atua (the gods). Likewise, Māori do not own the land, but are an intrinsic part of it; connected to Paptūānuku (Earth Mother) through their existence. Participation 'in' and 'as' the land is shared between the dead, the living, and the yet-to-be-born. It is a power that grows out of intergenerational Māori inhabitation and connection; one that is expressed through the political community of the hapū (sub-tribe). The hapū itself is understood as being derived directly from the land-as-living-being. Thus any authority over the land is inseparable from authority from the land. This sense of 'belonging to' is opposed to colonial as well as contemporary forms of territorial sovereignty that exert their dominion and 'control over' an externalised nature. The land is a vast ancestral church composed of the earth and the sky that encompasses all living entities. Authority derived from active participation 'in' and 'as' the land consequently involves responsibility towards maintaining relationships between past generations as well as those to come

---

1    Marshall McLuhan. *Understanding Me: Lectures and Interviews*, eds. Stephanie McLuhan and David Staines, (Cambridge, Massachusetts: MIT Press, 2003), 241–242.

The necessity of being in good relation is codified in a system of principles, protocols and values called tikanga.[2] Tikanga is derived from the term "tika" meaning "right" or "just" with tikanga being approximated by the word "justice" or "justness". Tikanga is the first law of Aotearoa although its existence as such was, and continues to be, denied by colonial powers. The denial of an existing system of law and the ability of self-governance is part of a technology of dispossession that was devised primarily by the political philosopher John Locke in 1690. In his writing 'On Property' which more accurately should have been called 'On Expropriation', Locke elaborates two key concepts: political society and property.[3] These concepts were defined in such a way so as to specifically disqualify Indigenous peoples from inclusion. Firstly, Indigenous forms of government were placed within the 'state of nature', and thus in the distant and surpassed history of Europe's own development. Secondly, Indigenous modes of life, our ways of inhabiting the land, were considered a prehistoric and proto form of European property rights and therefore were also excluded from counting as such. The operations of these two concepts works to render Indigenous forms of political organisation and our relationships with the land as inconsequential. Together they served to justify the expropriation and domination of Indigenous lands and peoples.

In a robust denial of Locke's tenets, 34 northern chiefs signed He Whakaputanga (a Declaration of Independence) in 1835. He Whakaputanga asserted that all sovereign power and authority resided with the hereditary chiefs and heads of tribes. It also outlined a process for hapū (sub-tribes) and iwi (tribes) to "make joint decisions on matters of common concern while respecting the mana of each participating polity. It was a constitutional transformation in which Iwi and Hapū would exercise an interdependent authority while retaining their own independence".[4] In 1840 the principles of He Whakaputanga were reaffirmed in the signing of Te Tiriti o Waitangi. Te Tiriti o Waitangi and The Treaty of Waitangi are the names for the Māori and English language versions of a treaty signed by around 540 Māori chiefs and the British Crown in 1840.[5] The vast majority of the rangatira (chiefs) signed the Māori language version and it is this text that is taken to be the authoritative text. Te Tiriti asserts that absolute sovereignty over Aotearoa was to remain with hapū and iwi. Given that this authority was a treasure passed down from the ancestors to be exercised in the present in service of the generations to come its alienation would have been absolutely unthinkable despite the claims by the Crown to the contrary. Instead, Te Tiriti outlines a relationship with the Crown premised on timeless Māori institutions of political authority whereby the Crown would assume a governance function over its own citizens, but absolute sovereignty would reside with the chiefs. That is, the Crown would be allowed independence within its own sphere of action, but this would be limited by the need to conform to the existing laws of Aotearoa: tikanga. Te Tiriti o Waitangi was never honoured by the Crown, but the legacy of Māori struggle has ensured it remains relevant.

2   Hana Burgess and Te Kahuratai Painting. 'Onamata, anamata: A whakapapa perspective of Māori futurisms,' in *Whose futures?*, eds. Anna-Maria Murtola and Shannon Walsh, (Tāmaki Makaurau Auckland: Economic and Social Research Aotearoa, 2020), 205–233.

3   John Locke. *Two Treatises of Government*, ed. Peter Laslett, (Cambridge: Cambridge University Press, 1999), 285–302.

4   'He Whakaaro Here Whakaumu Mo Aotearoa: The Report of Matike Mai Aotearoa - The Independent Working Group on Constitutional Transformation', Network Waitangi tautahi, 2016, https://nwo.org.nz/resources/report-of-matike-mai-aotearoa-the-independent-working-group-on-constitutional-transformation/, 44.

5   'Signing the treaty,' Ministry for Culture and Heritage, last modified July 1, 2016, accessed 29 October 2023, https://nzhistory.govt.nz/politics/treaty/making-the-treaty/signing-the-treaty.

**S. BARBER, A. RATA, W. ROESTENBURG, H. KOPEKE-TE AHO**

In 1975, the Waitangi Tribunal was created as a concession to growing discontent amongst Māori. Although symbolically important, the Tribunal was initially limited in its purview to breaches of Te Tiriti/The Treaty after 1975. This clause was vehemently criticised by Māori given that most of the land had, of course, been stolen long before this date. Under sustained pressure from Māori, the Crown conceded, and in 1985 legislation allowed the Tribunal to hear breaches dating back to the signing of the Treaty. The Tribunal process is ongoing and still drives a lot of politics in Aotearoa New Zealand. As a result of the Tribunal's findings, financial compensation has been made to a number of iwi, but by any calculations this amounts to a pittance in relation to what was stolen. However, one important outcome of the Tribunal process has been the emergence of significant relationships of co-governance between iwi (tribes) and the State in an attempt to honour the partnership outlined in Te Tiriti o Waitangi. For example, Te Urewera (formerly New Zealand's largest national park), and the Whanganui and Waikato rivers, have recently been granted legal personhood and have codified a relationship of co-governance with the relevant iwi in law.[6] While these arrangements mark a significant improvement they fall far short of the return of political autonomy and authority to Māori as outlined in Te Tiriti.

Most recently, the mantle of giving voice to the Māori constitutional imagination has been taken up by *Matike Mai Aotearoa, The Independent Working Group on Constitutional Transformation*. Matike Mai held over three hundred hui (gatherings) around the country seeking input and engagement from Māori on questions of constitutional transformation. The report that resulted from these engagements provides a profound record of the strength and vitality of Māori democratic practices and the energy and expansiveness of Māori political imagination. The report of the Working Group outlines six possible constitutional models that issued from the hui they conducted. The majority of the models suggest some variation on an arrangement whereby two separate spheres of influence, a Māori Rangatiratanga (chiefly authority and autonomy) sphere and a Pākehā Crown/Kāwanatanga (government) sphere, interact by way of a third relational sphere. The transformational effects of this new constitutional framework operates in two directions. On the one hand:

> rangatiratanga [chiefly authority and autonomy] would once again be a site and concept of our constitutional uniqueness rather than merely a means of accessing or trying to limit Crown policy. It could be exercised as an absolute authority in our sphere of influence because it has always been absolutely our power to define, protect and decide what was in the best interests of our people. As a taonga handed down from the tīpuna it could flourish by being sensitive once more to all of the relationships and tikanga that have shaped it in this place. It would be a conciliatory but independent authority no longer subject to the power of another, and the only constraints upon it would be those that tikanga has always imposed – that independence is only real when it depends upon the interdependence one has in relationships with others.[7]

> On the other, for the settler state, In its own sphere of influence it would still source its power in its history of Westminster sovereignty but it would no longer need to be conceived as a dominating power that is arrogant in its indivisibility

---

6    Andrew Geddis and Jacinta Ruru, 'Places as Persons: Creating a New Framework for Māori-Crown Relations,' in *The Frontiers of Public Law*, eds. Jason Varuhas and Shona Wilson Stark, (Chicago: Hart Publishing, 2019), 255–274.
7    Matike Mai, 'He Whakaaro,' 112.

*and unchallengeability. Rather it could find in its oft-professed good faith a more honourable power that prizes relationships more than conflict.*[8]

Arama Rata and Waireti Roestenburg's texts presented in this contribution emerged alongside a series of hui (gatherings) of Māori scholars and activists that were organised around picking up the challenge put down by Maitike Mai and developing paths towards constitutional transformation by 2040. They are a unique form of situated militant media. In order to be able to fully appreciate how these texts intervened in this struggle it is necessary to understand something of the onto-epistemological bases of te ao Māori (the Māori world).

Both authors speak of the way in which the struggle for a world before and beyond this one must be conceived of as having two aspects. For Māori, although our ancestors have passed away into the spiritual realm they remain alongside us and have continued presence within the physical world. The world beyond is a spiritual world that retains its intimate relationship with the current world of our existence. But the world beyond is also the world of generations to come. It is this aspect that is crucial, in that, we must imagine and breathe life into a world free of colonial domination before and beyond the world of our still-colonial present so as to "whaka-tika" or "make right" the injustices of the past.[9] It is to this beyond in the double sense—one which draws on our ancestors for strength and direction as well as for healing the damage done to them through our own flourishing for the sake of the generations to come—that Rata and Roestenburg share with us. Likewise, Huriana Kopeke-Te Aho, whose images accompany the texts has developed a visual language of protest that maintains the umbilical connection between the ways of the ancestors, the vitality of the present, and the generations to come.

Rata's text gives voice directly to the ancestors as they communicate with their present-day descendants. An ancestor calls out through the medium of a stone wall constructed by the forced labour of Māori from Parihaka who were convicted of the crime of attempting to live peacefully and independently on their own land. The Crown had invaded Taranaki in 1860 to provide land for settlers. Subsequently vast tracts of land were confiscated from Māori who were deemed to have been in sedition against the Crown for attempting to protect their own land from settler acquisition. An operation exemplary of the twin operations of law instantiating and law preserving violence in the settler colony. War and confiscation led to massive displacement of Taranaki Māori in the period. Under the leadership of Te Whiti o Rongomai and Tohu Kakahi, a large Māori settlement emerged at Parihaka to provide home to the dispossessed. Te Whiti and Tohu and the community at Parihaka promoted peaceful resistance, living in independence from the colonial regime, and egalitarian forms of self-governance.

One of the strategies at Parihaka for peaceful resistance to settler encroachment was ploughing settler land and fencing it off. Hundreds of those who undertook this work were imprisoned without trial and then sentenced to hard labour building infrastructure for the colony. In addition, the Crown enacted a series of laws that meant Māori could be imprisoned indefinitely and without trial while also claiming indemnity for itself. The spectacular—for its violence—conclusion of Parihaka was the Crown invasion of 1881. Fifteen hundred troops invaded the settlement, houses and gardens were destroyed, women

8  Matike Mai, 'He Whakaaro,' 112.
9  Moana Jackson, 'Decolonisation and the stories in the land,' *E-tangata*, 9 May 2021, https://e-tangata.co.nz/comment-and-analysis/moana-jackson-decolonisation-and-the-stories-in-the-land/.

**S. BARBER, A. RATA, W. ROESTENBURG, H. KOPEKE-TE AHO**

were raped, and livestock was slaughtered.[10] A flourishing Māori community who also refused to sell land was a humiliation the Crown could not conscience. In Arama's story, the convicted men maintain connection with the wall they were forced to build and call out to their descendants. Atua (gods) swirl amongst the day-to-day life in the now-settler city where she stands. The ancestors' message is one of an enveloping love as well as a call to a relationship not wholly mediated by the devastation of colonisation.

Waireti's text also describes the communication of the ancestors into experience. Visited by a painful recognition of the devastation colonisation has wrought on her people Waireti calls out to her ancestors for guidance. The ancestors respond by saying that they have given her this pain so as to open a path, and to set her on a path, towards healing her ancestors. Her text references a thinking-with or being called towards the Kawakawa plant and is the result of careful symbolic exchange with the world that is both one of close observation and communion. There is a saying in Māori: "Kei raro i nga ‾tarutaru, ko ngā tuhinga a ngā tūpuna" (beneath the herbs and plants are the writings of the ancestors) that provides powerful statement of the way in which thinking is an expression of the land of which we are part.[11] This way of being orientated towards the world and of being called into relationship with other entities is entirely consistent with Māori conceptions of thought that sees the self as co-constituted with the entirety of existence rather than the subject set apart from some remainder. As the philosopher Carl Mika explains:

> "whakaaro" which, alongside its common definition of "to think", can also mean a type of "orientation towards" something, prior to thinking or any other kind of cognitive engagement. Of central importance to this seemingly straightforward definition, though, is that one does not conduct one's own "orienting": I am in fact oriented towards something by the All because it constitutes me (and every other thing) in a material sense. Crucially, whakaaro can refer to an orientation taken by non-humans as well as humans.[12]

Thinking, then, is a complex interaction of the self and the world with its location distributed across different types of entities, different kinds of media—a kind of network effect. For example, in Waireti's account, thinking is distributed across the ancestors, the stomach and the heart, the concept of mā-hara (hurting and wholeness in interaction), the Kawakawa plant, the caterpillar that eats its leaves, the potency that is produced by the plant healing itself, the earth the plant is rooted in, the earth mother and sky father, te ao marama (the world of light and being that is born from the night of becoming), and ultimately te Aorangi (the cloak of the universe).

Whakapapa is perhaps the most fundamental concept in te Ao Māori. It describes the way in which everything in existence or that has ever been, both visible and invisible, is part of a vast cosmological whānau (family), the connections of which lead back to the cosmogenic embrace of the primordial parents, Pāpatūānuku and Ranginui. Within this totality, or the All as Mika terms it, it is mauri (life-force), one of the essential building blocks of the universe that makes possible an internal differentiation of beings within unity. In Māori Marsden's words, mauri is:

10   'Parihaka', Te Kotahitanga o Te Atiawa Taranaki, accessed September 26, 2023 https:// teatiawa.iwi.nz/history/parihaka/.

11   Waitangi Tribunal. *Ko Aotearoa Tēnei: Te Taumata Tuatahi: a Report into Claims Concerning New Zealand Law and Policy Affecting Maori Culture and Identity*, (Wellington: Legislation Direct, 2011), 105.

12   Carl Mika, 'Where Do We Stand When We Know? Mātauranga Māori and its Translation as "Science"', *The Philosopher* 109, no.2, https://www.thephilosopher1923.org/post/where-do-we-stand-when-we-know.

*the life-force which generates, regenerates and upholds creation. It is the bonding element that knits all the diverse within the Universal 'Procession' giving creation its unity in diversity. It is the bonding element that holds the fabric of the universe together.*[13]

In Rata's text it is the mauri of the stone that her ancestor handled that mediates the dialogue between the spirit world and the world of the living. For Roestenburg mauri is the way through which the world can speak into and through us. Both are examples of what the latter terms Māori Mauri Magic: our felicitous participation in the assembled powers of the earth in the struggle for the restoration of balanced relationships before and beyond those of domination.

## BRICK WALL
*by Arama Rata (Ngāruahine, Taranaki iwi,*
*Ngāti Maniapoto, Ngāti Apakura)*

*Hiiiii*
*Haaaaa*
*Hiiiiiiii*
*Haaaaaaa*
*Hiiiiiiiiii....*
I was once of flesh and blood and bone. Bound in machinery
of brain and body. Sharp sensations. Thirst and hunger.
Winter waters. Sun on skin. Sex. Labour, strenuous, tedious.
Endured for the drive stronger than all else: to be alive
alive alive.
Oh how I loved being alive! The precision of it. The certainty
of physics, artistry of body in motion, eloquence of speech,
physiology of laughter and tears.
The me that was. So terrified of death. How I gripped at life
as it slipped- as it was ripped from me.
And yet I recognise myself in you, strange reflection.
Shying from life. Inviting the abyss.
Seeking paradise between thoughts and breaths. Falling
off edges of conversation. The clumsy gestures of soul
discontent with bodily boundaries.
We two deny ourselves peace here and now, yearning
for otherwise.
I would not have guessed you would be one to recognise
me. You had never spoken my name, visited my bones,
or gathered among multitudes of mokopuna singing us home.
I, of course, recognised you. I see you- I am with you all.
Stonger in the places I linger. Though I am nowhere in
particular.
Perhaps you could think of me as a paraoa, rolling through
the clouds above the ever-growing city. Though at times
I am more of a stingray.
I often circle the hilltops, retracing steps taken in life. I sweep
though grasses where I was laid to rest, revisit scars left in

13  Māori Marsden and Te Ahukaramū Charles Royal. *The woven universe: selected writings of Rev. Māori Marsden*, (Otaki: Estate of Rev. Māori Marsden, 2003), 44.

the earth where I dwelt and laboured, brick by brick by brick.
I sometimes commune with plants and animals open to spirit.
But mostly I am more like the clouds themselves. Hovering.
Embracing all.
There is a sort of physics here too. The more everywhere
I am, the faster time circles.
The city heaves into life every morning and settles again
at night like giant lungs soaking up sunlight. Souls streak
through streets, dart in and out of buildings, cluster and disperse predictably. The patterns made evident by you:
exception proving the rule.
You climbed Ahumairangi most days and returned to your
whare in the evenings like so many others. But amid colony
ants, you were a bead of water, flowing and stopping, as
though not of your own volition.
One day, as city lungs exhaled, your water bead drew
near my bones.
From cloud I rolled into paraoa, to stingray and swept down
before you. You stared at me unseeing for a long moment,
motionless on the footpath.
Under your gaze, the feeling of your presence sharpened
into something akin to eyesight and I found myself almost
able to stare back.
Nearby a kurī barked and pawed at her fence and your
attention. You continued downhill, pulling me in your wake,
your ghostly whai aute: stingray kite.
From grounds where a prison once stood, you followed
the path I marched in chains. Of the brickworks where
I laboured, nothing remained.
But further ahead our brick wall still stood. Pulled in,
I swim through terracotta aquarium.
Without stopping, you pass by, the back of your hand
brushing course brick.
Skin gone a century tingles in response, savouring sensations
as you wander on by.
Daily our energies danced. Your touch became less tentative as time
progressed, everyday tracing the edges of me, finding fingerprints in
clay and the stamps in the bricks we made.
The day you approached from the West I was waiting. The wind
dropped suddenly, and silence descended. Your eyes fell upon a
plaque, and you read the line, "...the bricks were made by prisoners".
Ko te hinatore. A crack in cognition opens just wide enough
for spirit to enter. You fall to your knees, without knowing why,
hearing for the first time, tangi, as it pours through you.
Our ngākau align. We two, become one. You feel, as your own,
indignities: invasion, imprisonment, disease and death. I feel
chest heaving, body shaking, vocal vibration, the flow of hupe
and roimata, connecting us, dissolving us, so we can be
made anew.

**MĀORI MAURI MAGIC**

You hold your hand to the wall with longing and despair;
your lamentation growing softer as my bodily sensations fade.
And now, after this infinite pause, I let go to embrace eternity.
You gather your strength and slowly stand. And four thousand
tīpuna stand with you.
*Haaaaaaaaa.*

## KAWAKAWA AND MĀ–HARA KŌRERO
### By Waireti Roestenburg
*(Ngāti Kahungunu ki Te Wairoa, Ngāti Pāhauwera,*
*Rongomai Wahine, Ngāpuhi nui tōnu)*

*Compared to the presence of our tupuna, the white intrusion*
*in Aotearoa is but a blink in the eternity of time.*
*Donna Awatere*[14]

Prior to entering academia, I worked in a wairua-centric (spiritual) healing centre for 13 years. I also worked for the local Whanganui iwi as a Kaiatawhai or social worker. During this time, I had a profound 'decolonial' and Indigenous re-vitalisation experience, one that seemed to arrive from elsewhere. I felt it right in my heart and in my guts. It was from this experience that I understood in my puku (stomach) the devastation so few of our ancestors survived. I was grief-stricken and started crying. Two days later, I was still crying. On the second evening, I picked up a pūtātara (conch shell) and I blew it into the setting sun. I sent a karanga (sacred call) asking my Ancestors to tell me what was going on. I asked them why they had given me this great pain and what I was meant to do with it. They replied immediately. They said that they had given me this pain so that if I wanted to, I could heal them. They told me that healing them meant reinstating them, and that reinstating them meant finding the way of walking and being in the world today that they would be walking and being, had they been able to continue their life-courses on their own terms.

I said yes, and like magic—all the pain was gone. Somehow, I understood that I would go to university. I was drawn towards psychology. Even though I had four dependent children, I commenced full-time study within six months of this experience. I did not know why I was in psychology; I was just following where I felt I was being led. I guessed it was to find or bring Māori wairua-centric ways of working into Western psychology, so our people could be looked after in this way.

During that journey, I developed and carried a question. The question was: what would a Māori psychology our Ancestors could recognise look like? I only met three people who I thought may be able to answer this question: Dr. Rangimarie Te Turuki Rose Pere-Lambert (our Ngāti Kahungunu spiritual leader, academic and Nanny), a university Psychology department kaumatua, and a Kaiwhaikōrero (principal speaker) at Tokorangi Marae where a significant psychology gathering was hosted.

The healing centre I worked in operated in accordance with a particular spiritual lineage, one that is attached to Mere Rikiriki (1855–1926), a prophetess and healer who trained two people: Rātana and Te Mareikura. She sent Rātana off with the Bible to look after the people. He founded the Ratana movement and settlement. She sent Te Mareikura off with the pot to cook for the people. Maungarongo Marae in Ohakune

---

14  Donna Awatere, 'Māori Sovereignty: part two,' *Broadsheet*, no. 103 (October 1982), 26.

**S. BARBER, A. RATA, W. ROESTENBURG,
H. KOPEKE-TE AHO**

and the Māramatanga movement were established around his teachings. Both hahi (Māori religions) continue today. Along with the other Māori prophets, they led Māori into and through the darkest days of our near extinction. The healing centre where I worked was run by the grandchildren of Te Mareikura.

When we were welcomed onto the marae at Tokorangi I heard the Kaiwhaikōrero share that we were in one of Mere Rikiriki's wānanga marae. So, without any conscious awareness I found myself on the pulse of the spiritual lineage which I had been working under, and in, for years. On the first night they gave us the mana whenua kōrero (home peoples' narrative) about where we were and who they were. I approached the Kaiwhai-kōrero afterwards in the kitchen and told him my spiritual lineage to Mere Rikiriki, and so he was very open to me. I asked him my question: what might a Māori psychology that the Ancestors could recognise look like? He thought for a little while. Then he said to me that he believed a Māori psychology our Ancestors could recognise would be about mā-hara (recollection, thought, memory. He said mā is about our light, our vitalities, our goodness, and our healing. On the other hand, hara is about our hurting, trauma and "maemae"(pain, wound, injury). He believed a Māori psychology our Ancestors could recognise would be about helping our people re-find the ways to carry our healing, "mā", and our hurting, "hara", in balance and in harmony as we move through our lives: mā-hara.

A little while after this, I was in Mahia as part of a Matariki (Māori Lunar New Year) Manawahine (power, authority, status of Māori women) Wānanga (collective healing/knowledge emerging experience). That's when the Ancestors dropped into me an understanding of the way in which kawakawa (pepper tree, Macropiper excelsum) talks to and carries mā-hara. Kawakawa is one of our most recognised and well-known rongoā (medicines). What is not often known is that it is not the perfect leaves that hold the healing potencies. The healing power is an outcome of the interaction be-tween a caterpillar (rimurimu) and the leaf. As the caterpillar injures and eats the leaf, enzymes are released. In a kind of magical symbiotic relationship—the caterpillar, the injury, the enzymes, and the kawakawa—synthesise a healing potency.

So, rather than perfection, it is the process of mā-hara—hurting and wholeness in interaction—that produces the potency. I realised the "hara" or hurting, is represent-ed by the holes in the kawakawa leaf, and the "mā", or the healing, by the wholeness of the leaf and bush. Kawakawa and mā-hara, or te reo Māori (the Māori language), arise from the natural world and life itself. Together, kawakawa and mā-hara teach us the powerful healing potencies that are possible if we can find a way to hold our harming and healing in balance, because we also arise from the natural world. If we can find a way to recognise and understand our "hara" of historical/intergeneration trauma and soul wounding from past and ongoing colonisation, and hold this harming within the light and reality of our more expansive and natural Indigenous vitalities, then, like the injured kawakawa leaf a powerful healing potency is released.

Also, the holes of the leaf itself do not exist in isolation. Our pain does not exist in isolation. The leaf is on a branch with other leaves that are connected to a small leaf-let branch, that is connected to a stem. The stem is in turn connected to an extensive root system that ensures the bush is anchored in and part of the rhythms and flow of life itself. The kawakawa bush is rooted in Papatūānuku (Earth Mother) and embraced by Ranginui (Sky Father), and therefore is part of the whole life system that is te ao marama (the world of light), that is in turn also part of a wider system that is te Aorangi (cloak of the universe). So, what the kawakawa and mā-hara teach us is the impor-tance of knowing who we are, our whakapapa, our connections to each other, to the earth, and to the cosmos. And also, the importance of approaching our "hara" or hurting/trauma from a life-world position that is anchored in, emanates and honours the natural wholeness and healing vitalities of life itself.

I work with our Mongrel Mob-affiliated youth. As part of this work, we had a guy come and talk to our boys. This guy had made the ultimate sacrifice; he had taken the rap for someone else and been sentenced to life imprisonment as a result. Because of this he was notorious, a big guy in the Mob. Yet, he came to talk to our boys to urge them to do everything they could to avoid the pathway he had taken. At one point, he said that growing up as a Māori boy in Wairoa, he thought the world fucking hated him and he fucking hated the world right back. In relation to kawakawa, at this time in his life, the only thing that existed for him was the hole/trauma/pain. His entire world was the "hara", the hurting. The trauma of colonisation, both historical and ongoing, was so huge he thought he lived in a world of only hate and hurting. And that's what he got, and that's what he gave, so he was really trapped. The trauma was so thick and complex that there was no light for him, there was no healing. He had not way to balance his "hara" with his 'mā'.

One thing I want to make clear is that I am not inferring that being hurt is good for us. That is of course untrue, even if some trends within psychology (such as the ubiquitous language of 'resilience') take this position. For some of our people the darkness of colonisation is all they know: the hole and the harm are their entire universe. However, if we can take healing to them and if we can help them by igniting their understanding and experience of their 'mā' (light)—I find this especially with the Mongrel Mob boys and men that I work with, they have such good hearts—it doesn't take much to bring them alive to the notion of their light and healing. Colonization has ripped huge holes in our personal, collective and intergenerational hearts, minds, bodies, and souls. We have been systematically lied to and told that it is a civilizing and humanizing mission carried out by a superior civilization, for our own good. When in fact it was and remains a strategically designed and well tested elsewhere, death-centric technology and system of hurting, harming that results in the stealing of our lives, lands and livelihoods by a people capable of ghastly and superior brutality. The past and ongoing colonial process has ripped huge holes into our personal and collective being and lives. The truth has been hidden so that we have whānau (family) walking around in the world stuck in that darkness and they come to internalise it as their own fault and shame.

Healing involves grounding ourselves in the eons of truth bequeathed to us by our ancestors, in our Indigenous vitalities and our capacity to have dignity, potential, and goodness. Before colonization arrived, we lived in harmony with the natural and the 'other than human' worlds. Despite every attempt to destroy them the old stories and rhythms of this land, and the stories of our ancestors, have survived. The teachings of mā-hara and the kawakawa are examples of how the world can talk into and through us, how mauri (life force) can talk into and through us, how our Ancestors can talk into and through us and through that process illumine and inspire our hearts, hopes, healing, and minds. In poet Arapera Kaa Blank's words:

> Thus we are inheritors
> of interwoven dreams,
> whose paua-shimmering music ever
> echoes on the wind.

It is this paua-shimmering music or magic that I have come to call our Māori Mauri Magic (MMM), it is the vital and dynamic force that flows from our Ancestors into the present and reminds us that "even the greatest injustice need not destroy hope". It is from this that we draw our healing and our potency, and our insistence that colonisation is not all that there is to us.

**S. BARBER, A. RATA, W. ROESTENBURG,
H. KOPEKE-TE AHO**

## Works Cited

Awatere, Donna. 'Māori Sovereignty: part two', *Broadsheet*, no. 103 (October 1982), 24–29.

Burgess, Hana, and Te Kahuratai Painting. 'Onamata, anamata: A whakapapa perspective of Māori futurisms,' in *Whose futures?*, eds. Anna-Maria Murtola and Shannon Walsh. Tāmaki Makaurau Auckland: Economic and Social Research Aotearoa, 2020.

Geddis, Andrew, and Jacinta Ruru. 'Places as Persons: Creating a New Framework for Māori-Crown Relations,' in *The Frontiers of Public Law*, edited by Jason Varuhas and Shona Wilson Stark, 255–274. Chicago: Hart Publishing, 2019.

Locke, John. *Two Treatises of Government*, edited by Peter Laslett. Cambridge: Cambridge University Press, 1999.

Marsden, Māori and Te Ahukaramū Charles Royal. *The woven universe: selected writings of Rev. Māori Marsden*. Otaki: Estate of Rev. Māori Marsden, 2003.

Matike Mai, 'He Whakaaro Here Whakaumu Mo Aotearoa: The Report of Matike Mai Aotearoa-The Independent Working Group on Constitutional Transformation', Network Waitangi Ōtautahi, 2016, https://nwo.org.nz/resources/report-of-matike-mai-aotearoa-the-independent-working-group-on-constitutional-transformation/.

McLuhan, Marshall. *Understanding Me: Lectures and Interviews*, eds. Stephanie McLuhan and David Staines. Cambridge, Massachussetts: MIT Press, 2003.

Mika, Carl. 'Where Do We Stand When We Know? Mātauranga Māori and its Translation as "Science"', *The Philosopher* 109, no.2, accessed September 26, 2023, https://www.thephilosopher1923.org/post/where-do-we-stand-when-we-know.

Ministry for Culture and Heritage, 'Signing the treaty,'. Last modified July 1, 2016.https://nzhistory.govt.nz/politics/treaty/making-the-treaty/signing-the-treaty.

Jackson, Moana. 'Decolonisation and the stories in the land', *E-tangata,* May 9, 2021.https://e-tangata.co.nz/comment-and-analysis/moana-jackson-decolonisation-and-the-stories-in-the-land/

Te Kotahitanga o Te Atiawa Taranaki, 'Parihaka', accessed September 26, 2023. https://teatiawa.iwi.nz/history/parihaka/.

Waitangi Tribunal. *Ko Aotearoa Tēnei: Te Taumata Tuatahi: a Report into Claims Concerning New Zealand Law and Policy Affecting Maori Culture and Identity.* Wellington: Legislation Direct, 2011.

## Images

Illustrations on pages 107 & 109 by Huriana Kopeke-Te Aho. 'The national Māori flag'. https://nzhistory.govt.nz/media/photo/national-maori-flag.

The Te Tino Rangatiratana (Māori Sovereignty) flag was designed in 1989 by Hiraina Marsden, Jan Dobson and Linda Munn in preparation for the 150th anniversary of the signing of Te Tiriti o Waitangi. It became the official Māori flag in 2009. At inception the flag was accompanied by an explanatory text written by Walter Erstich:

Black–represents Te Korekore, the realm of Potential Being. It represents the long darkness from whence the world emerged. It represents the heavens. The male element is formless, floating and passive.

White–represents Te Ao Marama, the realm of Being and Light. It is the Physical World. White also symbolises purity, harmony, enlightenment, and balance.

Koru–the curling frond shape, the Koru, represents the unfolding of new life. It represents rebirth and continuity, and offers the promise of renewal and hope for the future.

Red–represents Te Whei Ao, the realm of Coming into Being. It symbolises the female element. It also represents active, flashing, southern, falling, emergence, forest, land and gestation. Red is Papatuanuku, the Earth Mother, the sustainer of all living things. Red is the colour of earth from which the first human was made.

# REHEARSING FREEDOM

## ACT I

I type into the search bar: #studentarrested, #nycschools, #schoolresourceofficers #schoolsecurity. I am on TikTok looking for videos of police officers committing violence against students. In one video posted on 21 December 2022, I am looking through the camera of a shaking phone held by someone (ostensibly a student) on a school bus full of (mostly) Black students.[1] A police officer enters the school bus, yelling, "Who's not getting off the bus?" twice. He asks the bus driver, "Which one do you need off the bus?" and begins walking down the aisle. Students around seem to try to cover for the student the police officer is looking for. A student says, "I think he got off," another, "Yeah, he got off". The police officer asks, "Where'd he get off at?" and continues walking. Some students mumble responses. The bus driver points to a student, and the police officer says sternly, "Get up. Off the bus". I watch as the police officer removes the student from the bus and proceeds to push him to the ground, and shove him against a metal railing outside. A chorus of students yell from inside the bus, "Bro, why y'all got to do him like that?" "Stop touching him!" "DJ, your mama on the way". The student eventually breaks from the officer's grasp and begins quickly walking away. The officer takes some kind of black object out of his belt. "Bruh, don't tase him, please!" another student screams. I'm one minute and 50 seconds in, and I can't stomach any more. I scroll.

Screenshots of a TikTok posted by @AshleyOSAMA (2022)

1   Trenchmamii (@AshleyOSAMA), 2022, 'Its the fact that this is really what this weird ass world has gotten to smhhh,' TikTok, 21 December 2022, accessed 7 August 2023, https://www.tiktok.com/t/ZT8NJBMJn/.

One Black student holds the camera in front of his face, and I see his friend over his shoulder.[2] Text across the screen reads, "If your School got this it's in the HOOD". Somewhat in sync, they yell, "If your school got this, it's in the hood! On my homie's grave!" The student holding the camera briefly promotes his StockX link and then returns to the content at hand. In the background, a picture of a metal detector pops up as the two students say simultaneously, "If your school got metal detectors, it's in the hood!" They do the same with school resource officers. The video is over in twenty-one seconds. I scroll.

Screenshots of a TikTok posted by @c3rtifiedbackup (2022)

In this next video, I hear stomping, a walkie-talkie, a voice saying, "Come in," and something jingling.[3] The camera points at five students gathered at the bottom of a flight of stairs. They feign surprise and run down the stairs. The person holding the camera follows. Text across the screen reads, "When u hear the keys and walkie in school". The video is only six seconds long. I find myself wondering how long the students took to rehearse such a performance. I scroll.

2    OFFICIAL M (@c3rtifiedbackup). 2022. 'THIS IS ALL JOKES TIKTOK.' TikTok, 15 December 2022, accessed 7 August 2023, https://www.tiktok.com/t/ZT8NJdapQ/.
3    MC (@dtb_jonel). 2022. 'lykyk,' TikTok, 30 October 2022, accessed 7 August 2023, https://www.tiktok.com/t/ZT8NJj8rm/.

Screenshot of a TikTok skit posted by @dtb_jonel (2022)

## ACT II

I spent many late nights scrolling TikTok, researching race and policing in New York City schools. At this point, I wasn't sure what form my project would take, but I knew I wanted to develop a method to meet students where they are already sharing about these topics organically.

TikTok allows users to create, edit, consume, and respond to short videos. The app is the offspring of a Chinese app (Douyin) that was available in 2016, and was made available internationally in 2017. To understand the power of the app, one has to understand the "For You" page. The "For-You" page (or "fyp," as it's known colloquially), where users spend most of their time, provides viewers with an infinite feed of videos that grow more and more tailored to their interests by tracking how long users watch certain videos, whether they like them, comment or if they rewatch them. Many users speak of the algorithm as if it is conscious, saying, among other things, that it "knows them".

TikTok is one of the most downloaded apps of the past ten years and is the most popular app for those under 25 years old.[4] Though there is an emerging field of TikTok studies, much analysis focuses on TikTok from a top-down perspective,

---

4    Andreas Schellewald, "Communicative forms on TikTok: Perspectives from digital ethnography," *International Journal of Communication* 15, (2021): 1438.

exploring its place in our socio-political landscape or how the algorithm works.[5] Less attention is paid to exploring why young people make TikToks, especially about social issues in their lives.

Adolescence, as a social category in America is defined by hyper-emotionality, reactivity, and risk. In *Black Age*, cultural theorist Habiba Ibrahim reminds us that, "What we think of as 'age,' the life stages of lifespans, changes over historical time, is socially mutable, and contains its own set of categorical differences along the lines of class, gender, sexuality".[6] Black children and youth are often denied the social protections afforded by the category of 'child'. Instead their adolescent behaviour is frequently criminalised.[7] Extending Simone Browne's theory of racialising surveillance, I argue that Black adolescence has become "a key site through which surveillance is practiced, narrated, and enacted," especially in structuring school discipline today.[8] In one of my interviews with a seventeen-year-old Black student, Z.R. (she/they), she described getting kicked out of class or suspended as early as fifth grade (students are typically ten or eleven years old) for behaviour such as not sitting up straight, not walking in a straight line, or speaking when she wasn't spoken to. They told me, "I felt like this, like, programmed child [...] I felt, I felt like I was in the world. And I wasn't even in the world yet for real. And I felt like I was just out there, you know?"[9] Z.R., as did all the students I interviewed, felt like they had never had a chance to be a child. To Z.R., being treated like a child meant being given the "benefit of the doubt" and the space to move freely.

As TikTok studies is a relatively new field, I've been trying to develop a methodology for understanding these TikToks in the context of my research project. I watched and collected over forty different TikToks and divided them into three categories: videos where students film interactions with police officers or surveillance technology; videos where students tell a story about an interaction they had or draw some kind of conclusion about policing/surveillance; and videos where students perform a skit about interactions with police officers or metal detectors in school (acting either as a student or an officer). While I came to TikTok searching for videos in the first category, it was videos from the third which most intrigued me. Particularly, I wanted to know where the impulse to re-enact these violent events on TikTok comes from.

5   A selection of relevant critical literature on TikTok: Natalie Collie, and Caroline Wilson-Barnao. "Chapter 11: Playing with TikTok: algorithmic culture and the future of creative work." *The Future of Creative Work: Creativity and Digital Disruption*, (Cheltenham, UK : Edward Elgar Publishing, 2020): 172.; Yachao Li, Mengfei Guan, Paige Hammond, and Lane E. Berrey. "Communicating COVID-19 information on TikTok: a content analysis of TikTok videos from official accounts featured in the COVID-19 information hub." *Health education research 36*, no. 3, (March 2021): 261-271.; J. Vázquez-Herrero,, M.-C. Negreira-Rey, and X. López-García, "Let's Dance the News! How the News Media are Adapting to the Logic of TikTok", *Journalism* 23, no.8, (October 2020):1717-1735.; D. Zulli, and D.J. Zulli, "Extending the Internet Meme: Conceptualizing Technological Mimesis and Imitation Publics on the TikTok Platform", *New Media & Society* 24, no.1, (December 2020): 1-19.

6   Habiba Ibrahim, *Black Age: Oceanic Lifespans and the Time of Black Life*, (New York: New York University Press, 2021), 5.

7   A selection of relevant critical literature on the criminalisation of Black youth: Monique Morris, *Pushout: The criminalization of Black girls in schools*, (New York: The New Press, 2016); Tera Eva Agyepong, *The criminalization of Black children: Race, gender, and delinquency in Chicago's juvenile justice system, 1899–1945*, (Chapel Hill: UNC Press Books, 2018); Dorothy E. Roberts, "Criminal justice and black families: The collateral damage of over-enforcement." *UC Davis Law Review 34*, (2000); Kristin Henning, *The rage of innocence: How America criminalizes Black youth*, (New York: Knopf Doubleday Publishing Group, 2021).

8   Simone Browne, *Dark matters: On the surveillance of blackness*, (Chapel Hill: Duke University Press, 2015), 9.

9   Author's interviews with Z.R., a high school student from New York City, July 2023.

Given the long history of Black performance and dance as resistance, movements of Black joy—seen as gestures towards Black freedom—are especially criminalised in teens and adolescents. In another interview with seventeen-year-old student T. H. (she/they), she spoke to me about the difficulties that came with being one of the only Black students in her school's Gifted and Talented programme. She noted that she often heard her teachers make fun of the way "Black and brown" students outside their programme were acting, especially when it came to social media. T. H. said, "with the trends and stuff, and like when Musical.ly was coming out,[10] like, people would dance, they'd make Dubsmashes,[11] and teachers often, like made jokes about it, or they'd even give each other looks".[12] Hearing this, I was reminded of the work of André Lepecki, a performance studies scholar who developed the concept of 'choreopolitics' and 'choreopolicing'. In his theoretical work around spatialised movement, he describes the police not just as a collection of people, but as a choreographic force that designates what and whose movements are proper, normal, and permissible. Inescapably, this choreography, enacted even when the police are not present, reifies racial borders and boundaries. To Lepecki, it is the dancer who is most capable of "inventing movements of freedom". He writes, "Choreography as a planned, dissensual, and non-policed disposition of motions and bodies becomes the condition of possibility for the political to emerge".[13] What does it say, then, that Black teenagers are turning to (what was originally) a dance app to perform their experiences with state violence in school? What if we read these choreographed TikToks as movements of freedom, agency, and counter-surveillance that allow students to both defy police conformity and define the contours of the state violence they are subjected to?

## ACT III

In trying to answer these questions, I made the decision to include TikTok actively in my interview methodology; conducting four two-hour interviews with students ages seventeen to nineteen and devoting the last third of each interview to TikTok. Drawing on the methodology of the ethnographic scroll,[14] I collected a playlist of twelve TikToks from the second and third categories (TikToks where students tell a story or perform a skit) and gave them blank pieces of paper to write down their thoughts about each video. At the start of this exercise, I left the room to give each student some privacy. Still, the sound of my interviewees' giggles often found their way across the glass and into the hallway. When I returned to ask each student questions about what they watched, I felt as though some gap between us had closed. Students' posture relaxed, and their speech became less formal. Looking down, I would see paragraphs of written notes.

10  Musical.ly was an app created in 2014 that allowed users to create short lip-syncing music videos. The app was merged into TikTok in 2018.
11  Dubsmash was an app created in 2014 that also allowed users to lip-sync videos. It was shut down in early 2022.
12  Author's interviews with T. H., a high school student from New York City, July 2023.
13  André Lepecki, 'Choreopolice and Choreopolitics: or, the task of the dancer,' TDR/The Drama Review 57, no. 4 (2013): 22.
14  I first encountered the "ethnographic scroll" in this piece: Harry Rodgers and Emily Christine Lloyd-Evans, 'Intimate Snapshots: TikTok, Algorithm, and the Recreation of Identity', Anthways, 18 September 2021.

A note taken by student T. H. during an interview with the author

I always started by asking the students whether they had seen these kinds of TikToks before (they all had) and whether they made them (only one had). For all of them, watching these TikToks was helpful in processing their own experiences and knowing that they didn't endure this violence in isolation. In the words of S. C. (she/her), a nineteen-year-old student, watching TikToks about school policing and surveillance aid in "recognising, like, this was like, really wrong, because like, even though, like, we laugh about it, you also have that moment where you're like, 'Wait, this is wrong. This is like really not okay,' like, 'Why did I relate to that?'" On the other hand, all the students I interviewed also hoped that the TikToks were also reaching adults and would eventually change public opinion about school policing. In their eyes, re-enacting incidents added more believability to their stories. S. C. said,

> In terms of the skit, I feel like it provides so much context because when you're hearing and seeing it, it's way different than if you just read about it. Because visual, visual and auditory stimulation, like that together, will automatically make you feel like you're in that position/place you there more presently, which I feel like has more of an effect in terms of the viewer feeling more like empathy, or receiving more like understanding out of the situation.[15]

These students intimately understand the ways that they are read by adults as Black teenagers: as hyper emotional, untrustworthy, and unaware. In re-enacting the (often traumatic) interactions with police officers that these students experience in school, they created a space for both students and adult viewers to confront their awareness.

A note taken by student T. H. during an interview with the author

The 2 April 2018 issue of *TIME Magazine* features a cover displaying an image of five Parkland, FL, students and March for Our Lives organisers. The word "ENOUGH" is emblazoned across their torsos. That past February, a former student entered their school, Marjory Stoneman Douglas High School, and shot seventeen students and teachers to death. According to this article, these five non-Black faces represent "the school shooting generation".[16] While conversations about school violence in the U.S. media begin and end with school shootings, the fight for safer schools, led by non-

15  Author's interviews with S. C., a college student from New York City, July 2023.
16  Charlotte Alter, 'How Parkland Teens Are Leading the Gun Control Conversation,' *Time*, 22 March 2018, https://time.com/longform/never-again-movement/.

white students, goes unnoticed. The students I spoke with are very aware of this difference. "Like when we start talking about these things, we get turned off the TV, we get, you know, swiped up on Instagram. Like nobody wants to take the time to listen to it, because it's just more 'Oh, these students just complaining about something'" (Author's interviews with Z. R., a high school student from New York City, July 2023) said Z. R. For these teenagers, social media feels like one of their only outlets to share their stories beyond their communities.

I forgot we had to take our jackets off when we we pulled aside! They also pat us down.

A note taken by student S. C. during an interview with the author

Today, as I think of spaces to share and honour these students' words, I am only more certain about the necessity of incorporating young people into research methods, not just focusing on them as the subjects of research. Why is it always on young people to meet us where we are, rather than on us to find ways and places to meet them? It is easy to dismiss young people's activities on social media as vacuous, but important opportunities for learning are lost if researchers don't take seriously the ways that young people make meaning for themselves in the world, especially those who are denied representation within dominant media forums (such as *TIME Magazine*). Radical possibilities reveal themselves when we not only legitimate, but also activate, Black adolescents' affective responses and performances.

At the end of all my interviews, I asked students to draw the blueprint of a school that would make them feel safe. Now, looking over my desk, I see it covered in blueprints for a new choreography of Black educational experience. I am more confident than ever that, if there is anyone who will show us how to transform spaces of control into spaces of freedom, it is Black children, who imagine new ways to dance every day.

# Works Cited

Agyepong, Tera Eva. The criminalization of Black children: Race, gender, and delinquency in Chicago's juvenile justice system, 1899–1945. Chapel Hill: UNC Press Books, 2018.

Alter, Charlotte. 'How Parkland Teens Are Leading the Gun Control Conversation,' Time, 22 March 2018. https://time.com/longform/never-again-movement/.

Browne, Simone. Dark Matters: On the Surveillance of Blackness. Chapel Hill: Duke University Press, 2015.

Collie, Natalie and Caroline Wilson-Barnao. "Playing with TikTok: algorithmic culture and the future of creative work." The Future of Creative Work: Creativity and Digital Disruption. Cheltenham : Edward Elgar Publishing, 2020.

Henning, Kristin. The rage of innocence: How America criminalizes Black youth. New York: Knopf Doubleday Publishing Group, 2021.

Ibrahim, Habiba. Black Age: Oceanic Lifespans and the Time of Black Life. New York: New York University Press, 2021.

Lepecki, André. 'Choreopolice and Choreopolitics: or, the task of the dancer.' TDR/The Drama Review 57, no. 4 (2013): 13-27.

MC (@dtb_jonel). 2022. 'lykyk.' TikTok, 30 October 2022, accessed 7 August 2023. https://www.tiktok.com/t/ZT8NJj8rm/.

Morris, Monique. Pushout: The criminalization of Black girls in schools. New York: The New Press, 2016.

OFFICIAL M (@c3rtifiedbackup). 2022. 'THIS IS ALL JOKES TIKTOK.' TikTok, 15 December 2022, accessed 7 August 2023. https://www.tiktok.com/t/ZT8NJdapQ/.

Roberts, Dorothy E.. 'Criminal justice and black families: The collateral damage of over-enforcement.' UC Davis Law Review 34 (2000).

Rodgers, Harry, and Lloyd-Evans, Emily Christine. 'Intimate Snapshots: TikTok, Algorithm, and the Recreation of Identity', Anthways, 18 September 2021.

Schellewald, Andreas. 'Communicative forms on TikTok: Perspectives from digital ethnography.' International Journal of Communication 15 (2021): 21.

Trenchmamii (@AshleyOSAMA). 2022. 'Its the fact that this is really what this weird ass world has gotten to smhhh.' TikTok, 21 December 2022, accessed 7 August 2023. https://www.tiktok.com/t/ZT8NJBMJn/.

Vázquez-Herrero,J., M.-C. Negreira-Rey, and X. López-García, 'Let's Dance the News! How the News Media are Adapting to the Logic of TikTok', Journalism 23, no. 8 (October 2020): 1717-1735.

Yachao Li, Mengfei Guan, Paige Hammond, and Lane E. Berrey. 'Communicating COVID-19 information on TikTok: a content analysis of TikTok videos from official accounts featured in the COVID-19 information hub.' Health education research 36, no. 3 (March 2021): 261-271.

Zulli, D. and D.J. Zulli, 'Extending the Internet Meme: Conceptualizing Technological Mimesis and Imitation Publics on the TikTok Platform', New Media & Society 24, no. 1 (December 2020): 1-19.

# WAITING FOR TEAR GAS AGAIN

Image from Allan Sekula's *Waiting for Tear Gas*, 1999-2000. Slide projection plus
wall text; 81 35mm transparencies in sequence; 10 sec. each projection interval.
Courtesy of Allan Sekula Studio.

*We're fed up with being fucking poor. Minneapolis has some
of the most extreme racial and class disparities [...]
We're tired of living this way. People are putting together
all the big picture shit.*
Anonymous interviewee, Unicorn Riot

On 25 May 2020, a nine-minute video began to circulate on social media of a white
police officer kneeling on the neck of a Black man, later identified as George Floyd,
outside a convenience store in Minneapolis. That video was taken by Darnella Frazier,
a 17-year-old girl standing metres away. Within the day, stills from the video had
been broadcast on national and international media as the outline of the event itself
became clearer. The day after, people around Minneapolis congregated at the site of
Floyd's murder. They began to march in the direction of the police station where Derek
Chauvin, the police officer who murdered Floyd, worked.

At 5:26 pm on 26 May 2020, Niko Georgiades began to live stream from the
memorial site for George Floyd (close to the site of Floyd's death), a camera mounted
on his shoulder and a streaming rig in a backpack. Georgiades is a founding member
of Unicorn Riot (UR), a decentralised media collective which formed after the death
of Jamar Clark in March 2015.[1] UR live streamed for a week, from 26 May to 3 June, in

---

1     UR's first live stream consisted of the unrest after Clark's death (including graphic scenes of
Black protesters being shot by white supremacists) in Minneapolis. In the years since, Unicorn
Riot covered the protests at Standing Rock and the rise of the far-right in Europe and the U.S.,
although many of them live around Minneapolis.

              **SANJANA VARGHESE**

Minneapolis, often for up to fifteen hours a day (only a fraction of this was preserved and uploaded onto the UR website).[2] Viewer figures from social media indicate that at its peak, 300,000 people tuned in to watch the live streams on consecutive nights, as Georgiades (and UR) were some of the first to broadcast what was happening in Minneapolis that week.

As cultural critic Tobi Haslett writes, the events in Minneapolis "felt like a fulcrum" of the protests that spread around the U.S., and even around the rest of the world following the murder of George Floyd.[3] He says,

"Something deeper and more disruptive had breached the surface of social life, conjuring exactly the dreaded image the conspiracy theorists refused to face. This was open Black revolt: simultaneous but uncoordinated, a vivid fixture of American history sprung to life with startling speed. One thousand seven hundred U.S. towns and cities–the number was absurd. Within a week, sixty-two thousand National Guardsmen were dispatched to support city forces as they lurched to regain control. But what emerged under the banner of Blackness was soon blended with other elements, flinging multiracial crowds against soldiers and police."[4]

The footage of those heady days was hard to avoid–those events became omnipresent, almost atmospheric. But as media outlets, as well as politicians in the U.S. struggled to make sense of what had happened in Minneapolis, and the political mimesis that it inspired,[5] UR's live streams documented the feelings, events, ineffable qualities of that week, from the ground.

Allan Sekula's projection of still images, *Waiting for Tear Gas* 1999-2000, consists of 81 35mm colour slides taken at the 1999 World Trade Organisation protests in Seattle, Washington. Sekula wrote in an accompanying text that he wanted to "move with the flow of protest [...] taking in the lulls, the waiting and the margins of events".[6] Sekula inserted himself into the fray and became a part of the crowd itself. In the image reproduced here, the blurry figure of a police officer, saturated in red, says more than a caption itself could. The feelings–the excitement, the tension, the confusion–are palpable.

In *Waiting for Tear Gas*, the "protest and the representation of it are inseparable".[7] Social movements and participants in protests have often strived for self-representation,[8] potentially as a counterbalance to portrayals of their aims and tactics in mainstream, implicitly, commercial media. With the advent of novel visual tools and platforms, these attempts to self-represent have often come in another form–the live stream.

2    There are roughly 30 videos on their website of that week, some of which were streamed on YouTube, while others streamed on Periscope and Facebook. The majority of the videos have the same name, and are differentiated only by their streaming date and duration. I have compiled all of the videos which I drew on into an Appendix which comes after the bibliography, labelled in chronological order.

3    Tobi Haslett, 'Magic Actions,' *N +1*, 7 May 2021, https://nplusonemag.com/online-only/online-only/magic-actions/.

4    Tobi Haslett, 'Magic Actions'.

5    Jane M.Gaines, 'Political Mimesis,' in *Collecting Visible Evidence*, ed. Jane M. Gaines and Michael Renov, (Minneapolis: University of Minnesota Press, 1999), 84–102. This is a term Gaines used to explain how images of people engaging in certain practices could move others to do the same.

6    Allan Sekula, *5 Days That Shook the World: Seattle and Beyond*, eds. Alexander Cockburn and Jeffrey St Clair, (London: Verso, 2000), unpaginated.

7    Stephanie Schwartz, 'Waiting: Loops in Time', in *In Focus: Waiting for Tear Gas 1999–2000 by Allan Sekula*, ed. Stephanie Schwartz, (London: Tate, 2016).

8    Yates McKee, '"Eyes and Ears" : Aesthetics, Visual Culture and the Claims of Nongovernmental Politics,' in *Nongovernmental Politics*, eds. Michael Feher, Gaelle Krikorian and Yates McKee, (London: Zone Books, 2007*)*, 335.

**WAITING FOR TEAR GAS AGAIN**

Activist groups, social movements, and protesters often agitate and organise with the aim of bringing something—a power relation, a long-standing claim of injustice, a discriminatory policy—into the light.[9] Live streaming was employed by activist groups and social movements long before people working for capitalist platforms were interested in its communicative possibilities.[10] Activist groups and 'fringe' organisations have been live streaming for decades, going as far back as the 1980s in the context of the US, where activists started a public access broadcast channel called Deep Dish Television in New York.[11] It combined public access television in the US with the insight of activists and video producers around the country, and while there were pre recorded segments, activists held panels and discussions live at sit-ins and demonstrations. These channels were also part of the radical documentary ecosystem – Deep Dish TV was part of a group of video activist groups and public access TV channels including the Damned Interfering Video Activist Television, the Film and Photo League, Paper Tiger Television and many others.[12] In the ensuing decades, many activist groups developed their own autonomous forms of live streaming using decentralised technologies around the world.[13] From 2010 onwards, commercialised platforms – such as Twitch, Periscope, Ustream – streamlined the model and moved it from niche to accessible.[14]

Following the Arab Spring and Occupy Wall Street in 2011, live streaming on social networks has become ever more central as a method of mobilisation for social movements and protest groups, by producing visibility and documenting unrest.[15] Live streaming within this context has also become more than just a form of documentation, but rather a kind of generative force. Judith Butler says, "the street scenes become politically potent only when and if we have a visual and audible version of the scene communicated in live or proximate time".[16] The temporality of the live stream—the fact that we are watching, just as the person streaming is—is what generates anticipation.

## MILITANT EVIDENCE

The Unicorn Riot livestreams often start during the day and continue well into the night. The live streams were shot mainly by Georgiades, occasionally accompanied by another member of UR, following marches and groups of protesters around the city. He narrates the events as he's filming, repeating why people have gathered and are marching, recounting what just happened on the stream. Georgiades also interviews participants and passers-by, often lucid and angry, often appearing for a few minutes and then disappearing into the ether. Over time, patterns emerge in the streams—the Minneapolis police force often circulate and circle protesters for hours in the daylight.

9 Yates McKee, "'Eyes and Ears'" , 330.
10 Sasha Costanza-Chock, Design Justice: Community-Led Practices to Build the Worlds We Need, (Massachaussetts: MIT Press, 2020), 203.
11 DeeDee Halleck, 'Deep Dish TV: Community Video from Geostationary Orbit,' Leonardo 26, no.5 (1993): 415-420.
12 Sarah Hamblin and Ryan Watson, 'Introduction : Radical Documentary Today,' Studies in Documentary Film 3, (2019):187-195.
13 Jeffrey S.Juris, 'The New Digital Media and Activist Networking within Anti-Corporate Globalization Movements,' The Annals of the American Academy of Political and Social Science 597, Cultural Production in a Digital Age (2005):191.
14 Costanza-Chock, Design Justice, 178.
15 Daniel Trotter and Christian Fuchs, 'Introduction,' in Social Media, Politics and the State: Protests, Revolutions, Riots, Crime and Policing in the Age of Facebook, Twitter and Youtube, eds. Daniel Trotter and Christian Fuchs. ( London and New York: Routledge, 2015), 1-10.
16 Judith Butler, 'Bodies in Alliance and the Politics of the Street,' in Sensible Politics: The Visual Culture of Nongovernmental Activism, eds. Meg McLagan and Yates McKee, (London and New York: Zone Books, 2012), 130.

Individual police officers engage with individual protesters or even sit idly by and watch as people march. Once the sun sets, the police escalate their tactics—firing rubber bullets and marker rounds, throwing tear gas grenades, kettling and arresting protesters.

These live streams from the ground produce what media scholar Ryan Watson calls "militant evidence".[17] Watson's conception of militant evidence is an iteration of Kodwo Eshun and Ros Gray's "militant image"[18] – images and sounds, produced by a range of filmic methods, "dedicated to the liberation struggles and revolutions of the late twentieth century".[19]

Within this term, "militant" refers to the ongoing struggle on the side of ordinary people to "intervene within their world"[20] depicting and emphasising the historical legacies and continuation of state violence, mobilising these images to move towards dismantling state power. In producing these forms of militant evidence, these images generate what Watson calls "affective radicality" – representing systemic problems while pushing those watching into practices of action against state violence – and effective radicality, which is a "jurisgenerative force in the cause of accountability and justice".[21]

As visual theorist Nicholas Mirzoeff writes, "police killings captured on cell phone video or photographs have become a hallmark of the United States' visual culture in the twenty-first century".[22] Contemporary discussions of this dynamic, particularly within the Global North, are closely related to the proliferation of images of Black suffering and Black death in the U.S., in particular.[23] These images are a reminder of the reality of life in America for Black and Brown people, particularly those who are poor. These images do not represent a new turn in white supremacy or racist violence, but rather constitute a new turn in rendering these structures visible. They are part of a lineage of violent imagery and the dehumanisation of Black and Brown people within the US. The images of bulldogs being released on Black civil rights protesters, the daguerreotypes of enslaved Black people with whip marks on their back, the recording of the beating of Rodney King – these images sit within the same genealogy, born out of specific ways that state violence is visibilised. But as writer Zoé Tsamudzi details, "Violence against black people occupies an understatedly important place of pleasure in the white racial imaginary, evidenced by the countless depictions of grinning whites and scenes of afternoon leisure

17  Ryan Watson, 'In the Wakes of Rodney King: Militant Evidence and Media Activism in the Age of Viral Black Death.' *The Velvet Light Trap 84 (2019)* 35, https://muse.jhu.edu/article/732636.

18  Kodwo Eshun and Ros Gray, 'The Militant Image,' *Third Text* 25, no. 1 (2011) 1-12.

19  Eshun and Gray's framework of the 'militant image' draws more specifically on cinematic traditions focusing on Third World Cinema, but this concept is instructive in thinking about the ecosystem of images of protest and insurgency which have become an increasingly ubiquitous part of contemporary digital and media landscapes. Moreover, the necessary flexibility with what constitutes evidence – from B-roll to pamphlets to short films – is similarly valuable in thinking about the many aftermaths of images of protest and riots, particularly in the last two decades.

20  Watson, 'In the Wakes of Rodney King,', *The Velvet Light Trap,* 37.

21  Watson, 'In the Wakes of Rodney King,', *The Velvet Light Trap,* 37.

22  Nicholas Mirzoeff, *The Appearance of Black Lives Matter,* (Miami: [NAME] Publications, 2017) 9. See also Christina Sharpe, *In the Wake: On Blackness and Being*, Duke University Press, 2016, Zoe Tsamudzi, 'White Witness and the Contemporary Lynching,' *The New Republic*, 2020, and Arthur Jafa's *Love is the Message, the Message is Death*, (2016).

23  The dissemination of the video of the Los Angeles Police Department beating Rodney King was widely considered to be the first viral video. Documentary scholars such as Bill Nichols and Jane Gaines converged on the term 'visible evidence' when situating the Rodney King tape within wider debates around race, policing and new media formats, such as the growth of cable news networks, at the time.

in twentieth-century lynching photographs."[24] She argues that their successors – videos shared on social media, clips which then circulate on cable news – produce a kind of traumatic evidence which is then collected. who we do not see : the harassment, the stop and frisk, those who are brutalised in ways which may not be possible to capture on a video camera (the minor traffic infraction, the generation of debt)?

The relationship between the mere documentation of an event and its ability to 'change' the conditions which led to the event (and others like it) is also less clear-cut than it may seem. The academic Thomas Keenan writes about the underlying assumptions of this belief, saying "Mobilizing shame presupposes that dark deeds are done in the dark, and that the light of publicity—especially of the television camera—thus has the power to strike preemptively on behalf of justice".[25]

Much has been written about the video taken by George Halliday of Rodney King being brutally attacked by LAPD officers. The Rodney King event was a manifestation of the structures and anxieties that structure life in the USA for many – it attracted widespread attention, and public opinion polling was unusually skewed towards sympathy for King.[26] But this video itself was freeze-framed, with select moments isolated and rendered into something like a film when it was presented during the trial of the LAPD officers involved in beating King, and the video's existence did not lead to a conviction for any of the police officers involved.[27] Peter Gabriel founded the organisation WITNESS after the dissemination of the Rodney King videotape, built on the idea that visibility on injustice leads to injustice faltering. Yet, despite the proliferation of these images and recordings, forms of accountability or significant change are still rare, often arriving years later, in a watered down form, if it happens at all. Derek Chauvin's conviction for the murder of George Floyd was notable for many reasons, one of those being the rarity of a conviction in this context.

As Susan Schuppli writes,"Evidence for events is never simply 'self-evident'".[28] Using this framework of "militant evidence" to think through the Unicorn Riot live streams of the week after George Floyd's death starts from recognising that these events themselves are not disseminated through or by individual texts, videos, or images, but rather through their accumulation and effects cumulatively and in relation to each other.

Framing this case study through engaging with "militant evidence" requires not thinking about this incident and its aftermath as isolated but also requires thinking about its previous instantiations – such as the killing of Eric Garner, whose death was filmed by Ramsey Orta, a bystander. The footage went viral and set off spates of protests, and Garner's last words became a rallying cry for the Black Lives Matter Movement.[29] Watson's conception of "militant evidence" is a lens through which to deepen our understanding of the social, political, and technological ecosystems of image production around viral Black death, and move our framing of these events out of their immediate, sensationalist networked circulation and into a longer genealogy of protest and resistance.

24   Zoé Samudzi, 'White Witness and the Contemporary Lynching,' *The New Republic*, 16 May 2020, *https://newrepublic.com/article/157734/white-witness-contemporary-lynching*.
25   Thomas Keenan, 'Mobilizing shame,' *The South Atlantic Quarterly* 103, 2/3, (2004): 435-449.
26   Louis-Georges Schwartz, *Mechanical Witness : A History of Motion Picture Evidence in US Courts,* (Oxford : Oxford Scholarship Online, 2009), 105-115.
27   Schwartz, *Mechanical Witness, 105-115.*
28   Susan Schuppli, *Material Witness,* (London: MIT Press, 2020), 7.
29   See David Joselit, 'Material Witness: Visual Evidence and the Case of Eric Garner,' *Artforum*, February 2015, https://www.artforum.com/print/201502/material-witness-visual-evidence-and-the-case-of-eric-garner-497 98.

Live streaming spread across the USA after 2014, particularly after the death of Michael Brown at the hands of police in Missouri–at the time, it was heralded as both the future of media and the future of activism.[30] Since Facebook implemented its Facebook Live feature (which allows any individual to press a button on a smartphone and stream live), videos of racialised violence, of Black and brown people being killed, assaulted, and apprehended by the police in the USA, spread faster than before. For some, such as Philando Castile, his girlfriend, Diamond Reynolds broadcast his last moments alive on Facebook.[31] The end of the live stream–where her phone was on the ground, filming upwards–also showed her arrest, only moments after Castile had been killed.[32]

The live streams' claim to 'real-time', the veridicality of its proximity to 'the event', spatially and temporally, are a critical element of their explanatory and narrative value. The temporal implications of the live stream are also bound up with the memory of the platform it is hosted on–i.e. how long will Facebook or Periscope allow individuals to access footage from an event several months ago, or fifteen years down the line? Korryn Gaines, a young Black woman, live streamed a police raid on her house, shortly before she was killed. The police department successfully petitioned Facebook and Instagram to have the video removed, as the raid was taking place, as Gaines' predominantly Black, predominantly female, followers were urging her to resist arrest.[33] In their article on dark sousveillance and live streaming, Mia Fischer and K. Mohrman detail how Diamond Reynold's narration over the encounter between the police and Castile makes systemic racism and structural violence difficult to ignore–these are articulated by Reynolds as she films.[34]

Here, I turn to Maya Binyam's phrase–"live streaming elucidates power's perforations".[35] Reading the Unicorn Riot live stream through this, viewers can see the 'real-time' brutality of the police–that as the sun begins to set, police forces seem to assemble in virtually every direction. Viewers see how power is seized and meted out, and see again who it is enacted on. By both documenting the events as they occur, and demonstrating how they are one part of a longer lineage of struggle against state violence in the USA, these live streams produce militant evidence. The documentation of these events also presupposes a future viewer–it assumes its historical importance. Live streaming serves a dual purpose–it records events as they happen, but it also functions as an archive. The metadata, the pixels, and the nature of the live stream produce an archival document that can be accessed over and over again.

While Georgiades captures images of spectacular violence, he also captures the lulls in between–protesters walking around, standing on street corners, buying water, the police standing impassively on a street corner, people having regular conversations because they haven't seen each other in months. For every image of a building on fire, there are several more protesters marching and chanting on empty

30  Adrien Chen, 'Is Live streaming the Future of Media or the Future of Activism?' *New York Magazine,* 7 December 2014, https://nymag.com/intelligencer/2014/12/live streaming-the-future-of-media-or-activism.html.

31  Philando Castile was killed by a police officer in 2016 and his girlfriend, Diamond Reynolds, had live streamed the event to Facebook. See : Philando Castile, Say their Names, https://exhibits.stanford.edu/saytheirnames/feature/philando-castile.

32  Mia Fischer and K. Mohrman, 'Black Deaths Matter? Sousveillance and the Invisibility of Black Life', *Ada: A Journal of Gender, New Media and Technology,* no. 10, (2016).

33  Maya Binyam, 'Against the Clock', *Real Life,* 30 August 2016, https://reallifemag.com/against-the-clock/.

34  Fischer and Mohrman, 'Black Deaths Matter?.'

35  Fischer and Mohrman, 'Black Deaths Matter?.'

roads, or people just standing around. These live streams are what Hito Steyerl calls "poor images".[36] Poor images are often low quality, distributed digitally through bad connections, pirated and iterative, reflecting the conditions of their own production. The live streams are pixelated because Georgiades is live streaming on the move across the city, dipping in and out of good network coverage. They blur and cut out because it's raining on the first night because Georgiades is in the hordes of people being pushed back by the police and struggling to find footing amidst tear gas. On day 1, Georgiades is pushed back by a police officer with a baton, who comes straight up to the camera, and the stream cuts out for two minutes.[37] On day 2, Georgiades tells the audience that UR has changed equipment to make the interruptions less likely to happen, speculating that irritants from discharged tear gas or jammers from the police force may have interfered with the feed.[38]

One feature of these images is integral to their affective register. These images produced by the UR live stream are in a curious double bind of visibility—their pixelation arises from the circumstances under which they are created. Still, they also obscure the features of protesters and police alike. The speed of the image transmission generates the anticipation of the diffuse thousands watching from around the globe. Viewers watching from home may see the hordes of police officers appearing as a mass of silhouettes, shapes emerging from their bodies that elicit screams from the crowd. They see a flash-bang grenade and the sudden movement of two teenage boys as the police appear around a corner. These images reflect the conditions of their making and their proliferation.

In this way, another way to read the livestream is to think of it as just another form of video footage, with the temporal regime which produced it eventually consigned to the past. The anticipation of the events that are yet to come, such as the potential arrest of protesters, is what generates the specificity of the live stream.

Media scholar John Durham Peters writes that "liveness matters for the living".[39] Even now, years on from the livestreams themselves, the less 'visual' furniture around them, such as dates and streaming time, are a bulwark, what Peters describes as an "assurance to truth and authenticity".[40]

Journalists Dhruv Mehrotra & Andrew Coutts explain how SITU, a research organisation based in New York, built a tool to organise videos of police brutality at Black Lives Matter protests in 2020.[41] Their tool, Codec, was used to mobilise a range of video inputs—timestamped social media footage, in concert with police body cam footage—to build a legal claim against the New York Police Department. Metadata from the footage, including that taken from live streams around various platforms, proved claims made by protestors of police violence, leading to 13 million dollars in damages eventually being awarded to protesters in the footage.

36  Hito Steyerl, 'In Defense of the Poor Image', e-flux, November 2009, https://www.e-flux.com/journal/10/61362/in-defense-of-the-poor-image/.

37  Unicorn Riot, '#LIVE: Minneapolis Responds To Police Murder of George Floyd,' 26 May 2020, video, 2:07:05, https://www.youtube.com/watch?v=XAa5xb6Jitl.

38  Unicorn Riot, '#LIVE: Minneapolis Responds To Police Murder of George Floyd,' 27 May 2020, video, 25:29 https://youtu.be/fHmoqQ86uxU.

39  John Durham Peters, 'Witnessing' in Media Witnessing: Testimony in the Age of Mass Communication, ed. Paul Frosh and Amit Pinchevski, (London: Palgrave MacMillan, 2009), 38.

40  Peters, 'Witnessing', 38.

41  Dhruv Mehtotra and Andrew Coutts, 'New Police Body Cam Data Exposes the True Scale of NYPD Violence Against Protesters', WIRED, 20 July 2023, https://www.wired.com/story/nypd-george-floyd-nyc-protester-settlement/.

**WAITING FOR TEAR GAS AGAIN**

When images of people using traffic cones to stop the emissions of tear gas are shared in news roundups and on social media, they create a recognisable gesture, and offer a blueprint to those who wish to reproduce it.[42] Several times throughout these live streams, people on and off screen respond to what is happening around them with humour and levity, thereby generating this affective evidence. On a live stream from Day 1, police officers stand guard in a ransacked liquor store (this is several minutes after many of them had brutalised and arrested a young man inside the store, all of which was captured on camera). People gather outside the door, standing on broken glass and ask the police officers if they wouldn't mind handing over some beer "if it's right there".[43] On Day 2, a group of young men come up to the UR camera and ask if they can rap for their thousands of viewers, shouting out their Instagram handle and commandeering the microphone until Georgiades asks for it back.[44] On Day 4, after Minneapolis mayor Jacob Frey imposes a curfew, a speaker with a megaphone asks for the time and then says to cheers, "How are y'all gonna tell a bunch of grown people to go in the house at eight o'clock?"[45] As artist Hannah Black explains, in 2020, a few months into the beginning of the Covid-19 pandemic, it seemed that these images "saved social life".[46] These images of so many people, mobilising through anger and grief, moving together on empty streets, with masks on and jugs of milk tucked into bags, chanting and holding up signs—these generated acts of "political mimesis".[47] By making these struggles visible, these images "produce a bodily swelling", 35 encouraging others to join these practices. Masks, hand sanitiser and water bottles became common practices at protests in the weeks after, as was the chant "fuck 12".[48] Media representations of protests are often one-note and unfamiliar, depicting looting and violence as the matter of sole concern—or even, as the event itself—while often failing to reckon with the larger issues behind the unrest. These live streams are something aside from a 'representation'—they are inside the protest itself.

42  At 6:33 in one of the livestreams on 28 May 2020, Georgiades describes the protesters adapting to police tactics – saying, 'moving like water, like in Hong Kong'. Also see: An Xioa Mina, 'Memes to Movements,' Interview by Danah Boyd. Databites: Data & Society, 19 January 2019. Audio, 54:02. https://datasociety.net/library/an-xiao-mina-memes-to-movements/.

43  Unicorn Riot, '#LIVE: Minneapolis Responds To Police Murder of George Floyd,' 26 May 2020, video, 1:22:16 https://www.facebook.com/unicornriot.ninja/videos/2584320961882544.

44  Unicorn Riot, '#LIVE: Minneapolis Responds To Police Murder of George Floyd,' 27 May 2020, video, 2:34:48 https://youtu.be/TQRywSylOUU, and Unicorn Riot, '#LIVE: Minneapolis Responds To Police Murder of George Floyd,' 29 May 2020, video, 5:25:42 https://www.pscp.tv/w/1LyxBNWvvYjxN.

45  Unicorn Riot, '#LIVE: Minneapolis Responds To Police Murder of George Floyd,' 30 May 2020, video, 3:09:45 https://youtu.be/jRcNwHPL-OM

46  Hannah Black, 'Go Outside,' Artforum, December 2020, https://www.artforum.com/print/202009/hannah-black-s-year-in-review-84376.

47  Much has been written about infographic activism, or the spread of easily digestible news through social media based platforms such as Instagram. But immediate tips, such as using milk to lessen the flow of tear gas, spread quickly on social media platforms as images from Minneapolis, and soon after, protesters from New York and Los Angeles, began to circulate too. These kinds of 'methodologies' of protest have been an area of inquiry for digital studies scholars in particular, but they generally remain outside the scope of this text.

48  Fuck 12, also meaning fuck the police, arises from an American TV show where a pair of cops had a callsign called 12. It is specific to police forces in the USA, and in a few of the videos, graffiti with the same phrase is spray painted over boarded up buildings. A patrol car with its windows smashed in has a sign on the front that says the same.

**WAITING FOR TEAR GAS AGAIN**

# THE PLACE FROM WHERE THE IMAGE COMES

Over the streams, Georgiades narrates. Georgiades' narration makes these relations, "the place from where the image comes,"[49] to borrow Akomfrah's phrase, explicit for a new audience, and are born out of a deep engagement not only with the physical location but the communities that form Minneapolis.[50] Georgiades spends much of the time when he's filming the lull between encounters detailing previous incidents of police brutality in the area, providing historical context to the lack of mass arrests in Minneapolis, as well as explaining what actions protesters and other demonstrators were taking off camera.[51] Georgiades details the specifics of the uniforms that police are wearing, marking out which are National Guard, which are Minneapolis Police, and which are Metro Transit Police. The presence of the National Guard (and the tanks which show up on the live streams on day five) are a reminder of the familiar policing tactics used to crush social unrest and insurgency, seen in other American cities in previous years too. Several times throughout the riots, individuals come to the camera to thank UR and, even more specifically, Georgiades for being at previous protests in the last five years. This relationship becomes pertinent later on that week, as Georgiades captures Louis Hunter (Philando Castile's cousin) being pushed back by police officers as they enter Castile's restaurant and confront him aggressively mid-interview.[52] In another interview on Day 2, a man with sunglasses and a mask speaks to the camera, noting that he recognised the name of the police officer who killed Floyd from another fatal shooting at a local housing project in 2011.[53]

One of Georgiades' interviewees explains to the camera that he hasn't watched the video of George Floyd because he's already seen too many versions of this exact incident.[54] As filmmaker John Akomfrah explains, "Anyone who turns up for demonstrations isn't just there because of George Floyd's death but because a year before, somebody else died in the same way. They have a narrative in their head that is trying to make sense of connecting the past and the present".[55] These live streams make explicit the link between not only the events of 2020, but what has already passed years ago, adding to the accumulation of what Watson calls "effective evidence"[56]. Many of the Black and Brown people who speak to Georgiades draw links between the murder of George Floyd and other incidents of racialised violence, including ones that they themselves have experienced. These encounters demonstrate that Floyd's murder is not an aberration to the rhythm of regular life for the racialised community of Minneapolis, and in doing so, place these new images into their wider historical and political context, working in concert with the accumulated footage, images, and texts from previous years of processions and protests.

49  John Akomfrah, 'John Akomfrah', interview by Devika Girish, *Caligari Press,* 6 April 2021, https://caligaripress.com/John-Akomfrah-interviewed-by-Devika-Girish.
50  Unicorn Riot, '#LIVE: Minneapolis Responds To Police Murder of George Floyd,' 30 May 2020, video, 50:52 https://youtu.be/B4yo0MbhUjE.
51  For example, Georgiades details how the Amalgamated Transit Union, which represents transport workers around the USA, backed its bus drivers right to refuse to transport protestors to police stations, in Unicorn Riot, '#LIVE: Minneapolis Responds To Police Murder of George Floyd,' 30 May, 2020, video, 50:52 https://youtu.be/B4yo0MbhUjE.
52  Unicorn Riot, '#LIVE: Minneapolis Responds To Police Murder of George Floyd,' 30 May 2020, live stream, 2:43:08 https://youtu.be/izQLrDO_bBE.
53  Unicorn Riot, '#LIVE: Minneapolis Responds To Police Murder of George Floyd,' 27 May 2020, live stream, 25:29 https://youtu.be/fHmoqQ86uxU.
54  Unicorn Riot, '#LIVE: Minneapolis Responds To Police Murder of George Floyd,' 26 May 2020, live stream, 2:07:05, https://www.youtube.com/watch?v=XAa5xb6Jitl.
55  John Akomfrah, 'John Akomfrah,' interview by Devika Girish, *Caligari Press,* 6 April 2021, https://caligaripress.com/John-Akomfrah-interviewed-by-Devika-Girish.
56  Watson, 'In the Wakes of Rodney King', *The Velvet Light Trap,* no. 84 (2019).

In April 2021, almost a year after Floyd was murdered, Unicorn Riot went live again at a protest over the killing of Daunte Wright in Minneapolis. Many of the familiar police tactics and strategies – pepper spraying protesters right to their face, waiting until the evening and then pushing back aggressively – were evident on the live stream. A month before, UR began an intensive live stream of the trial of Derek Chauvin. During the month-long trial, the video of George Floyd's murder was played over and over again in court. Several times over the course of the trial, UR's live stream was banned or taken offline as the video played, because it violated platform policies.[57] Witnesses on the scene—including Frazier—said that they still live with the memory of what they saw that day.

Unicorn Riot's streams were the first of many, and the images they produced became part of a much broader ecosystem of imagery of police brutality over the months which followed. These images draw on a longer lineage of unyielding struggles against state violence, but they beget more of these acts, such as the destruction of the Edward Colston statue in Bristol. Militant evidence is not formed through individual images which are dissected, but through their accumulative effect, generating outward action within and outside of politics.[58]

57  Adi Robertson, 'Broadcasting George Floyd's death violates Twitch rules, even during a murder trial,' *The Verge,* 30 March 2021, https://www.theverge.com/2021/3/30/22356973/twitch-george-floyd-death-video-derek-chauvin-trial-unicor n-riot-suspension.
58  Watson, 'In the Wakes of Rodney King', 36.

## Works Cited

Akomfrah, John. 'John Akomfrah,' interview by Devika Girish, *Caligari Press,* 6 April 2021, https://caligaripress.com/John-Akomfrah-interviewed-by-Devika-Girish.

Black, Hannah. 'Go Outside,' *Artforum,* December 2020, https://www.artforum.com/print/202009/hannah-black-s-year-in-review-84376.

Butler, Judith. 'Bodies in Alliance and the Politics of the Street,' in *Sensible Politics: The Visual Culture of Nongovernmental Activism,* edited by Meg McLagan and Yates McKee. London and New York: Zone Books, 2012.

Chen, Adrien. 'Is Live streaming the Future of Media or the Future of Activism?'. *New York Magazine,* 7 December, 2014. https://nymag.com/intelligencer/2014/12/live streaming-the-future-of-media-or-activism.html.

Costanza-Chock, Sasha. *Design Justice : Community-Led Practices to Build the Worlds We Need.* Cambridge, MA: MIT Press, 2020.

Durham Peters, John. 'Witnessing' in *Media Witnessing: Testimony in the Age of Mass Communication,* ed. Paul Frosh and Amit Pinchevski. London: Palgrave MacMillan, 2009.

Eshun, Kodwo, and Ros Gray. 'The Militant Image,' *Third Text* 25, no. 1 (2011) 1-12.

Fischer, Mia and K. Mohrman, 'Black Deaths Matter? Sousveillance and the Invisibility of Black Life,' *Ada: A Journal of Gender, New Media and Technology,* no. 10 (2016).

Gaines, Jane M. '*Political Mimesis*' in *Collecting Visible Evidence,* edited by Jane M. Gaines and Michael Renov, 84–102. Minneapolis: University of Minnesota Press, 1999.

Halleck, DeeDee. '*Deep Dish TV: Community Video from Geostationary Orbit,*' Leonardo 26, no. 5 (1993): 415-420.

Hamblin, Sarah and Ryan Watson. '*Introduction : Radical Documentary Today,*' *Studies in Documentary Film* 3, (2019): 187-195.

Haslett, Tobi. '*Magic Actions,*' N +1, 7 May, 2021. Available at https://nplusonemag.com/online-only/online-only/magic-actions/.

Joselit, David. 'Material Witness: Visual Evidence and the Case of Eric Garner,' *Artforum, February 2015.* https://www.artforum.com/print/201502/material-witness-visual-evidence-and-the-case-of-eric-garner-4998.

Juris, Jeffrey S., 'The New Digital Media and Activist Networking within Anti-Corporate Globalization Movements,' *The Annals of the American Academy of Political and Social Science* 597, *Cultural Production in a Digital Age (2005).*

Keenan, Thomas. '*Mobilizing shame,*' *The South Atlantic Quarterly* 102, 2/3, (2004): 435-449.

McKee, Yates. "*Eyes and Ears*": Aesthetics, Visual Culture and the Claims of Nongovernmental Politics,' in *Nongovernmental Politics,* edited by Michael Feher with Gaelle Krikorian and Yates McKee. London: Zone Books, 2007.

Mehtotra, Dhruv and Andrew Coutts, *'New Police Body Cam Data Exposes the True Scale of NYPD Violence Against Protesters'*. WIRED, 20 July 2023, https://www.wired.com/story/nypd-george-floyd-nyc-protester-settlement/.

Mina, An Xioa. 'Memes to Movements,' Interview by Danah Boyd. Databites: Data & Society, 19 January 2019. Audio, 54:02. https://datasociety.net/library/an-xiao-mina-memes-to-movements/.

Mirzoeff, Nicholas. *The Appearance of Black Lives Matter*. Miami: [NAME] Publications, 2017.

Robertson, Adi. *'Broadcasting George Floyd's death violates Twitch rules, even during a murder trial,'* The Verge, 30 March 2021. https://www.theverge.com/2021/3/30/22356973/twitch-george-floyd-death-video-derek-chauvin-trial-unicorn-riot-suspension.

Schwartz, Louis-Georges. *Mechanical Witness: A History of Motion Picture Evidence in US Courts.* Oxford : Oxford Scholarship Online, 2009.

Schwartz, Stephanie . *'Waiting: Loops in Time' In Focus: Waiting for Tear Gas 1999–2000* by Allan Sekula, edited by Stephanie Schwartz, (London: Tate 2016). Available at https://www.tate.org.uk/research/publications/in-focus/waiting-for-tear-gas-allan-sekula/loops-in-time.

Sekula, Allan. *5 Days That Shook the World: Seattle and Beyond.* edited by Alexander Cockburn and Jeffrey St Clair. London: Verso, 2000.

Steyerl, Hito. *'In Defense of the Poor Image'*. e-flux, no. 10 (2009), https://www.e-flux.com/journal/10/61362/in-defense-of-the-poor-image/.

Trotter, Daniel and Christian Fuchs. *Social Media, Politics and the State: Protests, Revolutions, Riots, Crime and Policing in the Age of Facebook, Twitter and YouTube.* London and New York: Routledge, 2015.

Watson, Ryan. *'In the Wakes of Rodney King: Militant Evidence and Media Activism in the Age of Viral Black Death'*. The Velvet Light Trap 84 (2019): 34-49.

### Videos Cited

Unicorn Riot, '#LIVE: Minneapolis Responds To Police Murder of George Floyd,' 26 May, 2020, video, 2:07:05, https://www.youtube.com/watch?v=XAa5xb6Jitl.

Unicorn Riot, '#LIVE: Minneapolis Responds To Police Murder of George Floyd,' 26 May, 2020, video, 1:22:16 https://www.facebook.com/unicornriot.ninja/videos/2584320961882544.

Unicorn Riot, '#LIVE: Minneapolis Responds To Police Murder of George Floyd,' 27 May, 2020, video, 25:29 https://youtu.be/fHmoqQ86uxU.

Unicorn Riot, '#LIVE: Minneapolis Responds To Police Murder of George Floyd,' 27 May, 2020, video, 2:34:48 https://youtu.be/TQRywSylOUU.

Unicorn Riot, '#LIVE: Minneapolis Responds To Police Murder of George Floyd,' 29 May, 2020, video, 5:25:42 https://www.pscp.tv/w/1LyxBNWvvYjxN.

Unicorn Riot, '#LIVE: Minneapolis Responds To Police Murder of George Floyd,' 30 May, 2020, video, 3:09:45 https://youtu.be/jRcNwHPL-OM.

Unicorn Riot, '#LIVE: Minneapolis Responds To Police Murder of George Floyd,' 30 May, 2020, video, 50:52 https://youtu.be/B4yo0MbhUjE.

Unicorn Riot, '#LIVE: Minneapolis Responds To Police Murder of George Floyd,' 30 May, 2020, live stream, 2:43:08 https://youtu.be/izQLrDO_bBE.

# THE DISOBEDIENT GAZE

How can knowledge about migration produce transformative effects in the politics of migration—understood as the contentious force field constituted by the practices and knowledges of multiple actors who together determine who can move and in what condition? In order to answer these questions as researchers, we believe one needs to adopt a self-reflective stance which does not see the practice of research as isolated from this force field, but rather acknowledges its entanglement with it. But refusing the scientific imperative of disengagement based on a 'critical distance' deemed necessary for thought is not enough. One should also ask: what are the potentials and dangers of this 'critical proximity'? What effects does it produce and how?

In this short text, excerpted from our 2013 essay 'A Disobedient Gaze: Strategic Interventions in the Knowledge(s) of Maritime Borders', we would like to probe these questions anew by discussing the project Forensic Oceanography, which we initiated in the summer of 2011.[1] This project used remote sensing and mapping technologies to document deaths and violations of the rights of migrants at the maritime borders of the European Union (EU). It did so in order to support the struggle for migrants' rights carried out by various groups through advocacy, litigations and activism of different kinds.

The death of illegalised migrants in the Mediterranean is, of course, a long-standing phenomenon. With the progressive introduction of a common European visa policy and the concurrent denial of legal access to non-European migrants, the latter have been forced to resort to dangerous means of entry, amongst others embarking on unseaworthy vessels. The increasing militarisation of maritime borders has furthermore resulted in the splintering of migration routes towards longer and more perilous points of passage. Finally, the refusal of coastal states to disembark migrants and the criminalisation of assistance have been a disincentive for seafarers to exercise their obligation of assistance to people in distress at sea.

As a consequence, between 1988 and May 2012, more than 13,000 deaths were documented at the maritime borders of the EU, and more than 6,000 in just the Sicily Channel.[2] Within this context, 2011 represented a tipping point in a number of respects. After years in which the transnational cooperation between Tunisia, Libya, Italy, Malta, and the EU had more or less effectively managed to block the arrival of large numbers of migrants on the European coasts of the Central Mediterranean, the so-called Arab Spring led to a temporary power vacuum in Tunisia that enabled over 28,000 people to cross the sea to Italy during that year. A similar situation in Libya was exacerbated by an entrenched civil war, NATO-led military intervention and the active role of Gaddafi's regime in forcing migrants onto boats, which led to the arrival of almost 26,000 people on the southern shores of Italy.[3] In this context, over 1,822 recorded deaths occurred in

---

1   Lorenzo Pezzani and Charles Heller, 'Disobedient Gaze: Strategic Interventions in the Knowledge(s) of Maritime Borders,' *Postcolonial Studies* 16, no.3 (November 2013): 289-298.
2   See: http://fortresseurope.blogspot.com.
3   It should be noted that, contrary to the alarming discourse of EU politicians, those fleeing Libya mostly remained within North Africa, with over 700,000 people fleeing to neighbouring countries and only 25,935 people arriving in Italy and 1,530 in Malta. See: United Nations High Commissioner for Refugees (UNHCR), 'Update no 13: Humanitarian Situation in Libya and the Neighbouring Countries,' 24 March 2011, http://www.unhcr.org/4d8b6a1f9.html.

the Central Mediterranean during 2011 alone.[4] However, this record number of deaths occurred in a context in which the militarisation of the EU's maritime frontier had taken on an entirely new dimension, with a large number of Western states' military ships and patrol aircraft deployed off the Libyan coast towards the international military intervention. This particularly dramatic situation, though, also offered the opportunity to non-governmental organisations (NGOs) and activist groups to contest anew (and with new instruments and arguments) the deadly militarisation of the sea. In June of that year, the migrants' rights organisation Groupe d'information et de soutien des immigrés (GISTI) sent out a call announcing that it would file a legal case against the European Union, Frontex and NATO for non-assistance to migrants at sea, arguing that given the heightened surveillance of the Central Mediterranean during the military campaign, it was impossible for military and border control personnel to have failed to witness the distress of migrants at sea.[5]

It was in support of this legal case and other similar initiatives that we launched the collaborative research project Forensic Oceanography. While we initially enquired into the larger condition in the Sicily Channel during 2011, we later focused specifically on what is now referred to as the 'left-to-die boat' case, in which 63 migrants who had left Tripoli on 27 March of that year died during 14 days of drift in the open sea despite having made contact with the Italian coastguard, several aerial and naval military assets and some fishermen's boats. In collaboration with the architectural practice Situ Studio, we produced a 73-page report which, by mobilising a wide range of digital mapping

and modelling technologies and by relying on an unorthodox assemblage of human and non-human testimony, reconstructed and mapped as accurately as possible what happened to this vessel.[6] The report was the basis for various legal actions, most significantly a legal complaint lodged in France, Spain, and Belgium against unknown parties for non-assistance to people in danger at sea. Since then, we have continued to collaborate with various networks, trying to use mapping and visualisation tools towards the documentation of violations at sea that are the structural product of the current border regime.

In this essay, we return to reflections on what kind of knowledge we produced, the conditions of its production and what this knowledge did in the world. Focusing, in particular upon the ways in which aesthetic regimes can produce new modes of militancy. The knowledge of the border collectively produced and shared by migrants themselves forms a 'mobile commons' that is central to their capacity to move and undermines the exclusionary logic denied legal entry to the European territory are forced to resort to means that avoid detection by state agencies. 'Clandestine', which comes from the Latin 'clandestinus' meaning 'secret, hidden', refers precisely to this condition. However, this desire to go undetected is always weighed against the risk of dying unnoticed at sea. When in distress, migrants may do everything they possibly can to be noticed and rescued. This is a first indication of the complex and ambivalent nature of the epistemologies of the border.

Consequently, from this perspective, agencies aiming at controlling or managing migration try to shed light on this act of border crossing in order to make the

---

4    United Nations High Commissioner for Refugees (UNHCR), 'Mediterranean takes record as most deadly stretch of water for refugees and migrants in 2011,' http://www.unhcr.org/4f27e01f 9.html.

5    'Le Gisti va déposer plainte contre l'OTAN, l'Union européenne et les pays de la coalition en opération en Libye,' *gisti*, last accessed 2 December 2021, http://www.gisti.org/spip.php?article2304.

6    The report can be found here: https://forensic-architecture.org/investigation/the-left-to-die-boat.

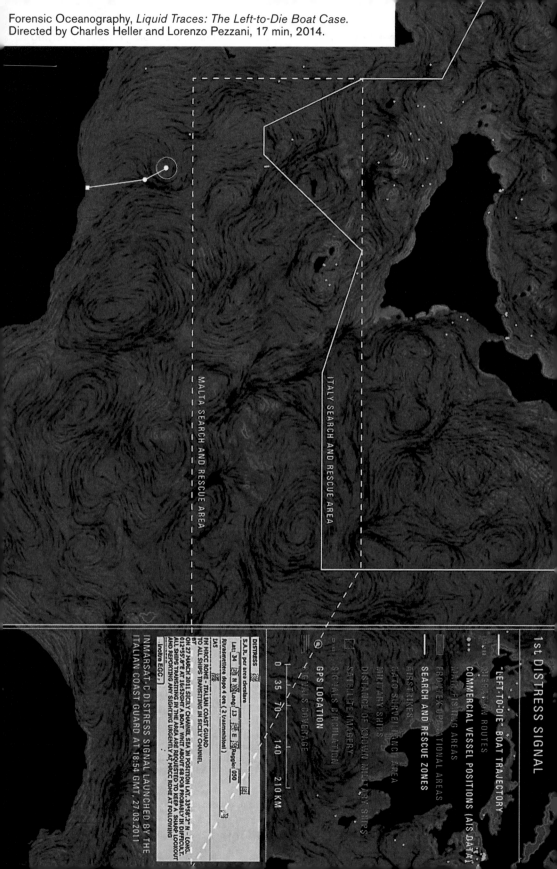

Forensic Oceanography, *Liquid Traces: The Left-to-Die Boat Case.*
Directed by Charles Heller and Lorenzo Pezzani, 17 min, 2014.

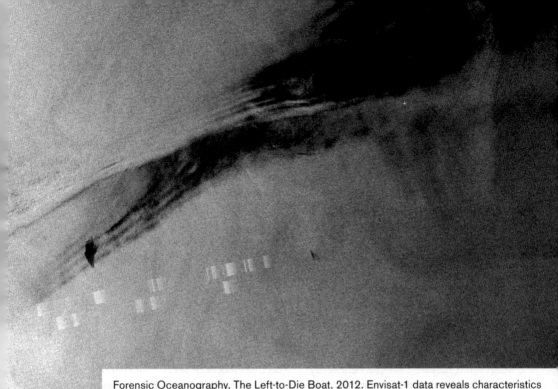

Forensic Oceanography, The Left-to-Die Boat, 2012. Envisat-1 data reveals characteristics present on the surface of the sea – different degrees of sea roughness and currents, returns indicating the presence of ships. The two bands are caused by a sensor-related error.

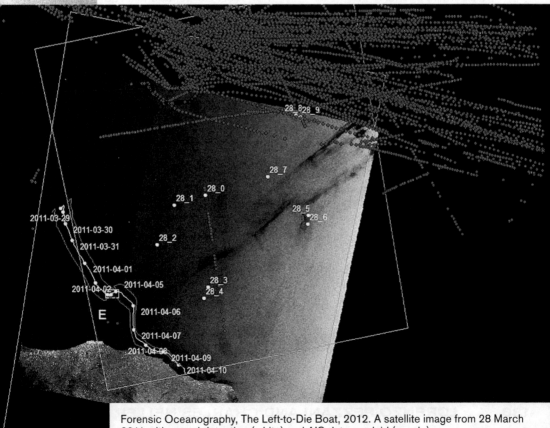

Forensic Oceanography, The Left-to-Die Boat, 2012. A satellite image from 28 March 2011 with vessel detection (white) and AIS data overlaid (purple).

phenomenon of migration more knowable, predictable, and ultimately governable. The enforcing of borders and management of migrations are clearly based on the information obtained by a wide range of actors (border guards, journalists, maritime traffic specialists, transnational military organisations) through a complex assemblage of sensing technologies (cameras, spotlights, radars, satellites, automated tracking systems, anomaly detection algorithms). This knowledge immediately translates into maps, graphs, reports, PowerPoints and policy papers that aim at making sense of the 'turbulent' character of patterns of mobility. This doubly networked knowledge—comprising both technologies and institutions across boundaries—produces less a representation of illegalised migration than a consubstantial of the border itself. For if the border only exists in its violation, the latter must first be detected either by human perception or by its various technological extensions.

While these agencies often claim a total monitoring capacity—a panoptical vision that would grant full spectrum visibility—this claim must be qualified in several respects. First, the agencies that operate maritime surveillance (NATO, coastguards, border police, Frontex, etc.) must recognise explicitly that the extension of the area and the high volume of traffic make such an objective into a chimera. The operational aim then is to identify 'threats' and sort them out from 'normal' productive traffic. As such, the surveillance machine operating in the Central Mediterranean operates as a sifting apparatus informed by what Bimal Gosh, one of the masterminds of migration management, calls a "softer, post-control spirit" that tries to regulate the porosity of borders rather than seal them.[7] Secondly,

the practice of making visible the maritime border is a controlled one. Because migrants cross a vast maritime space that is mostly out of reach of a civilian gaze, the knowledge and aesthetic products of the border are mostly in the hands of state agencies or of the journalists who accept to work 'embedded' in their operations. As such, the logic of border patrols at the maritime border operates a simultaneous unveiling and concealing. What is unveiled is the act of clandestine migration, what is concealed is the violent political and legal exclusion that produces this clandestinity in the first place, and the numerous legal violations the migration regime generates in turn.[8]

The knowledge ecology of the maritime border is thus a fundamentally conflictual and ambivalent one, and one of the main dimensions of this conflict hinges on conditions of visibility/invisibility. Illegalised migrants wish to go unseen to reach EU territory, but to be seen when they are in distress. Border agencies attempt to visibilise their clandestine mobility, but in a controlled way that simultaneously covers much of the reality and violence of the border. A fundamental question for activists and critical researchers alike is thus how to produce a strategic knowledge that operates within this conflictual and ambivalent epistemological and aesthetic field without risking to become part of the governmental attempt to manage migration by 'shedding light' on the border.

Thomas Keenan dubs this tactic of unveiling and monitoring used by activist and non-governmental groups "mobilising shame".[9] This dominant tactic within the field of human rights is based on the assumption that dark deeds are done in the dark, and that the light of publicity has an almost magical power to call for action on

7   Martin Geiger and Antoine Pécoud, eds., *The Politics of International Migration Management*, (Basingstoke: Palgrave Macmillan, 2010).
8   Nicholas De Genova, 'Spectacles of Migrant 'Illegality': the Scene of Exclusion, the Obscene of Inclusion,' *Ethnic and Racial Studies* 36, no. 7 (2013): 1180-1198.
9   Thomas Keenan, 'Mobilizing Shame,' *South Atlantic Quarterly* 103, no. 2/3 (2004): 435-449.

behalf of justice. Through a series of examples, he shows how, in fact, the knowledge of mass atrocities, human rights violations, and widespread violence alone does not necessarily trigger any form of political intervention or struggle, since many of them already happen blatantly in full light; thus exposure becomes at times part of the very violence being perpetrated.

This important insight has particular implications in our discussion of maritime border regimes, since at the border, "only detected, that is to say failed acts of illegal immigration become visible".[10] The practice of the activists on board the Cap Anamur provides a revealing example. In 2004, the Cap Anamur vessel, a humanitarian ship that started its activities by bringing help to the Vietnamese boat people in the late 1970s, rescued 37 African migrants who had got into distress in the Sicily Channel during their crossing to Europe. The ship was later denied permission to enter Italian territorial waters and kept off the coast of Sicily during a legal and diplomatic standoff that lasted more than two weeks, in which the fate of the asylum seekers bounced between competing claims and denials. During this time, the deck of the ship was transformed into a unique forum of sorts, in which numerous lawyers, journalists, photographers, politicians, priests, activists, and doctors publicly denounced the deadly effects of the European border regime. This exposure however failed to grant any salvation for the migrants or the crew. When the ship was finally allowed access to a Sicilian port, the migrants were immediately expelled and the representatives of the Cap Anamur were infamously indicted for favouring illegal immigration and turning the humanitarian emergency into a 'PR stunt' for their profit. Here, then, the attempt to 'scandalise' the death of migrants at sea and publicise assistance to them

had also uncovered the migrants' attempt to enter EU territory clandestinely, thereby contributing unwittingly to the logic of border control and thus exposing the risk of complicity that we mentioned earlier.

This episode reminds us that the risk implicit in the 'mobilising shame' paradigm is to ignore the productive role that openness and transparency can play within practices of power, and within the field of the politics of migration in particular. This situation puts activists and researchers alike at risk of participating in a production of knowledge that immediately becomes part of the governmental machine that attempts to regulate mobility. Because migrants need secrets, granting full spectrum visibility risks being counterproductive, and the Cap Anamur case is an example of how "showing what is hidden may sometimes lead to new forms of oppression".[11] This example is also crucial in reminding us that the complex and conflicting ecology of knowledge of/at the border is an immanent field, from which there is no exterior, and this is also why critical and militant research practices need to come to terms with this issue.

The strategy that we tried to mobilise in order to address this issue within the context of Forensic Oceanography was to exercise a 'disobedient gaze', which aimed not to disclose what the regime of migration management had attempted to unveil—clandestine migration; but rather to unveil that which it attempted to hide—the political violence it is founded on and the human rights violations that are its structural outcome. Applying this strategy to the Left-to-Die-Boat investigation entailed subverting the technologies of surveillance deployed by states in the frame of the war. By analysing vast amounts of digital data coming from ocean buoys, fishing, and commercial vessels' monitoring technologies, satellite

10  Christine Bischoff, Francesca Falk, and Sylvia Kafehsy, *Images of Illegalized Immigration: Towards a Critical Iconology of Politics*, (Bielefeld: transcript Verlag, 2010).
11  Bischoff, Falk, and Kafehsy, *Images*, 8.

phones, ships' logs, maritime distress signals, radars and satellites, we tried to transform the Mediterranean sensorium into a witness to interrogate.

But whereas all these technologies are usually part of the surveillance apparatus that routinely monitors the area in the attempt to detect migrants heading towards the coasts of southern Europe and other 'terrorist' activities, it was the violation perpetrated by the military that we attempted to reveal, rather than the act of clandestine migration. An example of this was provided by our use of satellite imagery to determine the position of military vessels in the Mediterranean. The relatively low resolution of the images we acquired did not allow for the location of migrants' boats (which are usually smaller wooden vessels) but only for that of the bigger military vessels. The resolution of the image became then a highly political issue, in that it determined the frontier between the visible and invisible, and separated the practice of a disobedient gaze from an uncritical act of revealing that risks complicity. Furthermore, we provided a detailed analysis of the sensing technologies used by the different military assets in order to prove that the naval assets in operation at the time had the means to detect the drifting migrants' boat. In this we were proving the claim that the states could not fail to witness the migrants' distress and thus were responsible for failing to assist them. The knowledge generated by surveillance became evidence of guilt.

Let us return to our initial questions: how can knowledge about migration produce transformative effects in the politics of migration? What are these effects and what are their potentials and dangers? Firstly, we need to inscribe militant knowledge production within a broader ecology of knowledges, focusing on migrant networks, border agencies and human rights activists and critical researchers. One key dividing line within this contentious and ambivalent ecology is 'aesthetics'. While illegalised migrants wish to go unseen to reach EU territory, but to be seen when they are in distress, border agencies attempt to visibilise their clandestine mobility but in a controlled way that simultaneously covers much of the reality and violence of the border. Yet shedding light on clandestine migration in order to denounce violations, often ends up being complicit with the border regime. In response we argue that militant knowledge of/at the border needs a more nuanced and selective 'disobedient gaze', one that simultaneously refuses to disclose clandestine migration and reveals the violence of the border regime.

How does the space of the EU's maritime border operate? How can knowledge production contribute to reconfiguring it? Let us not close these questions then but open them further by quoting Jacques Rancière's assertion, confronting the injunction of the police, "Move along! There is nothing to see here!",[12] politics should aim to transform the space of circulation into a space for the appearance of a subject: the people, the workers, the citizens (and, we might add, the migrants). Politics then, for the French philosopher, "consists in refiguring the space, of what there is to do there, what is to be seen or named therein".[13] Militant knowledges of/at the maritime border, all of the militant knowledges that attempt to counter in some way the border regime, from that of activists to more theoretical contributions, contribute to refiguring the space of the sea. Together, they contest the claim to the monopoly of the definition of the Mediterranean by states and capital, with their imperative to securitise its waters so as to foster 'wanted' forms of mobility and deny freedom of movement to non-EU nationals, who nonetheless seize this freedom at the risk of their life.

12  Jacques Rancière, Dissensus: On Politics and Aesthetics, (London: Continuum, 2010), 37.
13  Jacques Rancière, 'Ten Theses on Politics,' Theory and Event 5, no. 3 (2001).

**LORENZO PEZZANI AND CHARLES HELLER**

Forensic Oceanography, The Left-to-Die Boat, 2012. Dan Haile Gebre, a survivor from the boat, sketches details of his story in an interview with Lorenzo Pezzani.

## Works Cited

Bischoff, Christine, Francesca Falk, and Sylvia Kafehsy, *Images of Illegalized Immigration: Towards a Critical Iconology of Politics*, Bielefeld: transcript Verlag, 2010.

De Genova, Nicholas. 'Spectacles of Migrant' Illegality': the Scene of Exclusion, the Obscene of Inclusion.' *Ethnic and Racial Studies* 36, no.7, (2013): 1180-1198.

Forensic Architecture. The Left-to-Die-Boat. 2012. http://www.forensic-architecture.org/publications/report-on-the-left-to-die-boat/.

Fortress Europe. http://fortresseurope.blogspot.com.

Geiger, Martin, and Antoine Pécoud, eds. *The Politics of International Migration Management*. Basingstoke: Palgrave Macmillan, 2010.

Groupe d'information et de soutien des immigrés (GISTI), 'Le Gisti va déposer plainte contre l'OTAN, l'Union européenne et les pays de la coalition en opération en Libye', last modified 2 December 2021, http://www.gisti.org/spip.php?article2304.

Keenan, Thomas. 'Mobilizing Shame,' *South Atlantic Quarterly* 103, no.2/3, (2004): 435-449.

Pezzani, Lorenzo, and Charles Heller. 'Disobedient Gaze: Strategic Interventions in the Knowledge(s) of Maritime Borders.' *Postcolonial Studies* 16, no.3, (November 2013): 289-298.

Rancière, Jacques. 'Ten Thesis on Politics.' *Theory and Event* 5, no.3, (2001).

——— *Dissensus: On Politics and Aesthetics*, London: Continuum, 2010.

United Nations High Commissioner for Refugees (UNHCR). 'Update no 13: Humanitarian Situation in Libya and the Neighbouring Countries.' 24 March 2011, http://www.unhcr.org/4d8b6a1f9.html.

United Nations High Commissioner for Refugees (UNHCR). 'Mediterranean takes record as most deadly stretch of water for refugees and migrants in 2011'. http://www.unhcr.org/4f27e01f 9.html.

# DIGITAL AUTONOMIA

It's January 2022, and I find myself sitting inside a McDonald's in South London. The hygienic lighting and an uncomfortable stool remind me that the space is designed for constant turnover. Around me, the only other people not constantly moving are the delivery workers in their mismatched uniforms, waiting for their orders to be dispatched. My research focuses on platform-based labour to understand how work, knowledge, and cooperation have been transformed by algorithmic management. As a large and diffuse network of logistical workers is increasingly managed computationally—relentlessly matching supply with demand—spaces of contestation to the labour conditions shaped by platform companies are emerging. These sites, often scattered in the warehouses and car parks of fast-food joints, have become the locations of my fieldwork.

Many scholars have investigated how digital technologies changed the social relations of labour in the past decades.[1] To investigate this condition, I've drawn inspiration from the autonomia operaia, an Italian political movement that emerged in the 1970s. The *operaistas* asked how the subjectivity of workers froam the south of Italy was transformed by their experiences in the automated factories of the north. To do so, they adopted a practice that involved carrying out research alongside workers and through the organisation of workers' autonomy in what they called a process of *conricerca* (co-research). Carrying out research alongside workers generated new and unexpected insights from the situated perspective of a class of workers whose labour practices were transforming in real-time. Differing from ethnographies or sociological methodologies, *conricerca* is a practice of subjectivation, organisation, and rupture, where the production of knowledge is the production of struggle.[2]

*Operaistas* differed from traditional unions in two ways that are pivotal in my practice. Firstly, they departed from the workers' experience of automation to challenge the neutrality of technology and expose its role within the capitalist project. While factory owners described automation as an "external rationality" that could reorganise work more efficiently, *operaistas* understood automation as a web of machines, methods, and organisational techniques that reinforced the subordination of workers inside and beyond the factory boundaries.[3] They aimed to uncover the social relations embedded in the form and operatives of technology to explore how these relations could be subverted. Secondly, they noticed how capital began to draw more from the labour of precarious and less organised social groups outside the factory floor. This perspective suggested that every moment of the circulation process contributed to the production of value.[4] This transformed *operaismo* into *autonomia,* bringing together different groups, from women's movements to the unemployed, that were engaged in different instances of anti-capitalist practice. *Autonomistas* sought to understand how class was composed beyond the workshop, displacing their inquiry from the factory gates to the social factory,

1   Nick Srnicek, *Platform Capitalism,* (London: Polity Press, 2016); Tiziana Terranova, 'Free Labor: Producing Culture for the Digital Economy,' Social Text 18, no. 2, (Summer 2000): 33–59; Phoebe V.Moore and Jamie Woodcock, *Augmented Exploitation: Artificial Intelligence, Automation And Work,* (London: Pluto Press, 2021).

2   Gigi Roggero, 'Romano Alquati -- Militant Researcher, Operaist, Autonomist Marxist – Has Passed Away, Age 75.', Tumblr, *Tumblr* (blog), accessed 17 June 2023. Carrying out research through workers' inquiry has gained interest in recent years with initiatives like Notes From Below from the UK, Into the Black Box in Italy, or Plateforme d'Enquêtes Militantes in France.

3   Raniero Panzieri, 'The Capitalist Use of Machinery: Marx versus the Objectivists,' Libcom, 2005, https://libcom.org/library/capalist-use-machinery-raniero-panzieri.

4   Steven Wright, *Storming Heaven: Class Composition and Struggle in Italian Autonomist Marxism,* (London: Pluto Press, 2017).

**JÚLIA NUENO GUITART**

where the worker is reproduced. By contesting the nature of technology and of value production, *autonomistas* proposed a radical transformation of work and life.[5]

> *With machine learning [there] is not even a manager assigning orders. They've literally said how do you make an algorithm distribute work as efficiently as possible? You just get data from workers, like we are the ones doing all the value. It's not a manager, it's not coders setting it up. What do riders do ten million times over? And we'll try to predict it and make those predictions match demand and supply. Everything produced is being produced by us as a collective of riders.*[6]

In late 2021, I reached out to the Independent Workers of Great Britain (IWGB) union, established in 2012, primarily by outsourced and self-employed migrant workers in the UK. This radical union led the first campaign for collective bargaining rights for self-employed delivery workers, reflecting the changing face of the UK's workforce. Delivery workers are predominantly young men, with a significant number from migrant or ethnic minority backgrounds in London.[7] I was interested in understanding the cases that IWGB was taking on with delivery workers, and IWGB was interested in my ability to help with Spanish translation for Latin American members. The union suggested I meet with two delivery riders who were experiencing difficulties with the Stuart app.[8]

When the delivery riders arrive at McDonald's, they show me several screenshots illustrating how the navigational system of Stuart works. While navigational apps, such Google Maps or Citymapper, have reached an astonishing degree of accuracy, Stuart is perhaps unique in using a navigational system provider that takes riders on impossible routes, through parks and playgrounds instead of streets and alleys, routes that should only be taken by pedestrians. Shortening the virtual journey time by taking riders through parks instead of the city streets, which is what they inevitably end up doing, maximises profits for Stuart while reducing the riders' pay.

This first meeting will end up turning into a campaign, led by two riders, Kevin and Mercin, and supported by IWGB union. Over time, it will bring together forty workers in South London and another fifteen in Plymouth, to denounce how such flawed and impossible routes are severely reducing their income.[9] Over the next few months, meetings and conversations on picket lines begin to reveal how the app, data collection, algorithms, and the cloud have all combined to restructure work processes, focusing on measuring, predicting, and improving each worker's behaviour. This requirement of individualised constant engagement and improvement has been identified by logistics scholars as an extension of production management from the factory floor onto larger supply chains.[10] Under logistical capital, the assembly line transcends localised sites of production, and extends into the sphere of circulation, becoming a site of extraction of surplus value.[11]

5   Paolo Virno, *A Grammar of the Multitude: For an Analysis of Contemporary Forms of Life,* Semiotext(e) Foreign Agents Series, (Cambridge, Massachussetts; London: Semiotext(e), 2003).
6   Excerpt from an interview with a delivery worker, 2022.
7   Trades Union Congress, 'Seven Ways Platform Workers Are Fighting Back,' 5 November 2021, https://www.tuc.org.uk/research-analysis/reports/seven-ways-platform-workers-are-fighting-back.
8   Stuart is a food delivery platform headquartered in France that coordinates riders and their delivery points.
9   Eve Livingston, 'Food Delivery Drivers Fired after 'Cut-Price' GPS App Sent Them on 'Impossible' Routes,' *The Observer,* 2 July 2022, https://www.theguardian.com/business/2022/jul/02/food-delivery-drivers-fired-after-cut-price-gps-app-sent-them-on-impossible-routes.
10  Stefano Harney and Fred Moten, *All Incomplete,* (London; New York: Minor Compositions, 2021).
11  Charmaine Chua, 'Logistics,' in *The SAGE Handbook of Marxism,* ed. Beverly Skeggs, Sara R. Farris, Alberto Toscano , et al. 1st ed., (Thousand Oaks: SAGE Inc, 2021), 1444–1462; Wright, *Storming Heaven: Class Composition and Struggle in Italian Autonomist Marxism.*

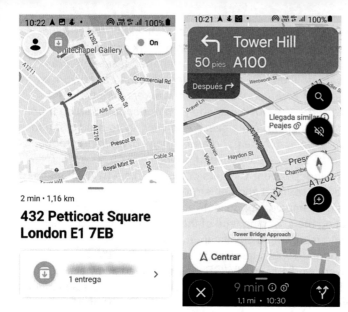

Directions given by Stuart app (2 min, 1.16km for delivery)
Directions for the same delivery in Google Maps (9 min, 1.78km).
Screen captures taken by a delivery worker in South London

Digital technologies optimise each task of this extended assembly line by establishing a pool of flexible workers who individually change their location and pace to adapt to real-time market changes. Rather than workers in a fixed position waiting for the same repetitive task, delivery platforms expect workers to move and adapt to tasks as they emerge. What's new is not the mobility of workers, which has been at the heart of the expansion of racial and logistical capital over the last two centuries, the distinctiveness now lies in the immediacy and nature of this mobility: a direct, just-in-time adjustment of workers' behaviour to meet market needs.[12] As many critical platform scholars have pointed out, lean platforms shift the costs of the job onto workers, such as equipment or insurance.[13] Data-based management serves to further disaggregate and externalise its losses onto workers, for example, the costs of idle waiting time.

The algorithmic model that organises work is based on a set of assumptions and constraints that are designed to fulfil profit for platforms by extracting surplus and externalising costs and losses to workers.[14] This is evident in several ways, including the calculation of fees based on the distance between a restaurant and a customer. Deliveroo and Uber calculate distance as the crow flies, from point A to point B in a direct line, while other apps, such as Stuart, calculate distances in a grid-like path. These metrics reduce the question of the calculation of fees to a spatial problem when, for the worker, it is actually a temporal one. The time spent waiting for an order to be received or prepared, the actual travel time on the road, the time spent searching for a specific

---

12  Just-in-time is a process of supply chain management that ensures that commodities arrive exactly when and where they're needed to cut down on warehouse costs. When transportation becomes an assembly line under just-in-time production, labour-power is the commodity that must be operational at all times, finding all possible strategies to minimise its associated costs.

13  Srnicek, *Platform Capitalism*; V. Moore and Woodcock, *Augmented Exploitation. Artificial Intelligence, Automation And Work*; Jeremy Anderson, 'Labour Struggles in Logistics,' in *The SAGE Handbook of Marxism*, ed. Beverly Skeggs, Sara R. Farris, Alberto Toscano , et al. 1st ed. (Thousand Oaks: SAGE Inc, 2021), 1463–1484.

14  Anderson, 'Labour Struggles in Logistics'.

apartment within a large complex, or waiting for an unresponsive customer–all these temporal aspects are disregarded in favour of a simplified spatial calculation.[15]

By using distance as an objective metric, platforms shift the cost of unproductive labour time to the worker, while also obscuring compensation for the actual time spent working. Inaccurate predictions show that biases are inherent in the system, but can also become externalised losses loaded onto workers. For instance, Stuart's motorcyclists are given impossible routes going through parks or one-way streets and must reroute to avoid fines without compensation.[16] In addition, the projected routes are shorter than the actual trip, so the final fee, which is based on distance, is reduced.

As part of our campaign, we informally contacted an engineer at Stuart via Twitter. In a direct-message conversation a senior manager told a union member: "Stuart has an internally built directions service and it's not great. We used to use Google Maps directions but they put the price up 10x". We understood that Stuart had changed the supplier of the mapping system since, economically, it was more advantageous for them. However, they did not formally respond to any of the complaints sent by drivers, or to a letter with more than 150 signatures from workers, potentially because publicly acknowledging the issue might require addressing it.

A flawed navigation system that makes incorrect predictions might seem a technological problem, but it is, in fact, a political one. As the geographer and media scholar Louise Amoore explains, "Algorithms are not unaccountable as such, instead, they are giving accounts of themselves all the time".[17] In this case, impossible routes are acceptable as long as they protect Stuart's income and only damage workers' income. Losses are externalised to the workers and are not charged to the platforms. Data-based management inscribes capitalist labour relations that, on the one hand, shift fixed costs of infrastructure onto workers and that, on the other hand, externalise losses onto their workers.

> Flexibility is not a concession to workers. Everywhere in the media it will say: "Delivery workers enjoy flexibility, so correspondingly they shouldn't have rights". It's not here because we demanded it, it's here because the companies need it. Logistically it's much better to have free log in. We manage the logistics; we know when it's better to log in. I always check the weather; I always know where it's busy and we are all doing those decisions collectively. Collectively, we are much more efficient as a group of riders with a capacity to log in and log out than a worker model. That's why it's there not because we wanted it.[18]

Kevin and Mercin agree to meet me again in a Greggs car park to speak with other drivers experiencing similar navigation problems with Stuart's app. The problem is acknowledged by all, but as Stuart pays better than other platforms, not everyone is prepared to take it further. We set a date for a first public meeting to discuss a plan– about ten riders turn up. In the meeting, we decide to continue spreading the campaign by approaching workers in different restaurant locations and inviting them to a second assembly. It is quite difficult to get confirmation of attendance, as the riders generally don't know what part of town they will be working in on the proposed date – and, as Kevin tells me, if they get a well-paid order, they are likely to leave halfway through the meeting.

15  Karl Marx, *El Capital,* Vol I, section IV, (Madrid: S.XXI, 2017)
16  Júlia Nueno, 'Riding the Algorithm. Repurposing Delivery Workers Data into a Digital Commons,' 2022.
17  Louise Amoore, *Cloud Ethics: Algorithms and the Attributes of Ourselves and Others,* (Durham: Duke University Press, 2020), 19.
18  Excerpt from an interview with a delivery worker, 2022.

Through consolidating riders' locations and consumer behaviour patterns, platforms create an extended and flexible assembly line that continually adjusts to meet changing demands, which leads to drivers' location fluctuating and impacting their ability to come to organising meetings. A system of individualised metrics, boosts, incentives, and penalties is used to predict and modify workers' behaviour. Individualised metrics push them to achieve productivity targets, and soften their attitudes to fulfill high customer ratings. They are prompted to adjust their location based on incentives in areas with high customer demand. In the highly commodified fee structures of food delivery services, such as those of Deliveroo, incentives are directly linked to prioritising orders that are running behind schedule, requiring riders to develop the ability to interpret fees to maximise income.[19] Conversely, when demand is low, delivery fees plummet in the expectation that riders will log out of the platform. Letting an algorithm set a worker's salary based on real-time market needs epitomises the concept of a self-regulating free market. However, behind this illusion, it is evident that to earn their salaries, workers increasingly need to understand and manage the complexities of the market that platforms are constantly reshaping.

Through this gamified system, riders learn which zones and routes are likely to offer more work, adapting the virtual platform to the material conditions of their labour.[20] Incentives and penalties also train riders, in much the same way that datasets train models, to modify their schedules to meet changes in demand. On the one hand, this adjustment of workers' behaviour echoes the techniques of reinforced learning, a subfield of machine learning. Reinforced learning focuses on how agents can learn to make decisions and take actions in an environment to maximise a cumulative reward.[21] Originally inspired by the cognitive ability of humans and animals to adapt to their environment, the frequency and coordination of adjustments required of delivery drivers has led to increased anxiety, fatigue, and a high number of road accidents.[22] On the other hand, management algorithms learn and rely on riders knowledge on how to navigate the city to optimise their services. There is a skill both in knowing how to choose the best orders, those that pay the most and require to travel the least, and on getting around a city in the fastest way: what roads have the least traffic lights, which have more accidents, which intersections often deploy migration enforcement points, and so on.

Riders told me they try to play off maps and glitches like companies do. For example, they will tamper with the GPS signal or work across multiple platforms in parallel by offsetting the thresholds of location detectability of each algorithm. They will use airplane mode to find out the routes of orders, then log in and log out multiple times to refuse an order without being penalised. These new strategies of resistance to algorithmic subordination emerge in a space of digitalised labour. However, as performance is tied to remuneration, some of these strategies mean that some workers

---

19  In the case of London, the four main food delivery apps – Deliveroo, Uber, Stuart and JustEat– categorise into four different pricing structures. JustEat, the only company that employs its riders, has a fixed hourly rate. UberEats and Stuart have a bracketed system according to different milage. Deliveroo has the most elastic and flexible pricing system based on machine learning, with fees changing according to distance, weather conditions, traffic, according to their website. However, the perception of delivery workers is that the fees are calculated by shifts in supply and demand, which are influenced by the conditions stated in Deliveroo's website.

20  Gamification is a management practice which uses rankings, and rewards to engage the worker in a particular task, resembling the design of traditional games.

21  Pedro Domingos, *The Master Algorithm: How the Quest for the Ultimate Learning Machine Will Remake Our World*, (Bristol: Allen Lane, 2015).

22  Focus on Labour Exploitation, 'The gig is up: Participatory research with couriers in the UK app-based delivery sector, ' 2021, https://labourexploitation.org/app/uploads/2021/11/ FLEX_TheGigIsUp_v4_0.pdf.

take on more tasks. Individual forms of resistance result in some riders accumulating the income normally distributed between all, turning the tools of resistance against other riders, while the platform's revenue remains the same.

The externalisation of the cost of unproductive labour has led to riders waiting outside restaurants where they engage in conversations about their labour conditions. These social gatherings have turned into assembly spaces—such as McDonald's for Stuart riders—prompting workers to organise and lead campaigns for better labour conditions and publicly expose the operatives and effects of data-based decision-making. Paradoxically, the savings achieved through externalisation may ultimately lead to significant losses for platform companies. Notably, in June 2023, after years of mobilisation, a minimum wage was introduced for over 60,000 delivery riders working in New York City.[23] Last year, in Sheffield, the longest gig work strike led by couriers and the IWGB won paid waiting time for riders working for JustEat.[24] Similarly, in Hong Kong, FoodPanda riders, whose platform is run by the German-owned Delivery Hero, went on a strike to protest against a faulty navigation system that used a Western-style city grid to calculate distances in Hong Kong's complex geography. Riders succeeded in getting FoodPanda to introduce a new navigation system and compensate them for underpaid routes.[25] Their struggle illustrates how delivery platforms reproduce forms of neo-colonial dispossession and exploitation under a global value chain by treating all geographies as equal. They also show how it is possible to articulate political demands based on understanding and challenging technological assumptions.

Back in London, we organised our campaign around the flawed navigation system in the spring of 2022. Along with riders, we began to reflect upon the aggregate and relational qualities of large data systems that define their labour conditions. What makes data about a rider valuable to a platform is the ability to make predictions or change behaviour based on relevant information about other riders and customers. There is an inherently relational quality to data-based systems and a value in aggregation as the assemblage of data amplifies the effects of relationality.[26] Riders explained to me how the sum and relation of their data contributes to the creation and management of the market, which platforms portray as neutral grounds for competition amongst workers. As I've already suggested, the platform's reliance on riders to manage this system also creates opportunities for leverage and even collectivisation on the part of riders.

> *[The algorithm] really knows how to send you stuff you will take. But at the same time when it becomes that commodified all that over-hiring becomes more pronounced. Because over-hiring literally drives down fees because the supply of riders is raised, and demand is the same. In the past, over-supply of riders was only about the amount of work we would receive, now it's also about the price for the work that we do. They have literally incentivised to over-hire to drive down fees, [the algorithm] is much more sophisticated.[27]*

23  Stefanos Chen, 'New York City Sets New Minimum Wage for Food Delivery Workers', *The New York Times*, 12 June 2023, https://www.nytimes.com/2023/06/12/nyregion/nyc-delivery-workers-minimum-wage.html.

24  Sam Gregory, 'Is This Sheffield Strike the Most Exciting Workers' Movement in the UK?', *Now Then*, 10 February 2022, https://nowthenmagazine.com/articles/is-this-sheffield-strike-the-most-exciting-workers-movement-in-the-uk.

25  Ben Wray, "Riders' Rights Concern Group: Why Europeans Should Care about the Struggle of FoodPanda Couriers in Hong Kong,' *Brave New Europe* (blog), 16 March 2022, https://braveneweurope.com/riders-rights-concern-group-why-europeans-should-care-about-the-struggle-of-foodpanda-couriers-in-hong-kong.

26  Salomé Viljoen, 'A Relational Theory of Data Governance,' *The Yale Law Journal* 131, no. 2 (November 2021): 370–781.

27  Excerpt from an interview with a delivery worker, 2022.

As critical finance scholar Michel Feher explains, trade unions often reflect capitalist structures. For over a century, unions have "mirrored the bosses' agreements to fix wage levels" on workers' articulation of wage demands.[28] In his work, Feher identifies the turn of markets towards credit attribution instead of value extraction. He proposes a form of "investee activism" that focuses on intervening in the revaluation of investors' portfolios. Investees aim to sink the creditworthiness of companies and generate disinvestment through reputational damage. His work also shows that "speculation" is an operation not only present in millionaire financial markets, but can also be a method of restructuring social relations.[29]

Meeting with delivery riders voting on strike-action during campaign against Stuart in London. Photo taken by the author.

The aggregation of workers' data, comprised of the history of their geolocation coordinates and all interactions with the app, is used to parametrise and predict their behaviour, becoming an expression of speculative social relations. In our conversations with delivery riders, we began to think about counter-speculative possibilities in relation to riders' data-points: How might the collection of data be reappropriated by those already subject to its coercive effects to influence decision-making processes? Can workers' data be

28  Michel Feher, *Rated Agency: Investee Politics in a Speculative Age*, Near Futures, (New York: Zone Books, 2018), 85.
29  Feher, *Rated Agency*.

**JÚLIA NUENO GUITART**

re-purposed to challenge the power relations established by platform-based labour? In a data-dense environment, can labourers optimise algorithms to switch their allegiance?

The main strategies for obtaining data are Subject Access Requests (SARs) under the UK General Data Protection Regulation (UK-GDPR)—to safeguard individuals' privacy—and information leakages.[30] The current data access model is weak for three reasons. Firstly, it recognises that data belongs to platforms and can only be requested (or hacked) rather than being seen as the collective intelligence that users, and in this case workers, generate, and should have free access to. Secondly, obtaining data retroactively means that it cannot be used to intervene in real-time, although it is sometimes used to highlight power asymmetries. Thirdly, it fails to consider the relational and aggregate qualities of data: a horizontal relation that is established between workers rather than a vertical relation between workers and management.[31] Individual data records fail to show how a system of surveillance and labour exploitation is put in place by the relation of data of its users.

The root of these limitations lies in the dominant legal framework for the control of data, which is based on the individual rights-bearing subject.[32] GDPR overlooks how the assembly of data is more than the sum of its parts, becoming a form of collective intelligence, or 'general intellect' as Marx identified it in his observations on the deskilling of workers in automation processes. As philosopher and autonomist Paolo Virno develops, when general intellect does not become "a public sphere, a political community, it then drastically increases forms of submission".[33] Algorithmically managed cooperation is used to grip on surplus extraction from workers. Instead, can the cooperation of data points between workers become a *political community*, a form of collective intelligence used by workers to build their autonomy from platform capitalism? Challenging the power imbalance between workers and platforms would require that workers be able to aggregate and relate their data to each other in real-time. This would allow them to collectively bargain in the system they are part of, returning their collective intelligence to the political sphere.

These principles, around what I've come to call a "data commons", were the driving force behind exploring forms of digital organising with delivery riders in South London and the IWGB union. What I define as "data commons" differs from ideas of "platform cooperativism", and economic alternatives that promote fair forms of platform services.[34] It is instead a medium to repurpose workers' data to create organising opportunities with the aim of increasing their autonomy from the ruling platform class.

30  In June 2022, *The Guardian* obtained over 124,000 confidential Uber files, including leaked data. Under UK law, individuals can request their personal data through a SAR. While SARs are crucial for understanding algorithms and protecting worker rights, companies frequently evade these requests.

31  The upcoming Data Protection and Digital Information bill set for Parliamentary consideration in November 2023, which is poised to replace the UK-GDPR, tightens the provisions for individuals seeking access to their data. Additionally, it represents a step back in collective rights, notably by removing the GDPR provision that enables class action suits against companies collecting data.

32  Becka Hudson and Tomas Percival, 'Carceral Data: The Limits of Transparency-as-Accountability in Prison Risk Data,' *Secrecy and Society* 3, no. 1, (10 August 2023). Demands of transparency relying on the creation of a data double – a copy of the data subject file – under GDPR have shown to foreclose possibilities of radical change in carceral contexts. Similarly, in the case of delivery platforms, I try to outline the limitations of accessing individual subjects data as a way to seek accountancy.

33  Virno, *A Grammar of the Multitude*, 41.

34  Trebor Scholz and Nathan Schneider, *Ours to Hack and to Own: The Rise of Platform Cooperativism, A New Vision for the Future of Work and a Fairer Internet,* (New York: OR Books, 2016).

If cooperation between workers is no longer defined by their physical proximity, but rather by their digital connection, what does the digital space offer to build on emancipation? A "data commons" brings together unionised and non-unionised workers, trying to experiment with the boundaries of organisational structures. The ultimate goal is to use this tool as a means to increase the leverage of workers against platforms – through actions such as helping workers to determine in which restaurants it is better to take strike action, or to coordinate their disconnection from a particular platform to pressure a company, or to assemble evidence for strategic litigation in IWGB.

Having experienced the limitations of our campaign against Stuart first-hand, a group of riders, and union members came together in the summer of 2022 to reflect and design a platform for a union "data commons". This is an experimental outcome of a *conricerca* process. Often, *conricerca* is translated into writing, turning experiences of work into a narration that can circulate to other workers, to create a shared account and stir the conditions for organisation. In our case, our observations turned into the design of a tool for delivery workers beyond our group to engage in *conricerca* of their own labour conditions. This platform eventually transformed into an app that we called Sabot, in reference to the first French saboteurs of the 18th Century who threw their wooden shoes or sabots into the textile looms to jam them when automation reorganised workshops.[35] The significance of the app is not limited to understanding data as collective property, as the general intellect that belongs to workers. Equally significant is the fact that it was designed along with delivery workers as the result of their labour experiences.[36]

Together, we identified four tools that would be useful to back the organisation of delivery workers. Firstly, an alternative map enables riders to map each other's locations, usually hidden by platforms. This serves to visualise the magnitude of the workforce dispersed under different platform companies. The map also allows riders to report and display road accidents (for which companies do not publish any numbers), and sites of migration enforcement that often target a precarious and largely migrant workforce. This map acknowledges that delivery labour highly exposes and unprotects migrated workers, understanding like *autonomistas*, that political subjectivity is built during work and outside of it. A second tool assists riders in assembling evidence for campaigns and strategic litigation by collecting data on their actual routes and their logged-in hours that can be used to support their pay or worker status claims. A third feature is a poll system to identify in which restaurants would riders agree to take collective action. The combination of multiple platform companies, operating over a large urban area, complicates the identification of collective organising opportunities for a small union like IWGB. A system of polls can help to identify particular places in which workers are experiencing discrimination, or abuse, and respond accordingly. Lastly, a feature for counter-speculative purposes, aims to use the principles of dynamic pricing that regulate demand and supply in favour of workers. For example, if machine learning cuts down fees during periods of high customer demand, riders can use the tool to coordinate logging out and logging back in, potentially creating surge prices in areas where rider supply is scarce. As delivery platforms increasingly rely on workers to manage the logistics of the market, workers are in a new position to interrupt the mechanisms of market-making to build leverage.

35  Elizabeth Gurley Flynn, 'The Conscious Withdrawal of the Workers Industrial Efficiency,' (Chicago: IWW Publisher Bureau, 1912).

36  Find the open-source repository of Sabot, along a downloadable beta version for Android, and a detailed explanation of the code and collection of the conversations with delivery workers during design process: https://github.com/julianueno/Sabot/.

As the riders' app project continues to develop, the current focus is on developing an agreement among riders about the conditions of data sharing. Present legal frameworks fall short in safeguarding collective rights, leaning heavily on individual privacy. With a rider's "data commons", individual strategies of resistance, the knowledge accumulated by riders on how to subvert the algorithm, can be turned into collective tools. That is the ideal outcome of a co-research process, one that can turn the production of knowledge in the production of struggle. As *autonomistas* showed, contesting the nature of technology is a means to return it to a terrain of dispute. Their legacy perhaps serves as a reminder that researchers should not only describe and interpret the world, but that we must also make sense of the world we want to transform.

## Works Cited

Amoore, Louise. *Cloud Ethics: Algorithms and the Attributes of Ourselves and Others*. Durham: Duke University Press, 2020.

Anderson, Jeremy. 'Labour Struggles in Logistics,' in *The SAGE Handbook of Marxism*, edited by Beverly Skeggs, Sara R.Farris, Alberto Toscano, Svenja Bromberg, 1st ed. Thousand Oaks: SAGE Inc, 2021.

Chen, Stefanos. 'New York City Sets New Minimum Wage for Food Delivery Workers'. *The New York Times*, 12 June 2023, https://www.nytimes.com/2023/06/12/nyregion/nyc-delivery-workers-minimum-wage.html.

Chua, Charmaine. 'Logistics.' In *The SAGE Handbook of Marxism*, edited by Beverly Skeggs, Sara R.Farris, Alberto Toscano, Svenja Bromberg, 1st ed. Thousand Oaks: SAGE Inc, 2021.

Domingos, Pedro. *The Master Algorithm: How the Quest for the Ultimate Learning Machine Will Remake Our World*. Bristol: Allen Lane, 2015.

Feher, Michel. *Rated Agency: Investee Politics in a Speculative Age*. Near Futures. New York: Zone Books, 2018.

Focus on Labour Exploitation, 'The gig is up: Participatory research with couriers in the UK app-based delivery sector,' 2021, https://labourexploitation.org/app/uploads/2021/11/FLEX_TheGigIsUp_v4_0.pdf.

Gregory, Sam. 'Is This Sheffield Strike the Most Exciting Workers' Movement in the UK?' *Now Then,* 10 February 2022. https://nowthenmagazine.com/articles/is-this-sheffield-strike-the-most-exciting-workers-movement-in-the-uk.

Gurley Flynn, Elizabeth. 'The Conscious Withdrawal of the Workers Industrial Efficiency'. Chicago, IWW Publisher Bureau, 1912.

Harney, Stefano, and Fred Moten. *All Incomplete*. London, New York: Minor Compositions, 2021.

Hudson, Becka, and Tomas Percival. 'Carceral Data: The Limits of Transparency-as-Accountability in Prison Risk Data,' *Secrecy and Society* 3, no. 1 (10 August 2023).

Livingston, Eve. 'Food Delivery Drivers Fired after 'Cut-Price' GPS App Sent Them on 'Impossible Routes'. *The Observer*, 2 July 2022. https://www.theguardian.com/business/2022/jul/02/food-delivery-drivers-fired-after-cut-price-gps-app-sent-them-on-impossible-routes.

Marx, Karl. *El Capital*. Madrid: S.XXI, 2017. Nueno, Júlia.

Space are missing. 'Riding the Algorithm. Repurposing Delivery Workers Data into a Digital Commons,' 2022.

Panzieri, Raniero. 'The Capitalist Use of Machinery: Marx versus the Objectivists,' 2005. https://libcom.org/library/capalist-use-machinery-raniero-panzieri.

Roggero, Gigi. 'Romano Alquati -- Militant Researcher, Operaist, Autonomist Marxist -- Has Passed Away, Age 75.'*Tumblr* (blog). Accessed 17 June 2023. https://fuckyeahmilitantresearch.tumblr.com/post/502186794/romano-alquati-militant-researcher-operaist.

Scholz, Trebor and Nathan Schneider. *Ours to Hack and to Own: The Rise of Platform Cooperativism, A New Vision for the Future of Work and a Fairer Internet*. New York: OR Books, 2016.

Srnicek, Nick. *Platform Capitalism*. London: Polity Press, 2016.

Terranova, Tiziana. 'Free Labor: Producing Culture for the Digital Economy'. *Social Text* 18, no. 2 (Summer 2000): 33–59.

Trades Union Congress. 'Seven Ways Platform Workers Are Fighting Back', 2021.

Viljoen, Salomé. 'A Relational Theory of Data Governance'. *The Yale Law Journal* 131, no. 2 (November 2021): 370–781.

Virno, Paolo. *A Grammar of the Multitude: For an Analysis of Contemporary Forms of Life*. Semiotext(e) Foreign Agents Series. Cambridge, Mass; London: Semiotext(e), 2003.

V.Moore, Phoebe, and Jamie Woodcock. *Augmented Exploitation: Artificial Intelligence, Automation And Work*. London: Pluto Press, 2021.

Wray, Ben. 'Riders' Rights Concern Group: Why Europeans Should Care about the Struggle of FoodPanda Couriers in Hong Kong.' *Brave New Europe* (blog), 16 March 2022. https://braveneweurope.com/riders-rights-concern-group-why-europeans-should-care-about-the-struggle-of-foodpanda-couriers-in-hong-kong.

Wright, Steven. *Storming Heaven: Class Composition and Struggle in Italian Autonomist Marxism*. London: Pluto Press, 2017.

# FEAR OF THE SYNTHETIC IMAGE

Recent debates on the dangers of AI-generated images,[1] or "synthetic media",[2] are gripped by the fear that an image might lose its evidential value as a representation of real events. Investigative journalists and researchers are used to the demand that photos and videos of atrocities must remain verifiable and traceable to their source, even as they break the news, go viral, and fall through the cracks of NDAs. But while some images have had to be smuggled out of conflict zones,[3] others must be carefully reconstructed,[4] composited,[5] or even generated out of pixels alone.[6] My research traces the production of images from military simulations to technical interfaces, in order to ask if we can begin to identify the political order produced by such synthetic images.

A blurry video is gaining traction on Facebook. One by one, military vehicles are targeted and destroyed as a convoy passes through a dark road. While users are cheering the explosions of what they believe to be NATO forces in Ukraine, the unmistakably low fidelity of the 3D graphics makes me question whether the comments themselves are authentic. How can anybody trust the veracity of the footage, in which the vehicles cast no shadows over two-dimensional grass? This and other screen grabs from the video game, Arma 3 (2013), go viral again and again, framed as real-life war footage. In 2018, Turkey used the game to generate misinformation in its assault on Afrin in Syria.[7] In 2022, once again, pro-Russian accounts faked Russia's advances in Ukraine using Arma 3. According to Pavel Křižka, PR manager of Arma 3 developer, these videos were used to spread misinformation about military operations in Afghanistan, Palestine, and even along the border zone

1     Dan Milmo and Kiran Stacey, 'AI-Enhanced Images a 'Threat to Democratic Processes', Experts Warn,' *The Guardian*, 3 August 2023, https://www.theguardian.com/technology/2023/aug/03/ai-enhanced-images-a-threat-to-democratic-processes-experts-warn; Jon Bateman, 'Deepfakes and Synthetic Media in the Financial System: Assessing Threat Scenarios,' *Carnegie Endowment for International Peace*, 8 July 2020, https://carnegieendowment.org/2020/07/08/deepfakes-and-synthetic-media-in-financial-system-assessing-threat-scenarios-pub-82237; Kyle Walter, 'New Research Reveals Scale of Threat Posed by AI-Generated Images on 2024 Elections,' *Logically*, 27 July 2023, https://www.logically.ai/press/new-research-reveals-scale-of-threat-posed-by-ai-generated-images-on-2024-elections.

2     Synthetic media is an all-encompassing term for the computer-generated media that is currently associated with AI, sometimes used synonymously with AI-generated media. UneeQ Blog, 'What Is Synthetic Media, and How Is It Distinguished from Digital Human Technology?,' Digital Humans, 22 February 2023, https://www.digitalhumans.com/blog/what-is-synthetic-media-digital-human-technology; Victor Riparbelli, 'The Future of (Synthetic) Media | Synthesia,' Synthesia.io, 6 September 2023, https://www.synthesia.io/post/the-future-of-synthetic-media#what-is-synthetic-media; Bateman, 'Deepfakes and Synthetic Media in the Financial System: Assessing Threat Scenarios'.

3     Human Rights Watch, 'If the Dead Could Speak | Mass Deaths and Torture in Syria's Detention Facilities,' *Human Rights Watch*, 16 December 2015, https://www.hrw.org/report/2015/12/16/if-dead-could-speak/mass-deaths-and-torture-syrias-detention-facilities.

4     Sajib Bhawal and Mehnaz Tabassum, 'Forensic Image Reconstruction Based on Efficient Morphological Operational Model,' (paper presented at IEMIS, Kolkata, 2018), https://www.researchgate.net/publication/323771450_Forensic_Image_Reconstruction_Based_on_Efficient_Morphological_Operational_Model.

5     Graham E. Pike et al., 'Advances in Facial Composite Technology, Utilizing Holistic Construction, Do Not Lead to an Increase in Eyewitness Misidentifications Compared to Older Feature-Based Systems,' *Frontiers in Psychology* 10 (August 28, 2019).

6     Ellen Verolme and Arjan Mieremet, 'Application of Forensic Image Analysis in Accident Investigations,' *Forensic Science International* 278 (September 2017): 137–47.

7     The Observers, 'Debunked: Viral video of 'Turkish drone' is from video game,' *France 24*, last modified 16 February 2018, https://observers.france24.com/en/20180216-debunked-afrin-video-drone-turkey.

0:50 / 3:30

Composite image showing the screen capture from Arma 3 used for the fake news report that went viral on Facebook. The fake news post is still available online: https://bit.ly/arma3nato. // Groupe Des Patriotes Du Mali, "UKRAINE: un convoi des conseillers militaires de l'OTAN détruit par l'armée russe_," Facebook post, 15 October 2022.

between India and Pakistan.[8] In a statement released to address the issue, the company referred to the specific popularity of the game as "flattering",[9] speculating that it stems from the realism of the 3D environments in the game. I wonder if the low-polygonal models from 2013 are the real reason, though. Despite Pavel Křižka's claim, the ability of the game to "simulate rain" seems an unlikely benchmark for the realism of 3D graphics in 2022.[10]

There is another reason not mentioned in these interviews. The mechanics of the entire Arma series is repurposed from an existing product: a military simulation called Virtual Battlespace used by the US Army, the UK Ministry of Defence and other armies of the Global North.[11] The core of Virtual Battlespace, from weapon interfaces to game characters, is modelled on tactical military documents, including United States Army Field Manuals.[12] Originally produced as a tool of war, it is no wonder that this simulation repeatedly re-enters the battlespace without any friction—it never truly left it in the first place. If you try to assess the authenticity of images from Arma 3, you will become trapped in an endless loop between misinformation and fact. The only way to escape this cycle is to approach the critical analysis of the game and the footage that it has generated from what it actually is—namely, a 'simulation'.

As political scientist Antoine Bousquet notes, one meaning of a simulation "invokes the notion of surface resemblance—a simulation is something that appears to

8   'Arma 3 footage being used as Fake News,' *Bohemia Interactive*, 28 November 2022, https://arma3.com/news/arma-3-footage-being-used-as-fake-news.

9   'Arma 3 footage being used as Fake News,' *Bohemia Interactive*, 2022.

10  The Observers, 'How a video game has been used to create fake news about the Ukraine war,' *France 24*, 12 February 2022, https://observers.france24.com/en/tv-shows/truth-or-fake/20221202-how-a-video-game-has-been-used-to-create-fake-news-about-the-ukraine-war.

11  Stepan Kment, 'Programming Worlds,' in *Simulation, Exercise, Operations*, ed. Robin Mackey, (Falmouth: Urbanomic, 2015), 25-30.

12  Kment, 'Programming Worlds,' 30.

## FEAR OF THE SYNTHETIC IMAGE

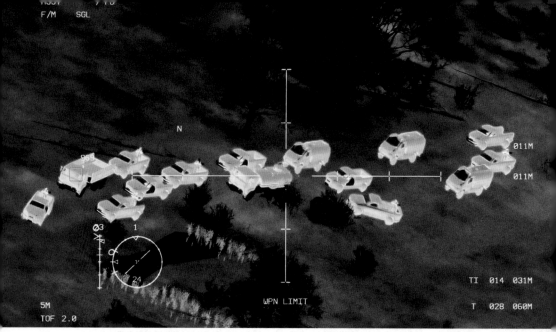

The screen capture of the thermal vision display in Arma 3. Such displays, like the ones claimed to be drone footage by the pro-Turkish social media accounts in 2018, are modelled on the software used by the US Air Force. This, in particular, is the Lockheed AC-130 gunship, a heavily-armed ground-attack aircraft. // Source: The YouTube Channel Compared Comparison, as a part of the screen capture 'ArmA 3 - AC-130 Gunship in Action - Firing Mission - Combat Footage - ArmA 3 Simulation,' 10 November 2020, https://youtu.be/IUAkReOygQE.

be what in fact it is not".[13] Today, this idea of a simulation as an empty copy of reality, popularised by philosopher Jean Baudrillard more than forty years ago,[14] runs short of explaining the feedback loop between military operations on the ground and their simulations. This older conception of simulation must be augmented by one that refers to the "dynamic representation of processes, operations, and situations [...] capturing in some depth whatever is being simulated, rather than simply its surface".[15] To achieve this complexity and depth, a simulation replicates the key characteristics of the system. These core qualities are determined by their importance for the system's operation rather than by surface resemblance. Such a difference between the two meanings of a simulation—a surface and a core process—is apparent in fighter jets' head-up displays (HUD). The planes today are so fast that pilots must be presented only with the "simplified terrain and mission targets", whereas all other parts of their reality must be "stripped out from the pilot's view"[16] as details would be a source of confusion or distraction. In this example, the simulation is "'realer' than the reality upon which it is putatively modelled".[17] This is not to say that the simulated image becomes more 'authentic' but rather that it becomes more tactically useful than the 'real' one. The fact that a synthetic image can be more relevant than the 'real' one makes me

13   Antoine Bousquet, 'A Short History of Wargames,' in *Simulation, Exercise, Operations*, ed. Robin Mackey, (Falmouth: Urbanomic, 2015), 13.
14   Jean Baudrillard, *Simulacra and Simulation,* (Michigan: University of Michigan Press, 1994).
15   Baudrillard, S*imulacra and Simulation.*
16   Bousquet, 'A Short History of Wargames,' 18.
17   Bousquet, 'A Short History of Wargames,' 19.

ANNA ENGELHARDT

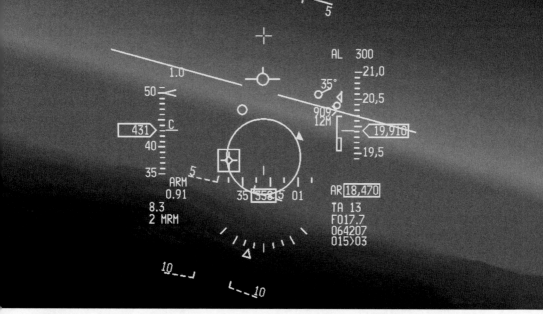

Screen capture of the F-16 Fighting Falcon jet fighter, made in the game Falcon 4.0. Falcon 4.0 is a combat flight simulation developed specifically as a realistic simulation of this jet fighter model. // The image is made by JC, the author of "Real and Simulated Wars" blog as a part of his playthrough debrief. JC, 'Falcon 4 BMS 4 - Early Morning of D1 - Sortie 4692 - Debrief (Complete Version),' 2 October 2011. https://bit.ly/450SaLQ.

question the fear of its "growing threat"as fully legitimate.[18] Such threat presents a growing distrust of evidentiary image,[19] assumed to have a pivotal role in politics. The fear of fake images implies an immense agency that evidentiary image possesses—one we should be scared of losing. How can we know that its use value is not merely consigned to representation in the hopes of inducing action or a humanitarian response? Maybe we are scared of the wrong image?

It is commonplace to assume that documentary images can work as evidence of injustice and, therefore, have potential agency to change the course of politics.[20] This expectation that images can effect change has eroded over the years.[21] Often, photographs of people who have been killed go viral under the pretext that "'decolonisation' and political change would happen through displaying horrific things empires have done".[22] In 2022, for instance, Kader Attia, curator of the Berlin Biennale,

18  Daniel Byman, Chris Meserole, and V. S. Subrahmanian, 'The Deepfake Dangers Ahead,' Wall Street Journal, 23 February 2023, https://www.wsj.com/articles/the-deepfake-dangers-ahead-b08e4ecf.

19  Andrew Schwartz and Tiffany Hsu, 'Distrust of Everything: Misinformation and AI,' Center for Strategic and International Studies, 18 July 2023, https://www.csis.org/analysis/distrust-everything-misinformation-and-ai.

20  Sean O'Hagan, 'Crime, Seen: A History of Photographing Atrocities,' The Guardian, 1 October 2015, https://www.theguardian.com/artanddesign/2015/oct/01/crime-history-photographs-atrocity-photographers-gallery-burden-proof; Micah Zenko Welch Emma, 'Imagery and Atrocity: The Role of News and Photos in War,' The Atlantic, March 30, 2012, https://www.theatlantic.com/international/archive/2012/03/imagery-and-atrocity-the-role-of-news-and-photos-in-war/255275/.

21  Thomas Keenan, 'Mobilizing Shame,' South Atlantic Quarterly 103, no. 2-3 (1 April 2004): 435–49.

22  M. Neelika Jayawardane, 'Art and the Limits of 'Awareness' Politics,' ArtReview, 11 November 2022, https://artreview.com/art-and-the-limits-of-awareness-politics-berlin-biennale-abu-ghraib/.

stated that "photos [of Iraqi torture and sexual abuse victims] must be seen for political change to take place".[23] As Rijin Sahakian rightfully responded, we can be confident that the imagined political change will not follow these photos because even at the height of their circulation, "there were no consequences, political or otherwise".[24] One can also recall the case of Alan Kurdi (born Alan Shenu), the boy fleeing Syria who drowned after being rejected for asylum by Canada in 2015. While many media outlets reported on the immense influence that the image had on Canadian politics, none of its migration laws and policies changed as a consequence. Alan Kurdi's family was still not allowed into Canada. In the words of Fatemah Alabed, commenting on the viral photos of her daughter's everyday life during the Russia-Assad assault on the Syrian population: "Apart from spreading the suffering of the people, the action is little".[25]

Does the problem lie in how the media frames these documentary images, the promise of intervention that their circulation holds out or, as Thomas Keenan has argued, in our misplaced belief in the operative role of the public sphere as the space of political debate?[26] The distinction made between evidentiary and synthetic images is helpful in beginning to answer this question. While photojournalists criticise Amnesty International for using AI to generate a backdrop for their report on police violence, their own (non-generated) photographs of arrested protesters are praised for their ability to document violence for others to witness.[27] "If the argument is that witnessing this violence is enough or is necessary to galvanize action, my single question is when? When will these acts become too unacceptable to simply continue to watch?" asks Zoé Samudzi.[28] "When" is a core term to consider here. By definition, the political agency of the documentary image is tied to its injunction to act in the aftermath of an event, but this implies that it is already too late by the time the image is produced. Consequently, the evidentiary image must have a direct material and temporal bond with an event of violence. This quality is what separates it from the synthetic image. When the role of an image is reduced to a representation of violence that has already occurred, such an image, regardless of how nuanced, doesn't have the agency to lead to "structural (that is to say, punitive) justice".[29] Does a synthetic image have the capacity to intercede before the event? In order to understand this temporal distinction, one should consider the tactical use of the synthetic image, its relationship with action.

The spectrogram of a radio receiver here depicts unencrypted communication between Russian militaries on the ground. The exchange is rendered inaudible, interrupted by noise. The green/yellow "dust" in the spectrogram is produced by various JPEG images such as signs, skulls, radioactive symbols, and memes when they are converted into sound, in order to muffle the communication between troops

23  Rijin Sahakian, 'Beyond Repair. Regarding torture at the Berlin Biennale,' Artforum, 29 July 2022, https://www.artforum.com/slant/regarding-torture-at-the-berlin-biennale-88836.
24  Ibid.
25  Andrew Katz, "What Has Changed?' The Role of Photography in Syria's War,' Time, 7 April 2017, https://time.com/4729560/syria-chemical-attack-photography-impact/.
26  Thomas Keenan, 'Mobilizing Shame,' South Atlantic Quarterly 103, no. 2-3 (1 April 2004): 435–49.
27  Luke Taylor, 'Amnesty International criticised for using AI-generated images,' The Guardian, 2 May 2023, https://www.theguardian.com/world/2023/may/02/amnesty-international-ai-generated-images-criticism.
28  Zoé Samudzi, 'White Witness and the Contemporary Lynching,' The New Republic, 16 May 2020, https://newrepublic.com/article/157734/white-witness-contemporary-lynching.
29  Samudzi, 'White Witness and the Contemporary Lynching,'.

Spectrogram of a radio receiver depicting communication between Russian militaries disrupted through JPEG images transmitted over the same frequency. The first wave of images was broadcasted in 2022 on UVB-76, a shortwave radio station of the Russian Armed Forces, also known by the nickname "The Buzzer", at 4625 kHz. Author unknown.

coordinating military actions.[30] The resulting audio noise is then broadcasted on the radio frequency on which the militaries have been communicating, saturating the chatter with visual data or what Harun Farocki coined "operational images".[31] Operational images are, in Farocki's words, "pictures that are part of an operation", implying the primacy of action and function instead of a picture to be seen and interpreted for meaning".[32] Operational image, instead of presenting itself for passive observation, "is tightly coupled with action, immediate or delayed".[33] Likewise, when someone superimposes "THE GAME" over a military transmission to confuse and interfere with the shooting on the ground, we cannot understand such an image without the action to which it is bound. The reference to "the game" only gains its meaning when the user utilises the image to enter the battlespace virtually, not having to put their own life at stake while engaging in combat. How such an image is defined through action brings me back to the logic of a simulation.

The goal of a simulation is to represent the core elements of the system in order to make those elements actionable. Recalling the fighter jet example, the

30  You can read more about the way the it works and also try it out via the link: https://www.skytopia.com/software/sonicphoto/.
31  Harun Farocki, Eye/Machine, 2000, video installation.
32  Parikka Jussi, *Operational Images: From the Visual to the Invisual*. (Minneapolis, Minnesota: University of Minnesota Press, 2023), 12.
33  Jussi, Operational Images, 12.

**FEAR OF THE SYNTHETIC IMAGE**

selected elements of terrain depicted to the pilot transform space into an actionable environment. Simulation, therefore, can be understood as the production of an information environment that can be operationalised (made actionable) in different ways. One way to operationalise such information environment is to resort to actions that have immediate and direct impact on the situation on the ground, for instance, by disturbing the radio landscape with image-noise. Another is to operationalise information environment, i.e., create a simulation, with the aim of a delayed effect, for example, acquiring new skills such as weapons-handling or team coordination. The latter type of simulation creates for the viewer a visual order in which the viewer, the image, and the action form a closely connected system. This system, radically different from passive witnessing of violence, interests me the most.

Air Training Corps cadets building recognition models. Creative Commons: CollectAir. https://bit.ly/3qrZ2mn.

Recognition models are an early example of such simulations. First introduced as 2D silhouettes of enemy planes in WWI, recognition models evolved into 3D maquettes to more accurately train the eye of "civilians and soldiers to tell friends from enemies during World War II".[34] These were considered an essential element of defence, "critical to the war effort".[35] Today, models are much larger, encompassing an entire building, site, or city.[36] With little risk or expense, one can use this form of simulation to memorise escape routes from a hostile environment and attain intuitive reactions to navigate them.[37] Extended further, these simulated landscapes can integrate open-source intelligence (OSINT) including satellite imagery, elevation data, and

34  Kurt Kohlstedt, 'Recognition Models: Scale World War Miniatures Used to Tell Friends from Foes,' 99% Invisible, 20 August 2018, https://99percentinvisible.org/article/recognition-models-scale-world-war-miniatures-used-to-tell-friends-from-foes/.
35  Kohlstedt, 'Recognition Models.'
36  Kment, 'Programming Worlds,' 26.
37  Kment, 'Programming Worlds,' 26.

**ANNA ENGELHARDT**

Satellite image of the electricity substation of Russian air base Baranovichi, Brest, Belarus. The infrastructure of the substation is referenced with on-the-ground photographs and tagged. Bottom left: Work-in-progress CGI reconstruction of the substation. Bottom centre: The process of virtual cinematography within the CGI reconstruction. IPad movement is being tracked and interpreted as camera movement inside the CGI environment. Background: The electricity substation as seen in the film. // Still from the film *Onset*, Anna Engelhardt and Mark Cinkevich, 2023. Source: the artists.

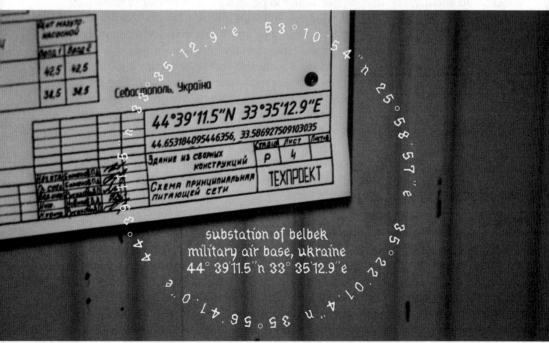

Close-up of the information board in the electricity substation of Russian air base Belbek, Crimea, Ukraine. The numbers forming the circle geolocate the electricity substations of Russian military air bases: Baranovichi in Belarus, Khmeimim in Syria, and Belbek in Ukraine. // Still from the film *Onset*, Anna Engelhardt and Mark Cinkevich, 2023. Source: the artists.

**FEAR OF THE SYNTHETIC IMAGE**

architectural reports to form a base for computer-generated reconstruction.

Similar method was used as a starting point for the video *Onset*, which I made with Mark Cinkevich in 2023. The film explores recent Russian invasions by looking into the life cycle of one of their core elements—the ubiquitous military base. An unsettling CGI environment was reconstructed from satellite images of Russian air bases: Khmeimim in Syria, Baranovichi in Belarus, and Belbek in Ukraine. By following how their initial deployment leads to the later devastation of the wider sovereign state, the film introduces a parasitic point of view—one that extracts energy to destroy the countries from within. It delves into the power grid of the military—an intensive consumer of energy and presents terror as an energy-intensive state.

The act of producing the film replicated the process of constructing a simulation. During research, Mark and I traced the energy sources that feed the Russian military that are classified due to their pivotal role in the invasions. We relied on OSINT tools, calculating the energy consumption via data gleaned from civilian airports,[38] cross-referencing spikes in generation and consumption, and by geolocating anomalies, to sketch out the exact outline and coordinates for the simulation. We then reconstructed the digital environment of the electricity substations in collaboration with CGI artist Eduard Morocho-Baias. The resulting simulation locates the viewer within an environment where the link between these energy sources and the violence it enables is not just explained and spelt out but is operationalised. In short, it represents the core elements of the system to make them actionable.

Such visual order defies the fears that follow synthetic media. It bypasses widespread antagonistic framing between the politics of 'authentic' and generated image. Its synthetic images are not at odds with satellite imagery, photographs, and footage from the ground. Defying concerns, they are bound in a symbiotic relationship, linked to form an interconnected system. Still, as many sceptics warned, the perceived importance of evidentiary image is indeed in decline. Its feared 'distrust' becomes real, since its value does not reside anymore in the evidentiary quality alone. The organising principle shifts from purely indexical to operational. Indexical image does not suffice as a means to an end—to gain political significance, it must be tied to an action, it must be operationalised as a part of a larger system.

The crisis, therefore, is not one of disbelief in the evidentiary image itself, but of disillusionment in its effect on politics. Its indexical link with a physical reality, recalibrated within a simulation, is utilised anew. Can it be used to hijack the violence as it unfolds?

38 During our investigation, we found out that the majority of Russian air bases abroad are converted from civilian airports into military facilities.

**ANNA ENGELHARDT**

# Works Cited

Bateman, Jon. 'Deepfakes and Synthetic Media in the Financial System: Assessing Threat Scenarios.' *Carnegie Endowment for International Peace*, 8 July 2020. https://carnegieendowment.org/2020/07/08/deepfakes-and-synthetic-media-in-financial-system-assessing-threat-scenarios-pub-82237.

Baudrillard, Jean. *Simulacra and Simulation.* Michigan: University of Michigan Press, 1994.

Bhawal, Sajib, and Mehnaz Tabassum. 'Forensic Image Reconstruction Based on Efficient Morphological Operational Model,' 2018. https://www.researchgate.net/publication/323771450_Forensic_Image_Reconstruction_Based_on_Efficient_Morphological_Operational_Model.

*Bohemia Interactive.* 'Arma 3 footage being used as Fake News.'28 November 2022. https://arma3.com/news/arma-3-footage-being-used-as-fake-news.

Bousquet, Antoine. 'A Short History of Wargames.' In *Simulation, Exercise, Operations*, edited by Robin Mackay. Falmouth: Urbanomic, 2015.

Byman, Daniel, Chris Meserole, and V. S. Subrahmanian. 'The Deepfake Dangers Ahead.' *Wall Street Journal*, 23 February 2023. https://www.wsj.com/articles/the-deepfake-dangers-ahead-b08e4ecf.

Farocki, Harun. *Eye/Machine.* Video installation, 2000.

Ha, Tu Thanh. 'Family of drowned boy did not apply for asylum: Ottawa.' *Globe and Mail*, 3 September 2015, https://www.theglobeandmail.com/news/national/syrian-family-whose-children-were-found-on-turkish-beach-tried-to-come-to-canada/article26202571/.

Human Rights Watch. 'If the Dead Could Speak Mass Deaths and Torture in Syria's Detention Facilities.' *Human Rights Watch*, 16 December 2015. https://www.hrw.org/report/2015/12/16/if-dead-could-speak/mass-deaths-and-torture-syrias-detention-facilities.

Jayawardane, M. Neelika. 'Art and the Limits of 'Awareness' Politics,' *ArtReview*, 11 November 2022, https://artreview.com/art-and-the-limits-of-awareness-politics-berlin-biennale-abu-ghraib/.

Katz, Andrew. ''What Has Changed?' The Role of Photography in Syria's War,' *Time*, 7 April 2017, https://time.com/4729560/syria-chemical-attack-photography-impact/.

Keenan, Thomas. 'Mobilizing Shame.' *South Atlantic Quarterly* 103, no. 2-3 (1 April 2004): 435–49.

Kohlstedt, Kurt. 'Recognition Models: Scale World War Miniatures Used to Tell Friends from Foes,' *99% Invisible*, August 20, 2018, https://99percentinvisible.org/article/recognition-models-scale-world-war-miniatures-used-to-tell-friends-from-foes/.

Kment, Stepan. 'Programming Worlds.' in *Simulation, Exercise, Operations*, edited by Robin Mackay,. Falmouth: Urbanomic, 2015.

Milmo, Dan, and Kiran Stacey. 'AI-Enhanced Images a 'Threat to Democratic Processes', Experts Warn.' *The Guardian*, 3 August 2023. https://www.theguardian.com/technology/2023/aug/03/ai-enhanced-images-a-threat-to-democratic-processes-experts-warn.

O'Hagan, Sean. 'Crime, Seen: A History of Photographing Atrocities.' *The Guardian*, 1 October 2015. https://www.theguardian.com/artanddesign/2015/oct/01/crime-history-photographs-atrocity-photographers-gallery-burden-proof.

Parikka, Jussi. *Operational Images: From the Visual to the Invisual.* Minneapolis, Minnesota: University of Minnesota Press, 2023.

Pike, Graham E., Nicola A. Brace, Jim Turner, Hayley Ness, and Annelies Vredeveldt. 'Advances in Facial Composite Technology, Utilizing Holistic Construction, Do Not Lead to an Increase in Eyewitness Misidentifications Compared to Older Feature-Based Systems.' *Frontiers in Psychology* 10 (28 August 2019). https://doi.org/10.3389/fpsyg.2019.01962.

Riparbelli, Victor. 'The Future of (Synthetic) Media | Synthesia.' *Synthesia*, 6 September 2023. https://www.synthesia.io/post/the-future-of-synthetic-media#what-is-synthetic-media.

Sahakian, Rijin. 'Beyond Repair. Regarding torture at the Berlin Biennale,' *Artforum*, 29 July 2022, https://www.artforum.com/slant/regarding-torture-at-the-berlin-biennale-88836

Samudzi, Zoé. 'White Witness and the Contemporary Lynching,' The New Republic, 16 May 2020, https://newrepublic.com/article/157734/white-witness-contemporary-lynching.

Schwartz, Andrew, and Tiffany Hsu. 'Distrust of Everything: Misinformation and AI.' *Center for Strategic and International Studies*, 18 July 2023. https://www.csis.org/analysis/distrust-everything-misinformation-and-ai.

Taylor, Luke. 'Amnesty International criticised for using AI-generated images,' *The Guardian*, 2 May 2023, https://www.theguardian.com/world/2023/may/02/amnesty-international-ai-generated-images-criticism.

The Observers. 'Debunked: Viral video of 'Turkish drone' is from video game,' France 24, last modified 16 February 2018, https://observers.france24.com/en/20180216-debunked-afrin-video-drone-turkey.

The Observers. 'How a video game has been used to create fake news about the Ukraine war,' *France 24*, 12 February 2022, https://observers.france24.com/en/tv-shows/truth-or-fake/20221202-how-a-video-game-has-been-used-to-create-fake-news-about-the-ukraine-war.

UneeQ Blog. 'What Is Synthetic Media, and How Is It Distinguished from Digital Human Technology?' *Digital Humans*, 22 February 2023. https://www.digitalhumans.com/blog/what-is-synthetic-media-digital-human-technology.

Verolme, Ellen, and Arjan Mieremet. 'Application of Forensic Image Analysis in Accident Investigations.' *Forensic Science International* 278 (September 2017): 137–47. https://doi.org/10.1016/j.forsciint.2017.06.039.

Walter, Kyle. 'New Research Reveals Scale of Threat Posed by AI-Generated Images on 2024 Elections.' *Logically*, 27 July 2023. https://www.logically.ai/press/new-research-reveals-scale-of-threat-posed-by-ai-generated-images-on-2024-elections.

Welch, Micah, and Emma Zenko. 'Imagery and Atrocity: The Role of News and Photos in War.' *The Atlantic*, 30 March 2012. https://www.theatlantic.com/international/archive/2012/03/imagery-and-atrocity-the-role-of-news-and-photos-in-war/255275/.

# LEGAL INVESTIGATIONS AS A FORM OF PEDAGOGY

*This short methodological text discusses a workshop I co-facilitated with Mariana Karkoutly on 6 March 2023 around our professional work as legal investigators developing gender-sensitive case files for war crimes and crimes against humanity committed in Syria. The workshop was an experiment in human rights pedagogy. Specifically, it provided an opportunity to reflect upon the potential applications of legal and investigative competencies within a more speculative paradigm, in order to discuss their relevance to a spectrum of research projects beyond the mandate of civil society organisations and legal institutions. Understanding how to teach, in relationship to doing political work, underscores the relationship between knowledge production in academia and its role and stakes in human rights work.*

Reflecting upon the use and value of a legal methodologies as a teaching medium offers an opportunity to address concerns commonly raised in investigative rather than pedagogical contexts such as confidentiality, security, ethics, "do no harm," and many of the other associated challenges that arise when working directly with affected communities.

Intended as an introduction to legal investigations for master's level students, the workshop's main pedagogical aim was to think collaboratively about elements and challenges pertaining to such investigative practices that might also be relevant to practical considerations of students' research projects.

The workshop was organised around two main areas: investigation planning and witness interviewing and involved collaborative case-study analysis by the students, as well as group discussions reflecting on their insights, lessons learned,

and queries. The case-studies were all developed specifically for the workshop in collaboration with my Huquqyat colleague, Mariana Karkoutly.

### INVESTIGATION PLANNING
The workshop began with an initial discussion about the investigative work that Huquqyat and others do on Syria; focusing on the ways that Huquqyat develops case files around atrocity crimes for the purposes of strategic litigation. In our investigation planning, we must take into account the issue as to existing access to legal institutions and whether universal jurisdiction can be used to bring cases in front of national courts in the absence of any alternative legal avenues. Consequently, different investigative methods must be adopted depending on the intended outcome and investigative body: perpetrator-centred, survivor-centred, structural investigations, and so on.

Following this initial introduction, each group was tasked with developing an investigation plan and given a fictional case study with specific circumstances aimed at enabling discussions around key elements. These included considerations around how to identify witnesses, how the presence of a witness in a specific country can influence their willingness to participate or the investigators' ability to prioritise that testimony over another, how gender and socio-economic dynamics play a role, how issues pertaining to reliability, liability, jurisdiction as well as chain of custody or authenticity of evidentiary material all combine to shape the investigation plan. The purpose was to familiarise students with the practical challenges and processes that are key in the developing planning, and analysis of case-work, alongside factors related to the mitigation and management of risk.

A template investigation plan was developed specifically for this exercise highlighting the basic steps of any investigation plan.

## WITNESS INTERVIEWING

The second part of the workshop focused on best practice in witness interviewing. It began with a short presentation of the PEACE model for witness interviewing and included gender-sensitive survivor-centred approaches to conducting investigations. Our discussions also touched upon the core ethical principle of any investigation; namely that of "do no harm". We then went on to explore the different ways in which "informed consent" might be understood, defined, and ultimately given. This has to include considerations of the health and security concerns that witnesses may have.

Once the fundamentals were established, we followed-up with another group exercise in which students were asked to participate in the process of conducting witness interviews for each of the fictional cases. One student was allocated to each role: lead investigator, second investigator, and witness. While the fictional investigating team prepared the interview questions with the help of one of the facilitators, the fictional witness worked with the other facilitator to create a backstory for their character, deciding what their account of the events is, how truthful they are willing to be, and why. Then, fictional witness and investigators met for the interview and were asked to play out the scenario according to what each side had prepared.

This kind of training exercise is typical in preparing potential legal investigators for upcoming situations in order to improve their interview skills as well as highlight good and bad practices. Within the context of the Centre for Research Architecture, this exercise and the use of improvisation as a teaching strategy was multi-fold. It served to encourage students to identify and acknowledge similar dynamics and concerns that may arise as part of their research practice. Specifically, it shaped discussions around the ways that that contentious issues, ethical dilemmas, and potential risks can be mitigated. At the same time, it also helped in raising the students' awareness around the unexpected challenges that may arise within the context of interviews. Despite the fictional aspect of the interviews, it brought the performative aspects of our roles as investigators or researchers to the fore.

As the situations we developed for the case studies involved elements of role-play and improvisation, there were inevitably moments when the students broke out of character and laughed nervously, thereby breaking the usual bounds of a witness interview. There were also times during which those actively engaging in the exercise willingly created uneasy situations to bring others out of their prepared roles and into unexpected territories. Since hypothetical witnesses and investigators are prepared separately, none of the participants ever know the other's backstory. This is the case in all normal witness interview scenarios as well. Enabling a form of productive 'unpreparedness' creates space for improvisation and for emergent scenarios that couldn't otherwise have been foreseen in the phase of investigation planning and witness preparation. The improvisational and performative nature of the workshop, thus served as a useful pedagogical tool for exploring how such dynamics can help students remain responsive to the changing conditions and contours of their research activities, while simultaneously helping them to cope with the potential challenges and pitfalls that might come their way.

## DOCUMENTING:
## TO RECORD OR NOT TO RECORD

One of the most important topics we covered during the workshop pertained to best practice in recording sensitive information. In particular, whether and how to record witness interviews and personal information pertaining to the witness. Internal policy at Huquqyat, as it stands at this time of writing, dictates that witness interviews are normally only recorded in a written memorandum outlining the main points discussed and not through sound or video recording. Our policy also stipulates that witnesses have a right to initially testify anonymously.

This decision was initially taken from a concern to record only information that was strictly necessary to the case at any existing stage of the proceedings. This was in order to best protect witnesses and uphold the highest possible standard of security, as witnesses generally need to give their testimony again to national authorities at later stages. Although this is how Huquqyat currently records information, other organisations working in the field of legal investigations make different decisions as to how to record their interviews and evidentiary material, such as via audio or video recording. Factors that guide the decision on whether and how to record sensitive information generally involves a security assessment and the minimisation of possible risks to information, witnesses, and investigators. These factors and how they may differ depending on the goals, priorities, methodology, and of course available resources. Within the context of academic research into human rights abuses and war crimes, such protocols also need to be established. Where they do already exist, it may be the case that current research ethics frameworks will require ongoing modification and adaptation.

## TEACHING
## LEGAL INVESTIGATIONS

Legal investigations are a difficult topic to teach because they require many complex elements to come together. Investigative and legal skills alone won't enable someo-
ne to lead their own investigation because access to, and understanding of, affected communities is required as well as access to relevant institutions, including training and support to manage delicate situations, such as trauma-sensitive survivor-centred witness interviewing. Although our workshop aimed to generate increased awareness into how such investigations are led, its aim was not to enable the students to immediately make any direct use of these skills in launching their own legal investigations. Rather, our workshop focused on developing new methods for planning and engaging with research that may involve affected communities in politically-charged environments and fraught legal landscapes. This is an ongoing pedagogical balancing act: how to teach students to lead their own investigations whilst recognising that methods of workshopping and skills development are not wholly adequate to developing competencies in dealing with real-world experiences and contexts. Ultimately our group discussions around the challenges associated with working on sensitive topics with affected communities focused on ways of managing expectations, prioritising community needs, and upholding high standards of ethics and care, all the while aiming to produce a positive outcome regardless of how strenuous, stressful, and even re-traumatising the process might be.

Template Investigation Plan

1.    Overview of event or events to be investigated
      a.    Details
      b.    Chronology
      c.    Gender analysis and other socio-economic aspects relevant to the case
2.    Contextual information and background
3.    Terms of reference

**Profile of potential defendant(s):**
*Identify those* **possibly** *responsible for the alleged violations, their alleged allegiance, and their mode of liability.*

**Institution(s)/entity of interest:**

**Working theories:**
1.    Underlying crime base
*Identify which crimes the conduct could possibly amount to in the Rome Statute and the relevant elements of crime that would need to be evidenced, including contextual elements.*

2.    Liability theory:
*Identify who did what to whom in which capacity. Ex: Liability Theory 1: Direct Participation: X* ▓▓▓▓▓▓▓▓▓▓▓▓▓ *OR Liability Theory 2: Command Responsibility: X gave* ▓▓▓▓▓▓▓▓▓▓▓ *orders to* ▓▓▓▓▓▓▓
▓▓▓

3.    Legal avenues/potential jurisdiction:
*Where would the case be submitted and what are their grounds for jurisdiction.*

**Sources (OSINT, documents, contact, key connector) and potential witnesses (victim, direct, indirect, expert):**

**Evidence/information collection plan:**
*This section should list the initial tasks that are to be undertaken by the investigation team.*

Task / Type of assignment / Tasked to do / Due date / Date completed / Result / Next step

**Risk assessment and mitigation:**
*Identify risks pertaining to mental health, physical security, digital security, other that could harm the case, the organisation, or the individuals involved in the investigation in any capacity. If time allows, you can try and fill the risk assessment matrix provided. For each risk, identify:*

Risk:
Likelihood:
Impact:
Mitigation strategy:

---

Centre for Research Architecture                                                      1

Simplified version of the template investigation plan developed specifically for the purpose of the CRA workshop. All materials developed by the author and Mariana Karkoutly. The template was supplemented with additional resources enabling students to fill (Rome statute, handouts on legal frameworks and modes of liability, a risk assessment matrix, and diverse resources on human rights investigations).

Contextual information:

The case takes place in a country called ███ that is undergoing a popular uprising and against the long-standing dictatorship of ███████████ , a one party system under which ████████████████████ . The popular unrest has reached the threshold of non-international armed conflict (NIAC) and was declared as such ██████████ on ██████ ████████ . Under this dictatorship, individuals had been arbitrarily detained by the security forces on the basis of their political affiliation, real or alleged. Although the country has legal codes in place, the lack of separation of power leads to regular abuse of power where rights provided for in writing are not accounted for in practice.

███████████████████████████████████████████████████████
███████████████████████████████████████████████████████
███ individuals held in ██████ detention facilities are often subjected to physical violence, ███████████████████████████████████████████████████████
███████████████████████████████████████████████████████

Following the increase in violence, individuals started fleeing ██████ for a neighbouring country, ███████ , a country utilising universal jurisdiction to prosecute war crimes and crimes against humanity ████████████████████████████████████████████
███████████████████████████████████████████████ .

**LEILA SIBAI**

Case 1:

A video was shared on Facebook on ████████ by an account linked to what appears to be a gathering of media activists from ████ in ████. The video shows a group of armed men (█men) wearing military uniforms entering a religious site. The video is filmed from inside the religious site/building in question. In ████, a community prayer is held ████ ████████████ inside that religious site. The video appears to be shot during a ████ community prayer.

The video shows the █ armed men entering the site and men beating individuals present inside the building who appear to be trying to flee outside the building to escape the █ armed men. The people fleeing are dressed in civilian clothing and not carrying any weapons. The video shows one of the armed men giving orders to detain people while other armed men ████████████████████████████████████████. Some of those rounded up by the armed men appear to be very young people (possibly younger than 18 years old). All of the armed men are wearing a ████████████ uniform but it is difficult to identify any further details on the video.

The metadata is not available but the description explains that the events portrayed in the video took place in the main religious site of ████ on ████████. The video ███████████████████████████████████████████████████████████████ ███████████.

At first glance, the video appears to be unedited (one shot, no added visual/text/sound) and includes the voice of the person filming ████████ stating the date and place and that this is a video depicting the arbitrary arrest of peaceful civilians from ████ in ████ including █ of their friends all residents of ████ whom they name ████ ███████████████████████████████████████████████████.

The Facebook page of the group of activists is still active and responsive. They appear to be based in ████.

# GEO-ENDOSCOPIES

With the heavy rains of the winter of 2018, the landslides and sinkholes returned to Silwan in Jerusalem. One such sinkhole opened just behind the Ein Silwan Mosque in the Wadi Hilweh neighborhood. Within a short time, a truck arrived to fill the hole with cement. The amount of concrete needed seemed surprisingly large; the liquid cement continued pouring through the crack, a testament to the size of the underground cavity. Sinkholes and collapses are not a natural phenomenon in Jerusalem, a city built on solid bedrock, and yet the earth under Wadi Hilweh has been shifting. The first time such a hole opened up beside the mosque was nearly two decades ago, and since then, cracks have gradually started to appear across the neighborhood, in family homes, roads, public stairways, and walkways. That morning in December 2018, the opening of the road's surface revealed for a brief moment the officially unacknowledged connection between the violence, damages and quite literal undermining of Palestinian life and the City of David settlement.

This contribution traces a connecting line through the sensor ecology spreading through Silwan. Focusing mainly on Wadi Hilweh, we look at the role sensor infrastructures play in the site and its colonisation. While this is one of the most monitored areas in the world by NGOs and civic society groups, there is still a lack of spatial records and analysis of the tunnel locations, their impact on Palestinian homes, the CCTV surveillance networks, and the electronic restrictions in the air. Therefore, working with these NGOs and researchers, our project aims to use volumetric 3D model space to follow the expansion and entanglement of these three infrastructural layers of the occupation.

## UNDERGROUND

What is popularly referred to as the 'City of David' is a settlement and archaeological site of tourism, selectively amalgamating over 150 years of excavations, research, and history of inhabitation on this site of ancient Jerusalem. It is located amidst the houses, gardens, and fields of the centuries-old Palestinian village of Silwan, gradually displacing its population as part of the Judaification attempts led by the El'ad organisation and the Israeli state.

Registered as an NGO on 8 September 1986 by David Be'eri, a former Israeli commando officer,[1] El'ad proclaimed its commitment to "continuing King David's legacy as well as revealing and connecting people to Ancient Jerusalem's glorious past through four key initiatives: archaeological excavation, tourism development, educational programming and residential revitalization". El'ad's residential revitalisation plans, similar to those practised by settler organisation, 'Ateret Cohanim', meant a persistent process of terrorisation, forced buyouts and displacement of Palestinian families only then to repopulate their emptied homes with ideologically driven Jewish families. However, unlike other organisations, El'ad directed its public-facing activities through the Ir-David (City of David) foundation, a tourism-led body promoting Zionist and evangelical agendas through biblical archaeology.[2, 3]

As a result of this policy of settlement by tourism, tunnels now run underground across the entire length of Wadi Hilweh; some follow ancient pathways, and some are newly excavated. Contracted by El'ad and carried out by the archaeologists of the Israeli Antiquities Authority (IAA)–the precise number, depth and routes of this vast underground project are to this day undisclosed. It was only as the buildings, balconies, public stair-

1   Ministry of Justice, 'לארשי לש תותומעה רתא - ראטסדייג | דוד ריע לא - ד.ע.ל.א', accessed 26 February 2019, https://www.guidestar.org.il/organization/580108660.
2   Wendy Pullan and Maximilian Gwiazda, '"City of David": Urban Design and Frontier Heritage', *Jerusalem Quarterly* 39, (1 January 2009).
3   Nadia Abu El-Haj, *Facts on the Ground: Archaeological Practice and Territorial Self-Fashioning in Israeli Society,* (Chicago: The University of Chicago Press, 2001).

ways, and roads began collapsing that fragments of the project were forced into the spotlight. Yet the linkage between the hollowing out of the mountain under Wadi Hilweh and the ground-level damages is still unacknowledged. In a China Mieville-like synopsis, The 'City of David' settlement has grown into a sprawling mega-tourist site drawing over half a million visitors per year while writing out and pushing into opacity the presence and history of Wadi Hilweh, along with its close to 20,000 Palestinian residents.[4]

Digital theodolites, Lidar and photogrammetry survey scans provide accuracy and spatial orientation as never before. These kinds of three-dimensional imaging, along with tools such as structured light and photogrammetry, are used throughout the Holy Basin in various ways: by the Israeli state as part of its security and control apparatus; by the municipality in its planning, monitoring, and surveillance mechanisms;[5] by archaeologists in their inspection and recording of the 'City of David' site and its artefacts; and by El'ad in its methods of imaging, imagining, and narration of the 'City of David'. Large-scale terra-forming, tunnelling, climate control, acoustics, landscape design, as well as imaging, projection and modelling are all deployed to control degrees of vision, erasure and opacity.

Early scan data[6] from the 'City of David' comes from a survey of 'Area G' and its sloping structure.[7] What is immediately striking (yet consistent with this computational vernacular) is how, in the point cloud,[8] the site is detached from its surroundings and imported into a standard software environment—a floating object set against a virtual backdrop. The same ideology that erases all mention and trace of Silwan, Abu Tor, or Sheikh Jarrah from its official maps finds here a technology that can perform a similar erasure, but at the level of the data.[9] 'Less relevant' information is discarded. The point-cloud scan doesn't only show an isolated, abstracted archaeological model. Still, it is first and foremost an operational photographic entity, providing a 'design-ready' dataset streamlined into archaeological, engineering, and architectural workflows.

In 2008, for example, El'ad's Be'eri was filmed giving a tour of Beit Hama'ayan, the 'Fountain House', the new name given to the Palestinian sacred spring 'Ein Umm ed Daraj'.[10] As the group he leads descends underground, Be'eri describes how bit by bit, he and his family clandestinely dug through the floor of a house they bought at the top of the hill, down to the Gihon spring, time and time again, evading inspections by authorities. The events that Be'eri speaks of took place a few years before this filming, yet they were not achieved by Be'eri and his family alone. In fact, the site he is discussing had already been dug and developed by Archaeologist Ronny Reich of Haifa University (also in charge of the Herodian tunnel excavations). The Fountain House is now the largest and most technologically elaborate section of the 'City of David' tourist site, boasting a projection mapping-based 3D reconstruction of the biblical turned Zionist narrative. The former entrance to 'Ein Umm ed Daraj', now closed off, is also now situated physically adjacent to a fortified and heavily surveilled police control room, part of El'as's 'fountain house'. So, it is clear that despite the 'guerrilla' tactics Be'eri describes, his actions were always deeply acknowledged and embraced by the Israeli state and aided by its professional bodies.

4    "The City & the City – Wikipedia," accessed 11 October 2023, https://en.wikipedia.org/wiki/The_City_%26_the_City.
5    "מעמכ יומ - יעירית ירושלימ," accessed 13 November 2023, https://jergisng.jerusalem.muni.il/baseWab/?config=../gisviewerngsupport/api/InjectingConfig&locale=he.
6    "סירוקית תלת דמימ ריע דוד ירושלימ'," scan3d, accessed 10 October 2023, https://en.scan3d.co.il/david-city.
7    Israeli Antiquities Authority, "Projects - Preservation," accessed 8 March 2019, http://www.iaa-conservation.org.il/Projects_Item_eng.asp?subject_id=10&site_id=3&id=127.
8    Point-Clouds are data points, clustered together to represent a 3D object or shape.
9    "City of David Map – Map of City of David (Israel)," accessed 11 October 2023, http://maps-jerusalem.com/city-of-david-map.
10   "ד"עלא אתומע ר"וי, יראב דוד לש הטלפקה, 2008," https://www.youtube.com/watch?v=MiOPPPUD-Ok.

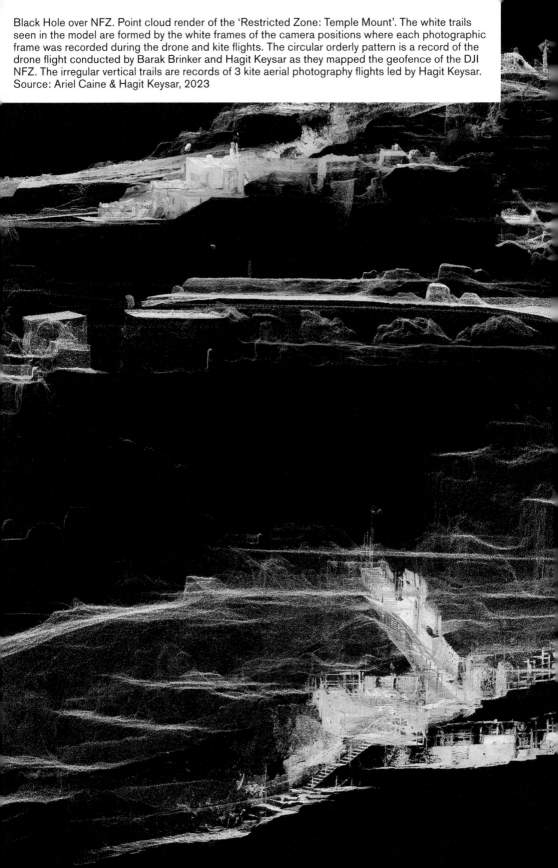

Black Hole over NFZ. Point cloud render of the 'Restricted Zone: Temple Mount'. The white trails seen in the model are formed by the white frames of the camera positions where each photographic frame was recorded during the drone and kite flights. The circular orderly pattern is a record of the drone flight conducted by Barak Brinker and Hagit Keysar as they mapped the geofence of the DJI NFZ. The irregular vertical trails are records of 3 kite aerial photography flights led by Hagit Keysar. Source: Ariel Caine & Hagit Keysar, 2023

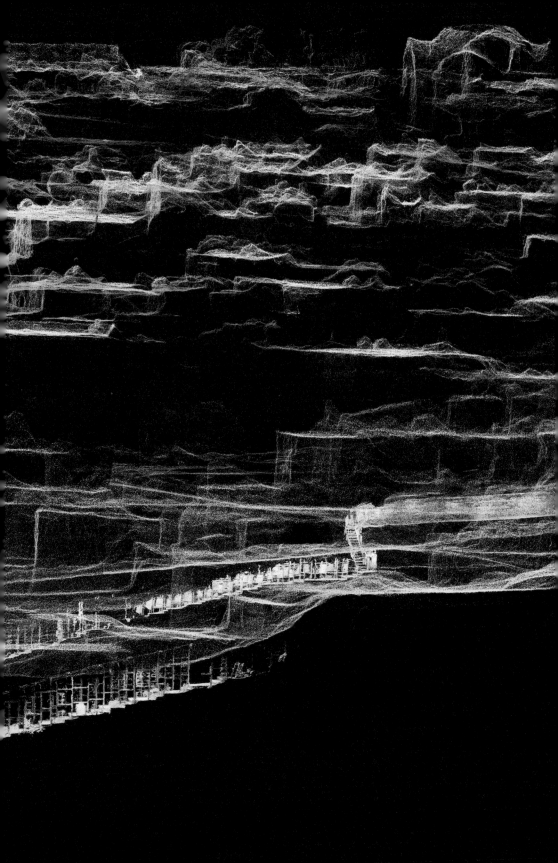

Cracks and structural damages caused to private home in Wadi Hilweh.
Source: Faiz Abu Rmeleh, 2018

> *Part of turāth Silwān (the heritage of Silwān) was to do the washing of the 'arīs (the groom) in the Silwān pool. You know, the day before the wedding, the friends take the 'arīs and shave him and wash him: the people of Silwān used to do that in the Silwān pool. It was like that in the old days, now we still try to do it when we can, but it has become almost impossible since the time they took the pool and closed it.*[11]

Yet the information linking the surface and the underground, used to conduct the operation is withheld from the public. In this site, the thin crust of the surface forms an optic and cognitive divide that enables the separation of narratives, archaeology, and dispossession. Damage to Palestinian properties and infrastructure are replaced by Jewish and evangelical narratives of heritage, exile, and return. Throughout the ongoing development, spatial imaging has been used to bridge the gap, to the point of conflation, messianic narrative, and scientific data between the existing and the planned.[12] El'ad's success is inextricably linked to its strategy of forming partnerships with civic, scientific, and commercial entities and its ability to present its operations through professional, technical and 'secular' discourse and not solely in ideological, religious terms. As the spatial photograph, with its calculable, parametric nature, is now part of the architectural and engineering mechanism of production, it is—just as much as the home, the road or the archaeological site—a form of settlement.

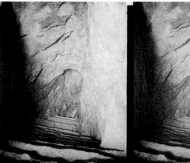

Police Station and Control centre adjacent to Fountain House. Ariel Caine, 2022 / Valleys of Jehoshaphat and Hinnom. Entrance to Siloam Tunnel at Virgin's Fountain. American colony Photographer, circa 1900

11   Resident of Wadi Hilweh, interviewed by Dr. Silvia Truini. Silwān, 20 May 2017. Silvia Truini, 'The Handmaiden of Settler-Colonialism: Archaeology and Heritage in Silwan, East Jerusalem,' (PhD diss., University of Exeter, 2020).
12   Nadia Abu El-Haj, *Facts on the Ground: Archaeological Practice and Territorial Self-Fashioning in Israeli Society*, (Chicago: The University of Chicago Press, 2001). See also: Raphael Greenberg, "Extreme Exposure: Archaeology in Jerusalem 1967–2007," *Conservation and Management of Archaeological Sites* 11, no. 3–4 (November 2009): 262–81.

Since the occupation and annexation of 1967, two processes have occurred simultaneously—a gradual inclusion of Palestinian residents into the municipal's physical and digital infrastructures. Second, primarily within the 'holy basin' area, Palestinian cultural heritage, historical markers, names and connection to physical sites are slowly being cleansed.

While they live within the Israeli boundaries of the separation wall, 10 minutes walk from the western city, Silwan's 19,570 residents have no voting rights. With virtually no planning permits for construction since the 1970s and no new neighbourhood planning by the municipality since the 'unification', practically all new construction carried out by residents in order to house the growth of over 13,000 people is deemed illegal. Under this regime of mass-illegalisation of a non-citizen population and economic, educational, and infrastructural impoverishment, Jewish-led settlement, infrastructures, and tourism in and around Silwan have flourished.

The expansion of settlement and tourism coincides with an expansion of surveillance infrastructure. A brief historical sketch can substantiate this.

In 1999, the C. Mer Group, an integrator in the areas of communications and security, won the Israeli police tender to establish the 'Mabat 2000' (Gaze 2000) project and the infrastructure surrounding it. An estimated 320 cameras were distributed across the entire old city of Jerusalem, covering its entry and exit points as well as the main routes.

A central computerised control centre was also set up within the old city, from where police personnel could observe and track the residents and tourists in high-definition live video. 'Mabat 2000' was a flagship project for the Israeli police. It was then expanded to 'Mabat Kedem' (gaze east), an expansion of the old city surveillance 'model' into further neighbourhoods in occupied east Jerusalem, such as Sheikh Jarrah in the north and Silwan in the south.

CCTV cameras installed at the entrance to the residential area of the settlement in Wadi Hilwe, Silwan.
Surveillance mast with police cameras, al Bustan, Silwan, Jerusalem. Source: Ariel Caine, 2022

Finally, in recent years, as part of the system upgrade we mentioned earlier with the C-Mer tender, another upgrade was undertaken, this time called: 'Mabat Yerushalayim' (which we translate to gaze Jerusalem). This encompasses the entire municipality. Here, the municipality and the security apparatus merge under a 'smart city' umbrella so to speak.

There is no full official mapping or verified number of cameras or technologies for this system however, some numbers gathered by researcher Ronen Eidelman list:[13]

1. A further 2,000 cameras to the approx. 320 of the Mabat 2000. This system was planned to expand to 3,000 by the end of 2022.
2. 850 security cameras installed by the municipality.
3. 250 LPR (license plate recognition) cameras were installed in 160 entrances and intersections across the municipality by the transport bureau.
4. A further undisclosed number of cameras is known to be installed and monitored by the Secret Service, the housing ministry, as well as cameras privately installed by institutions along the light rail project, universities, etc.

All cameras within the municipal network connect to the new municipal system, where they are funnelled into a purpose-built control centre in the Gilo settlement in south of Jerusalem. The 'KFIR' system as it's called, links all cameras, loudspeaker systems, sound and temperature sensors installed in conjunction with cameras.

> One goes out of the house and there are one hundred cameras spying on him, lurking [...] but even inside the house, I don't feel free to get undressed in my own house anymore. There are the guards on top of the settler house over there that look into my windows 24 hours, then the soldiers approach on the side and peek inside, and on this other side come all the foreigners and the tourists and look inside, the guard on that other side looks inside, and from the other part the cameras point into the living room [...] the house has become totally laid bare, not only during the day, but day and night.[14]

NGOs such as Peace Now, B'tselem, WhoProfits, and Amnesty have for years been monitoring the expansion and evolutions of the use of surveillance.[15] As of yet, these did not include spatial survey and analysis. To their efforts we aim to add spatial, time and classification detail within the area of Wadi Hilweh, out of an understanding that while we cannot gain direct access to these networked vision systems, their spatial and infrastructural configurations can teach us about their intent and capabilities.

In Silwan, the earliest and only complete dataset of camera numbers and locations we found is from 2008, compiled by Peace Now. Since the beginning of 2022, we have conducted our own regular ground survey, counting, and identifying the camera locations, types and estimated association with the many state and private actors in Wadi Hilweh. camera numbers have more than quadrupled, from 60 to around 243. We can see in our map that the distribution of cameras, the vast majority of these installed privately by the El'ad settler organisation, follows the main pathways, roads, settlements, and archaeologi-

---

13   Ronen Eidelman, 'Community Surveillance in the Public Sphere' (PhD diss., Hebrew University of Jerusalem, 2020).

14   Resident of Wadi Hilweh, interviewed by Dr. Silvia Truini. Silwan, 21 May 2017. Silvia Truini, 'The Handmaiden of Settler-Colonialism: Archaeology and Heritage in Silwan, East Jerusalem.' (PHD diss., University of Exeter, 2020).

15   See: WhoProfits, 'The Israeli Occupation Industry - "Big Brother" in Jerusalem's Old City,' accessed 10 October 2023, https://www.whoprofits.org/publications/report/44?big-brother-in-jerusalems-old-city, and 'Israel and Occupied Palestinian Territories: Automated Apartheid: How Facial Recognition Fragments, Segregates and Controls Palestinians in the OPT,' *Amnesty International*, accessed 10 October 2023, https://www.amnesty.org/en/documents/mde15/6701/2023/en/.

cal sites. But in key points, the 'City of David' camera presence also includes police masts mounted with PTZ type 360 rotating cameras with over x40 optical zoom levels and facial recognition capacities. These cameras, along with loudspeaker systems are connected to local control rooms as well as to the centralised 'Mabat Jerusalem' HQ in Gilo.

Camera systems at the street and house level have been installed side by side with the advancement of the process of occupation in which cultural heritage, tourism and the tourist bodies have been mobilised as drivers and justifiers.

### AERIAL: NFZ (NO-FLY-ZONE)

Rising from the ground into the sky, another infrastructure is in place. Centred on the Haram al-sharif, Temple Mount, spanning approx. 3km in diameter, this less known, cylindrical digital barrier known as a "geofence"[16] extends from the ground and up into the skies, set to prevent drone flights into or from within the area. This technologically restricted zone follows the geographic coordinates of an already present regulatory No-Fly-Zone (NFZ) that has been set and enforced by the Israeli security apparatus for more than two decades.

The "geofence" is a recent technological layer added to an increasingly dense infrastructural sensor stratigraphy in the city. It spans wide-ranging volumetric technologies, from underground seismic and waterflow sensors; through heat, sound and optical street-level monitoring systems to an assemblage of remote-sensing aerial and satellite-based geographic information systems. However, developed and exclusively controlled and managed by the Chinese drone manufacturer DJI, this geofencing technology serves as a unique example of an emergent mode of blended sovereignty between the airspace controlled by Israel and the drone flight regulation controlled by DJI. Particularly in urban contexts, data infrastructures are becoming increasingly dominant in directing the various layers of everyday life and rapidly shaping techno-political futures. It can be argued that one of the biggest challenges we face regarding the datafication of cities is the fact that algorithmic infrastructures are opaque and illegible to most of us, therefore, very hard to audit and critique. Should we understand these rapid and powerful changes as historical ruptures in our understanding of urbanism? Is there space and time for intervention, refusal, and resistance—or "slow urbanism" within the overwhelming acceptance of data-driven smart cities?

### CONCLUSION

Over the last four decades, Silwan has become one of the most entangled and densely surveyed areas in Palestine. From the underground to the skies, the volume of this site is networked with a myriad of sensory apparatuses, a dense constellation of electromagnetic computational media central to ongoing processes of civil and military occupation.

For each spatial register discussed in the text, a media method, response and set of collaborations has been developed over the last few years.

In the underground, where Israel's settler-archaeological tunnelling project runs in unknown depths and lengths beneath the village, georeferencing and structure from motion photogrammetry allowed us to piece the fragments of existing footage into a preliminary tracing of tunnel routes and their relation to the homes and collapses at street level.[17] Found video footage filmed above and below ground, uploaded by settlers, tourists,

16 'Geo Zone Map - Fly Safe - DJI,' accessed 20 January 2023, https://www.dji.com/uk/flysafe/geo-map.
17 'Structure from Motion Overview - MATLAB & Simulink,' accessed 14 November 2023, https://www.mathworks.com/help/vision/ug/structure-from-motion.html.

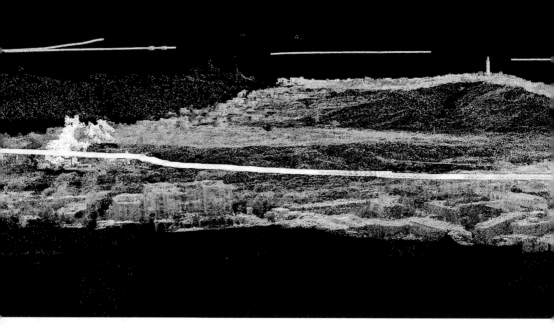

Black Hole over NFZ. Point cloud render of drone and kite mapping.
Source: Ariel Caine & Hagit Keysar, 2023

workers in the excavation project, as well as our own footage and that of Palestinian activists and residents allowed us to gain access to sections and momentary conditions of these sites. From these videos, broken into thousands of frame sequences, we computed a point cloud model of the tunnel routes. These were then anchored in geocoordinate space and depth using measurements at entrance and exit points of the tourist tunnels, as well as using points of opening in the digs where the excavated earth is vacated. As the terrain model and satellite images in Jerusalem (along with the rest of Israel/Palestine) are not accessible in high detail and drone flight is prohibited, our surface model was computed using kite-aerial-photography, jointly carried out by residents, mostly youth from Wadi Hilweh.[18] Once surface and underground point clouds were brought together into the same 3D model space, we could not only begin to see clearly where, and underneath what homes the tunnels pass, but we could now start a process by which we go back to the Silwan families testimonials of collapses and damage and start drawing a connecting line from their homes, into the tunnel beneath their feet.

At street-level, the ongoing monitoring of CCTV surveillance combined on-the-ground surveys, identifying and classifying the sensors installed across the neighborhood,

18   A community mapping project led by PublicLab organiser Hagit Keysar and co-founder Jeffry Warren along with Shai Efrati and youth from Silwan, 2011. See: Hagit Keysar, 'DIY Drones in Silwan - Hagit Keysar,' 2011, https://cargocollective.com/hagitkeysar/DIY-drones-in-Silwan; Hagit Keysar, 'Seeking New Ways of Seeing – Collaborative Mapmaking in Jerusalem,' Evidence & Influence Micromagazine (blog), 17 September 2013, https://micromag. evidenceandinfluence.org/article/mapmaking-in-jerusalem/, https://cargocollective.com/ hagitkeysar/Aerial-visions/Silwan.

**ARIEL CAINE AND FAIZ ABU-RMELEH**

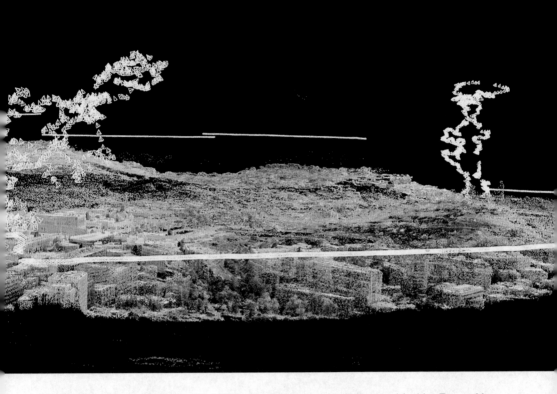

with the emerging mapping of settlement expansion datasets provided by Peace Now. For many years, it is known that surveillance is widespread and deep and this knowledge has almost fossilised it, accepting it as an amorphous techno-sovereign assemblage. We continued the work started by WhoProfits in trying to do the groundwork, count, position and classify each camera and then together with local and international partners, began a process, still underway, of reading both in and out of these camera networks, trying to understand how penetrating this surveillance is, and how this constellation extends from Silwan out into the larger smart-city network.[19] Overlapping the camera locations, tourism development, settlement expansion and archaeological excavation's 'layers' across time, we see how these infrastructures advance together alongside destruction, and dispossession.

Finally, together with Hagit Keysar, we began a third project aiming at making tangible the effects of electromagnetic restrictions in the air, on the possibility of vision. By using the tool these geofencing systems are aimed to impact, i.e., drones, Hagit Keysar and Barak Brinker conducted drone flights while traversing and 'crashing' against the circumference of the Temple mount 'No-Fly-Zone'. Nearly 10,000 images from these flights were processed and triangulated in our subsequent ongoing project to produce a preliminary point-cloud model of the black hole of vision data above the Haram al-Sharif. Using kites, balloons, non DJI drones and on-the-ground movement, we began experimenting with other ways through which this black hole of visibility could be made sensible and its complex politics of ethnic, juridical, and social control could be challenged.

19   Ronen Eidelman, 'Community Surveillance in the Public Sphere' (PhD diss., Hebrew University of Jerusalem, 2020); 'Israel and Occupied Palestinian Territories'; 'Post-Visual Security | VISUAL STUDIES LAB | Tampere Universities', VISUAL STUDIES LAB, accessed 14 November 2023, https://research.tuni.fi/visualstudieslab/projects/post-visual-security/.

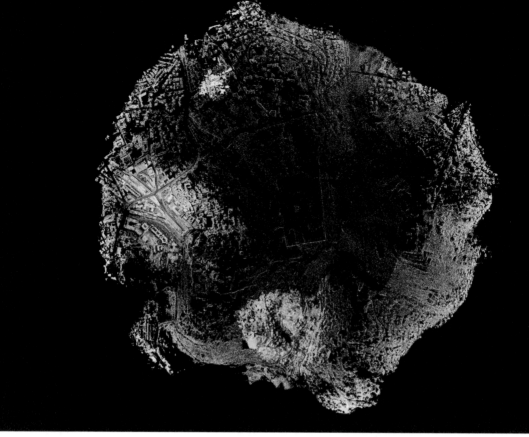

Black Hole over NFZ. Point cloud render of drone and kite mapping. Source: Ariel Caine & Hagit Keysar, 2023

Working between the physical site and the production of 3D models not only offer the possibility for changed forms of visibility but simultaneously calls for the development of methodologies for collective spatial practices of media. In this expanded sense, the model is an epistemological lens through which to critically engage with the complex interrelations that ground physical reality and the invisible infrastructural architectures of the sensed.

While, as we aimed to show, optical computational models are used by state and corporate actors, they also offer new possibilities for resistance and processes of accountability. We sought to explore the changing conditions of networked vision, its spatialization, the decision-making logic at its core, and some of the techno-social realities that form through and around its deployment. Drawing on a set of collaborations and spatial imaging methodologies, the visual project shown here offers some insight into infrastructures, their entanglement, and their implications, through unpicking the physical and sensory infrastructures that are either opaque or have not been made visible before. This spatial practice does not only produce model environments, as we propose; it should be seen as offering a framework for the development of communities of practice.

## Works Cited

Abu El-Haj, Nadia. *Facts on the Ground: Archaeological Practice and Territorial Self-Fashioning in Israeli Society*. Chicago: The University of Chicago Press, 2001.

Amnesty International. 'Israel and Occupied Palestinian Territories: Automated Apartheid: How Facial Recognition Fragments, Segregates and Controls Palestinians in the OPT,' Accessed 10 October 2023. https://www.amnesty.org/en/documents/mde15/6701/2023/en/.

'City of David Map - Map of City of David (Israel),' accessed 11 October 2023. http://maps-jerusalem.com/city-of-david-map.

Eidelman, Ronen. 'Community Surveillance in the Public Sphere'. PhD diss., Hebrew University of Jerusalem, 2020.

'Geo Zone Map – Fly Safe – DJI,' accessed 20 January 2023. https://www.dji.com/uk/flysafe/geo-map.

Greenberg, Raphael. 'Extreme Exposure: Archaeology in Jerusalem 1967–2007'. *Conservation and Management of Archaeological Sites* 11, no. 3–4, (November 2009): 262–81.

Israeli Antiquities Authority. 'Projects – Presevation'. Accessed 8 March 2019. http://www.iaa-conservation.org.il/Projects_Item_eng.asp?subject_id=10&site_id=3&id=127.

Keysar, Hagit. 'DIY Drones in Silwan - Hagit Keysar', 2011. https://cargocollective.com/hagitkeysar/DIY-drones-in-Silwan.

–––. 'Seeking New Ways of Seeing – Collaborative Mapmaking in Jerusalem'. *Evidence & Influence Micromagazine* (blog), 17 September 2013. https://micromag.evidenceandinfluence.org/article/mapmaking-in-jerusalem/.

Ministry of Justice. ''רתא - ראטסדייג | דוד ריע לא - .ד.ע.ל.א‎ לארשי לש תותומעה,'' accessed 13 November 2023. https://www.guidestar.org.il/organization/580108660.

Pullan, Wendy, and Maximilian Gwiazda. '"City of David": Urban Design and Frontier Heritage'". *Jerusalem Quarterly* 39 (1 January 2009): 29-48.

SCAN3D. 'City of David: 3D Documentation Laser Scanning'. Accessed 10 October 2023. https://en.scan3d.co.il/david-city.

'Structure from Motion Overview - MATLAB & Simulink,' accessed 14 November 2023. https://www.mathworks.com/help/vision/ug/structure-from-motion.html.

'The City & the City - Wikipedia,' accessed 11 October 2023. https://en.wikipedia.org/wiki/The_City_%26_the_City.

Truini, Silvia. 'The Handmaiden of Settler-Colonialism: Archaeology and Heritage in Silwan, East Jerusalem.' PhD. diss, University of Exeter, 2019.

VISUAL STUDIES LAB. 'Post-Visual Security | VISUAL STUDIES LAB | Tampere Universities,' accessed 14 November 2023. https://research.tuni.fi/visualstudieslab/projects/post-visual-security/.

Who Profits. 'The Israeli Occupation Industry - "Big Brother' in Jerusalem's Old City." Accessed 10 October 2023. https://www.whoprofits.org/publications/report/44?big-brother-in-jerusalems-old-city.

הטלקה לש דוד באר"י, ר תתומע אלע"ד, 2008. https://www.youtube.com/watch?v=MiOPPPUD-Ok.

''מערכת מפוי - יירי ת ירושלמי,'' accessed 13 November 2023. https://jergisng.jerusalem.muni.il/baseWab/?config=../gisviewerngsupport/api/InjectingConfig&locale=he.

# BURNING AN ILLUSION[1]

*In the autumn of 2022, the MA Research Architecture course undertook a five-week intensive investigation of the New Cross Massacre (1981), a house fire at a party in London that claimed the lives of thirteen young Black people.[2] Our aim was not to produce a singular narrative of the night itself nor come to any definitive conclusions regarding the cause of the fire. Instead, we hoped to expose the failures of the police and British establishment to conduct a thorough and fair investigation into the cause of the fire, while connecting this with a larger history of state violence and neglect towards Black communities in Britain. In other words, we sought to investigate the investigation.*

On the evening of 17 January 1981, partygoers gathered at 439 New Cross Road, South East London. The party was to celebrate the birthday of Yvonne Ruddock, and Angela Jackson, her friend. At around 5:40 in the morning of the 18 January, a fire raged through the house, claiming the lives of thirteen young Black people between the ages of 14 and 22, and later, one more victim who took his own life. Despite multiple investigations between 1981 to 2011, no one has been charged in connection to the fire. The victims of the fire were:

Andrew Gooding, age 14
Patricia Johnson, age 15
Rosaline Henry, age 16
Patrick Cummings, age 16
Owen Thompson, age 16
Glenton Powell, age 16
Yvonne Ruddock, age 16
Steve Collins, age 17
Gerry Francis, age 17
Humphrey Brown, age 18
Peter Campbell, age 18
Lloyd Hall, age 20
Paul Ruddock, age 22
Anthony Berbeck, who died later in 1983

In addition to the initial forensic analysis in 1981, three investigations were carried out: coroners' inquests in 1981 and 2004, as well as a second forensic investigation in 2011. Both coroners' inquests ended in an open verdict.[3] The initial police investigation determined that the fire started somewhere in the front room on the ground floor. On the first day of the initial investigation, the police suggested that the fire was started by a petrol bomb thrown through the front window. This theory was quickly dropped despite the high frequency of racially motivated fire attacks in the area

---

1    The title of our research, *Burning an Illusion*, was taken from the 1981 film by Menelik Shabazz, an intimate depiction of the political awakening of a young Black couple in London after their interactions with police violence and incarceration.
2    Though this event is sometimes referred to as the New Cross Fire, many community organisations refer to this event of violence as the New Cross Massacre. In solidarity with activists and community groups, this essay will make use of the term New Cross Massacre.
3    An inquest is a type of legal inquiry that seeks to determine the circumstances of death, particularly when there are doubts as to these circumstances. It is not a trial and does not ascribe liability to any party but is rather used to ascertain certain facts. An inquest must be held by the local coroner, and an open verdict can be returned in an inquest and implies a lack of sufficient evidence to understand the circumstances in which the person died.

and the wider city at the time.[4] The police narrative and investigation then promoted the theory that the fire started from within the house, suggesting an alleged fight was the cause of the fire. This theory was later ruled out by the second inquest in 2004.

An image of a thin-walled aluminium tube, approximately 125 mm long and 20 mm in diameter, which was found in the back garden. Donald Henderson, an investigator for Scotland Yard, admitted that he did not look for any wick or container that might be attached to the device, which would have indicated that the object was designed for arson. For the inquest in 1981, chemical tests were conducted by forensic analyst Peter Pugh and indicated the presence of sugar and chlorate (which is an incendiary mixture). The unidentified object reached Woolwich Explosive Laboratory on March 17, two months after the fire. By that time, the object had been flattened out into alumnium sheets. Strangely, when the object reached Walter Elliot, a scientific officer at Woolwich Explosive Laboratory, he found no traces of chlorate or sugar. In this case, as well as in the case of the seat of the fire, state authorities (including the police and forensic analysts) seemed to disregard evidence that might have indicated arson. Further, the subsequent absence of chlorate and sugar indicates the possibility of mishandling or tampering of evidence.

In response to the police investigation of 1981, the New Cross Massacre Action Committee (NCMAC) was formed within two days of the fire. Led by the Black Parents Movement, they founded a Fact Finding Commission, compiling evidence by conducting witness statements. The work of the NCMAC contradicts the unreliable, inadequate, and prejudiced official statements conducted by the police, some of which have been sealed in the National Archives until 2087.[5] Our investigation has drawn mainly on the George Padmore Institute, which contains the files of the NCMAC, as well as the Black Cultural Archives and the National Archives.

We organised our findings around five key themes: the role of the coroner, the details of the police investigation, the allocation and upkeep of housing by

4  As part of our investigation, we created a series of timelines, one of which maps the pattern of arson attacks on Black community spaces in South London preceding the New Cross Massacre, including the Black Panthers Unity Bookshop in 1974, the Moonshot Club in 1977, and the Albany Centre in 1978. These events demonstrate that the Massacre was not an isolated and irregular tragedy, but part of a pattern of racial violence that characterised the political and social landscape of Britain across the 1970s and 1980s. Just six months after the Massacre, Doreen Khan and her three children were murdered in their home in Walthamstow from a racially motivated petrol bomb attack. See our archives at https://burning-an-illusion.uk/.
5  Aaron Andrews, 'Truth, Justice, and Expertise in 1980s Britain: The Cultural Politics of the New Cross Massacre,' *History Workshop Journal* 91, no. 1 (January 2021): 184.

the council of Lewisham, the distribution of police resources by the city, and the media depoliticisation of the fire. Our investigation sought to expose how racism within powerful institutions such as the media, the police, and the coroner's office contributed to the inconclusive results of the investigation of the New Cross Massacre. In this essay, we will focus on several conclusions from our research; however, further documentation and evidence from our investigation are available on the online platform we developed for the project.[6]

The depoliticisation of the Massacre was institutionalised through the Hytner Report and the Scarman Report, both published in 1981, which were government inquiries analysing the cause of the uprisings in Manchester and London. The Hytner report concluded that the Moss Side uprising was a "spontaneous eruption(s) of hate," placing the event in an ahistorical vacuum by refusing to acknowledge the racial violence that grounded the uprising. The Scarman Report followed suit, which came to the same conclusion regarding the Brixton uprising. Ultimately, the summer of 1981 was a pivotal moment where the height of resistance action, police brutality, far-right groups, and state legislation coalesced to reveal how the state depoliticised mass uprisings against racism in Britain.

6    Website available at https://burning-an-illusion.uk/.

We created a 3D model of the house at 439 New Cross Road to understand the events of the evening, particularly how the fire spread. We simulated the fire, which began in the front room and spread in less than six minutes throughout the whole house, fatally trapping people upstairs. The model allowed us to situate testimonies within a spatial frame. Through this process, we could understand the fissures between community accounts and the official narrative produced by the police and circulated by the media. This model also aided our inquiry into how the building materials of the house exacerbated the fire, spotlighting the role of Lewisham Council and its systematic neglect in the housing of Black families.

## INQUEST INJUSTICE

A key aspect of our investigation showed that the structure of the inquest system allowed the negligence of Coroner Arthur Gordon Davies to obstruct legal processes. With the help of the Metropolitan Police, the inquest system was used to put the community itself on trial.

Three main complaints were issued against the coroner of the New Cross Massacre, Arthur Gordon Davies, and thus the inquest proceedings. These complaints concerned:

**1**

Misleading the jury as to potential verdicts that could be rendered.
The coroner directed the jury that three possible verdicts were available: unlawful killing, accidental death, and open verdict.[7] Coroner Davies directed the jury first to ascertain where the fire originated. He directed them that if the fire originated from the outside, the only possible verdict should be unlawful killing. If the fire's origin was inside the house, they should determine whether it was intentional (and if so, they should render an unlawful killing verdict) or accidental (and if so, they should render an accidental death verdict).[8]

    Through this framing—that the origin of the fire must be determined to infer intentionality—Davies foreclosed the possibility that evidence could point to an intentionally set fire without knowing where it originated. If this were the case, the verdict could have been unlawful killing, rather than an open verdict, and would have allowed for a criminal proceeding to take place, despite lingering ambiguities.[9] Inquest rules also allowed juries to render their verdict in phrase form, rather than by choosing a verdict from a list.[10] Coroner Davies boxed the jury into a rigid list of options that obfuscated the verdict of unlawful killing, as well as a more holistic, modified verdict.

**2**

The use of police statements during the inquest.
Many witness statements that the police collected during the investigation were taken under duress and later retracted. Despite the subsequent retractions, the coroner used many coerced witness statements during the inquest. Moreover, he used statements not entered into the record as evidence. Witness statements were read directly when questioning the witnesses rather than informing the line of questioning.[11] This practice is directly discouraged in the Recommendations on Procedure 1975 by the Coroner's Society of England and Wales, which states, "The coroner should not show the witness his police statement or read out the police statement and ask the witness if that is true".[12] Leading witnesses by reading from statements is counter-productive to the purpose of an inquest, which is to determine the circumstances and information around death with as much clarity as possible.

**3**

Davies' lack of note-taking during the inquest.
Coroner Davies did not take notes. Instead, he annotated witness statements taken by police and recorded the proceedings on a tape which was not transcribed. The official procedure states that "[I]t is essential that the coroner's notes show the true statement of the witness [...] It is also improper to use the police statements as the coroner's notes by putting in amendments as the witness gives evidence".[13]

7    The possibility of a narrative verdict was not added until 2004.

8    Unknown, 'No new inquest into Deptford fire deaths,' HO 299/135, The National Archives, London.

9    In the case of an unlawful killing verdict, the perpetrator(s) need not have been conclusively determined.

10    For more information, see: Letter from AMC Inglese to RJ Phillips, June 23, 1982, HO 299/135, The National Archives, London.

11    Frankie Rickford, '"I made errors"--fire coroner,' *The Star*, HO 299/135, The National Archives, London.

12    Coroner's Society of England and Wales, 'Recommendations on Procedure 1975,' HO 299/135, The National Archives, London.

13    Coroner's Society of England and Wales, 'Recommendations on Procedure 1975.'

Documentation of the trial is only available to the public because of the extensive media coverage and the efforts of activist and publisher John La Rose, who took notes at the trial.[14]

The harm caused by the inquest procedure and the British legal system did not begin or end with the New Cross Massacre inquest in 1981. As inquests and inquiries do not assign criminal liability, they provide the appearance of accountability and closure without any framework for convictions or consequences for potential perpetrators. In the case of the New Cross Massacre, not only was the initial inquest process led by a coroner who allegedly committed numerous violations of protocol, but it also reflected a structural failing whereby the possibility of a criminal investigation was foreclosed. Additionally, the 1981 inquest placed the community itself on trial, treating many of the victims of the fire as suspects rather than witnesses by coercing testimonies under duress and questioning minors without due supervision.

## KEY EVIDENCE:
## SHIFTING POLICE, MEDIA, AND
## WITNESS NARRATIVES

To investigate the forensic investigation, we created five key case files based on forensic evidence collected from various zones of the house: the incendiary device in the backyard, an unknown intruder who entered the house before the fire, the theory that a fight in the front room had led to the fire, the location where the fire started, and who had driven by in a car before the fire. We observed many shifting narratives among the police and media in the process of compiling these case files, as well as the possibility of evidence mishandling or tampering.

One such example from our five-pronged analysis was the seat of the fire. Our investigation showed that initial witnesses' statements, media, and police claims considered that an incendiary device landed near the window and started the fire. Early reports indicated that the fire had begun on the chair by the window and then spread to the drapes. After a short time, the police began to state that the fire had started in the centre of the room. Media narratives followed suit, therefore eliminating the possibility of arson, and strengthening the theory that the fire had started with a fight inside the party. Then, the police investigation in 2001 reverted to the original claim of the fire starting next to the window.[15]

During the first coroner's inquest in 1981, forensic scientists Donald Busby and Peter Pugh did a series of tests to determine the fire's origin.[16] Pugh claimed that the attack could not have been arson because the fire started in the centre of the room, and it would have been impossible to throw a projectile this far; however, in an earlier map of the fire, Pugh depicted the fire as having started by the window. This discrepancy went unexplained.

Busby attempted to replicate the introduction of an arson device into the house. He recreated a projectile thrown into the room from the outside via the front window. However, according to La Rose's notes, Busby did not have the time or resources

---

14  John La Rose (1927-2006) was a poet, writer and activist who served as the chairman of the New Cross Massacre Action Committee as well as the founder of the George Padmore Institute. La Rose also founded New Beacon Books, the first Caribbean publishing house in England.

15  Dee Lahiri, '"I don't think I can die before I find out what happened to my son",' *The Guardian*, 15 May 2001, https://www.theguardian.com/world/2001/may/15/race.london.

16  Analysis of forensic evidence presented, undated, NCM, NCM 2/3/1/4, New Cross Massacre Campaign 1980-1985, George Padmore Institute, London.

to recreate this event a sufficient number of times. Even Busby himself found the conclusions thus anecdotal.

In addition, the forensic simulations were only conducted with the drapes and curtains closed, even though eyewitness reports had been mixed on this matter—some witnesses said the drapes were open, and some witnesses stated they were partially open. It is possible that flammable materials could have spread differently had the drapes been open, casting doubts on the legitimacy of Busby's forensic analysis.

The contradictions in Busby and Pugh's investigations went unchallenged until June 2001, when the Metropolitan Police concluded that the forensic evidence for the seat of the fire in the centre of the room was insignificant and that the fire definitively began on the chair by the window.[17] This conclusion became the basis for the later inquests and investigations in the 2000s.[18] That such a crucial element of the investigation—where the fire had started—could be misconstrued in the initial inquest, contradicting the reports of many eyewitnesses, indicates the failure to conduct a thorough and fair investigation.

## POLICE AGAINST THE COMMUNITY

By mapping the relationships between relevant actors, we determined that across all levels—local, regional, and federal—police weaponised resources against racialised communities both in New Cross and further afield.

Locally, police officers interrogated and threatened children while over-policing Black neighbourhoods, rather than pursuing leads in the New Cross Massacre investigation. Meanwhile, the Met and Special Patrol Group deployed militarised and colonial police tactics and played heavy-handed roles in antagonising and harming residents in New Cross and throughout London.[19] Police activities perpetuated violence against the Black community, and in many cases, perpetrators were and continue to be rewarded.

One actor we analysed in this larger nexus of policing was Commander Graham Stockwell, the lead investigator of the New Cross Massacre. Under Stockwell's direction, the police interrogated the children present at the New Cross Massacre using extreme and coercive means. Excerpts from John La Rose's handwritten notes from the inquest in 1981 demonstrate the threatening nature of police questioning, as recalled by Wayne Downer. Downer, who was a teen at the time, describes being threatened with other charges, held in a cell, and forced to assent to the police's account. Coercive methods of interrogation were used to produce the police's false theory that a fight had broken out and started the fire. Downer's coerced testimony was used to name six key witnesses, including himself, from which the police extracted additional coerced statements to build the false narrative of the fight. Police also aggressively questioned

---

17   Aaron Andrews, 'Truth, Justice, and Expertise in 1980s Britain: The Cultural Politics of the New Cross Massacre,' *History Workshop Journal* 91, no. 1, (January 2021): 197.

18   Kehinde Andrews, 'Forty Years on from the New Cross Fire, What Has Changed for Black Britons?,' *The Guardian*, 17 January 2021, https://www.theguardian.com/world/2021/jan/17/forty-years-on-from-the-new-cross-fire-what-has-changed-for-black-britons.

19   The style of policing present in London at this time was the direct product of police and military violence in the colonies and Northern Ireland. Individuals such as Commissioner Kenneth Newman were critical in establishing the use of violent, colonial methods of policing in mainland Britain. Prior to 1948, Newman served as a colonial detective in the Palestine Special Branch [Adam Elliot-Cooper, *Black Resistance to British Policing. Racism, Resistance and Social Change* (Manchester: Manchester University Press, 2021)]. Afterwards, he was the Chief Constable of the Royal Ulster Constabulary (RUC) in Northern Ireland where he was pivotal in ceding army authority to the RUC [Cooper, *Black Resistance to British Policing*]. Later, Newman would deploy paramilitary policing for the first time in mainland Britain during the 1985 Broadwater Farm uprisings [Cooper, *Black Resistance to British Policing*.].

Denise Gooding (age 11) on the day she was released from the hospital for injuries sustained in the fire and her escape through the second-floor window.[20]

Commander Stockwell had a history of abusing his power in questioning witnesses, specifically when interrogating unaccompanied teenagers. On 22 April 1972, Michelle Confait, a transgender woman, was murdered in her South East London flat, which was later burnt down.[21] Stockwell, then Detective Inspector of the local Criminal Investigation Department (CID), and Detective Chief Superintendent Alan Jones interrogated three teenagers without adult supervision, legal counsel, or a tape recording.[22] These teens were Colin Lattimore (18), Ronnie Leighton (15), and Ahmet Salih (14). With prompting and leading questioning from the police, two of the boys confessed to the murder of Confait, and all three confessed to burning Confait's home.[23] Three years later, the teens were later exonerated through unequivocal alibis that were corroborated by the forensic timeline of the murder.[24]

The release of the boys occurred six years before Stockwell was brought on to the New Cross Massacre investigation. Stockwell was specifically sought for this case despite his history and, according to some, because of it.[25] That an authority figure with a demonstrated record of coercively interrogating teenagers would be chosen to spearhead the New Cross Massacre investigation casts doubt on the legitimacy of many claims made in the inquest in 1981. However, the violence inflicted upon this community was more systemic than just the actions of one proverbial 'bad apple.'

Just prior to the New Cross investigation, Margaret Thatcher raised police pay by 45 per cent, one of her first decisions as prime minister. Under her tenure, the police became known as "Thatcher's boot boys".[26] In the fiscal year of 1980, the nationwide budget for "police services" was £2,090 million (equal to £8,035 million in 2022).[27] To follow the money is, in this case, to see the rise of an increasingly militarised, well-funded British police force.

## THE PUBLIC FORUM
## AND THE EXPERTISE OF EXPERIENCE

On 30 September 2023, we held a closed forum at Goldsmiths, University of London, to share the findings of our investigation with those who had been affected by the New Cross Massacre. While acknowledging the complex and often adverse influence the university has had on the New Cross neighbourhood, the space bridged researchers, activists, students, and the local community. The forum invited new ways to frame our work, prompting the question: How do we represent our research material to those whose lives were irrevocably changed by the Massacre? The forum also provided

20  NCM, NCM 4/1/1, New Cross Massacre Campaign 1980-1985, George Padmore Institute, London.
21  Robin Bunce and Paul Field, 'Thirteen Dead and Nothing Said,' in *Darcus Howe: A Political Biography*, (London: Bloomsbury, 2014), 197.
22  Andrews, 'Truth, Justice, and Expertise in 1980s Britain,' 197.
23  Henry Fisher, 'Report of an inquiry into the death of Maxwell Confait,' (London: Home Office, 1977), 265. https://www.gov.uk/government/publications/report-of-an-inquiry-into-the-death-of-maxwell-confait.
24  Fisher, 'Report of an inquiry.'
25  Bunce and Field, 197.
26  Robert Chesshyre, 'Thatcher's "boot boys": When the unholy trinity of police, press and government took root,' *The Independent*, 15 September 2012, https://www.independent.co.uk/voices/comment/thatcher-s-boot-boys-when-the-unholy-trinity-of-police-press-and-government-took-root-8139816.html.
27  Christopher Chantrill, 'Time Series Chart of UK Public Spending,' *UK Public Spending*, https://www.ukpublicspending.co.uk/spending_chart_1980_2021UKm_17c1li011lcn_56t51t55t.

# When the black ti
# the thin blue lir

A wall of police riot shields contains marchers at the approach to

A coffin is carried shoulder-high at the march's head

## March: Calm start...

**Continued from Page One**

Tendency marched with anti-Nazi banners and shouted slogans against the far Right. Wordings on banners alleged 'massacre', 'murder' and 'police conspiracy'. White demonstrators included representatives from the Socialist Workers' Party and the Anti-Nazi League.

Thousands of police—supervising a march against themselves—were on the nine-mile route which wound from Deptford to Hyde Park, via the heart of London at rush-hour. Traffic came to a standstill all along the way.

The protesters, led by a coffin carried shoulder-high, marched to the beat of drums carried on the back of a lorry.

London demonstrators were reinforced by others from Birmingham, Coventry, Bristol and Manchester.

At the head of the march was one of the most active members of that Committee, Darcus Howe, a 38-year-old self-admitted Marxist.

Police escorting the protestors appealed to demonstrators over megaphones. 'Will you please follow the police van and the police horses. There is no other route.'

One officer said: 'We were told to bend over backwards to be fair to the marchers—and then to bend over a bit more.'

The march started peacefully, almost with good humour. Police allowed the black stewards to control the crowd as they spilled off the roadway and on to the pavements.

The first sign of trouble came as the demo approached Blackfriars Bridge. Young black troublemakers began throwing bricks piled up for building works.

Police, many with riot shields, formed a solid line in front of the demo, and hundreds more could be seen on the bridge behind them.

Within the procession people were fighting the police. Black organisers pleaded through megaphones 'Stop it! Please stop it.'

An organiser begged a reluctant senior police officer to let them march through. He pointed out that the crowd was angry and said the situation could deteriorate. Finally, the officer agreed.

More trouble came as the march passed Street, when window was goods taken.

In Kingsw got a bloody something stand was ki ther along, a shop wa leather coats other shop.

Teacher Jo was on his w lecture at th cl Economics passed him.

He tripped

## The militant in the l

THE man who headed the march, 38-year-old Darcus Howe, has been a leader of the radical black community since the early Seventies.

He was director of a group called Towards Racial Justice, whose professed aims, as part of the black revolutionary movement, were to overthrow the capitalist system.

Howe, from Trinidad, has professed himself to be a Marxist. When the group took over the magazine 'Race Today'

after a brief power strugg became editor.

He later became an or don's Notting Hill carni Notting Hill in May 1978 arrested and charged wit barrister after an altercati

He was jailed for thre the sentence was quashed Lord Justice Lawton sai might have been sparked remark against Mr Howe Howe had 'given valuabl community.

**MA RESEARCH ARCHITECTURE
STUDENTS 2022-23**

ly Mail, Tuesday, March 3, 1981    PAGE 19   Newsdesk: 01-692 1122   Tele-Ads: 01-692 7393

# met Mercury

RENTAPIANO
MORLEY GALLERIES

# They marched. They sang. They cheered. They jeered. Only a few hotheads spoiled a peaceful protest

● Above: The march sets off from New Cross led by a line of police.

**Bridge**    PICTURES: GRAHAM WOO

● Right: The feeling shows as the demo makes its way to the City.

## ngry finish

lack youths gathered round im, kicking his briefcase way and preventing him rom getting up.

An attempt was made to rob Daily Mail reporter John Passmore as he bent to help Mr Newton.

Anger erupted near Wimpole Street when one marcher was arrested. Suddenly others rushed to his rescue and fighting broke out in the middle of the inevitable traffic jam.

At the front of the jam was Dave Woolstaff with his builders van. Demonstrators leapt on the back, seized brooms, a pickaxe and a wheelbarrow, and threw them into the police lines.

Minutes later a young constable was dragged unconscious down the street after being hit on the head by a litter bin torn from a lamp post.

The march went on. In Regent Street a girl of around 20 stood sobbing after seeing a man knocked to the ground and his briefcase stolen.

In Cavendish Square a black policeman was taunted by several of the marchers. Police then tried to take away a young West Indian. He struggled and other marchers

tried unsuccessfully to preve his arrest.

The police who held h needed reinforcements horseback to stop the marche surging towards them.

Eventually the young marc and at least four other W Indian youths—were tak away to a waiting police co

As the marchers gathe at Hyde Park Corner to h speeches from black leade one of the stewards blam bands of 'kids' for the dis tion.

He said that in Fleet Str the protest had been joi by several gangs of you ters who started trouble.

But he also blamed the of police horses.

'I admit there were black kids causing trouble, but the polic d need to use their horses, said. 'Women and chil were frightened.'

One speaker told the that after 400 years of suppression now was the to fight back.

'We must make them re that we are here to stay said to loud cheers.

But there were cat when he said the mar must go back into the munity and organise a nt defence.

## DISCOUNT HER SHOP

½ Price SALE

SHEEPSKINS D LEATHERS

ROM MANUFACTURERS ➤

| | |
|---|---|
| eather coats | £45 |
| sheepskin style coats : | £45 |
| Sheepskin style coats | £43 |
| Leather jackets and full suits | £43 |
| nge of Furs from Rabbit | £59 |
| To Mink | £1250 |
| Sheepskin style coats (for ds) from | £26 |

reet, SE8 telephone 01-692 1122 and printed by Bucks

● The line of 3,0

**BURNING AN ILLUSION**

Moonshot. Black Youth
b. December 1977.

Albany Empire, black
ub, July 1978.

Asian Sub Post Office,
cember 1978.

Grocery shop just taken
er by Greek Cypriots,
ring 1980.

West Indian owned
rage, October 1980.

Two cars on Milton Court
tate, 18 January 1981.

No. 439 New Cross Road,
January 1981.

Car owned by black
amily, 2 February 1981.

MA RESEARCH ARCHITECTURE
STUDENTS 2022-23

March 1981  3

d rats
mper

th Jenkins

al Front's plans
ough Deptford
oss were
a Home Office

claim they
rotest against the
hite people were
for the deaths of
oss Thirteen.
e National Front
oating over those
Thursday they
nd local housing
king up posters
down. 2 million

ediately after the
nts of the dead
received
racist letters
r the deaths of
n.
r march banned.
urned up
ed to make their
two miles away
e of Lewisham.
an a hundred anti-
ainly from the
eague, who had
New Cross just in
tried to pull a
to Lewisham as
heard the Nazis

constantly moved
ussed by the
made it as
they could for us
he NF

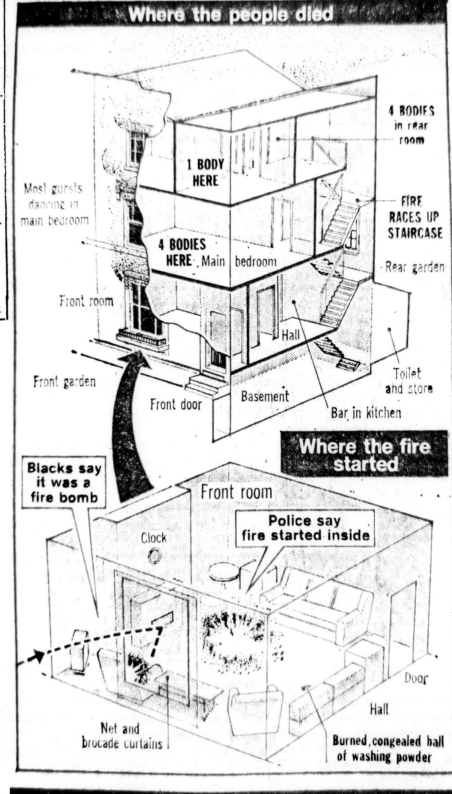

**Where the people died**

1 BODY HERE

4 BODIES in rear room

Most guests dancing in main bedroom

FIRE RACES UP STAIRCASE

Rear garden

4 BODIES HERE. Main bedroom

Front room

Hall

Front garden

Toilet and store

Front door

Basement

Bar in kitchen

Blacks say it was a fire bomb

**Where the fire started**

Front room

Police say fire started inside

Clock

Door

Net and brocade curtains

Hall

Burned, congealed ball of washing powder

an environment to understand how the project resonated with those who have spent decades undertaking their own research on the event, while acknowledging the gaps in our investigation.

As our methodology involved archival research and analysis of published media, we prioritised documents and other written material. We had limited access to oral histories, and witness testimonies remain sealed in the archives of the Metropolitan Police. The project represented material forensically, drawing on technological processes like 3D modelling, which cannot wholly capture the multiplicity of experiences surrounding the fire, nor its deep affective reverberations. To work within this forensic analysis is to use a certain logic of the courts and legal systems. The aim of ascribing a perpetrator as found within these systems leaves diminished space for the embodied "expertise of experience," as described by historian Aaron Andrews in his writing on the New Cross Massacre. Andrews writes:

The experiential expertise deployed by New Cross activists was wide-ranging, rooted in the experiences of living in Lewisham, being black in Britain, and encountering the carceral state. It enabled campaigners to deploy the recent history of structural racism in British society – especially mismanaged police inquiries and legal injustices – as the basis for their criticism of the investigation.[28]

*Burning an Illusion* is an investigative research project that acts as an archive and repository of information regarding the investigation of the Massacre. As such, this knowledge must become activated through participation. Sharing our findings with those affected by the fire and members of the NCMAC was a key step in shaping our investigation and understanding our role in relaying this information to a wider audience. Our investigation was only a partial attempt to understand that night in January 1981; it is an investigation that will remain incomplete until it is set in motion with the expertise of experience.

Our research revealed that numerous police and coroner failings formed the basis for the inquest in 1981. By investigating the investigation, it becomes clear that those affected by the fire found it difficult, if not impossible, to achieve the justice they seek and deserve. Coerced witness statements, a hostile media environment, insufficient arson replications, and a coroner who misled his own jury demonstrate that the 1981 inquest only had the pretence of a fact-finding process. The New Cross Massacre was paradigmatic of colonial histories of policing and governance, as well as the social and spatial exclusion of Black British people. These failings are not confined to individuals but permeate the whole web of actors and institutions involved. Institutional racism does not originate from a handful of authorities and their malpractice. Rather, it is a structural characteristic of the state apparatus.

### Acknowledgements

It is all too rare that such an endeavour can be undertaken over 40 years after an event took place. It is only through the energy and labour of the New Cross Massacre Action Committee, among other community-led organisations in compiling, archiving, and making available evidence that this project could exist. We thank Leila Hassan Howe, Kamara Scott, and Stafford Scott for their guidance and feedback.

28  Andrews, 'Truth, Justice, and Expertise in 1980s Britain,' 195.

## Works Cited

Andrews, Aaron. 'Truth, Justice, and Expertise in 1980s Britain: The Cultural Politics of the New Cross Massacre.' *History Workshop Journal* 91, no. 1 (January 2021): 182-209.

Andrews, Kehinde. 'Forty Years on from the New Cross Fire, What Has Changed for Black Britons?' *The Guardian*, 17 January 2021, https://www.theguardian.com/world/2021/jan/17/forty-years-on-from-the-new-cross-fire-what-has-changed-for-black-britons.

Bunce, Robin and Paul Field. 'Thirteen Dead and Nothing Said.' In *Darcus Howe: A Political Biography*. London: Bloomsbury, 2014.

Chantrill, Christopher. 'Time Series Chart of UK Public Spending.' *UK Public Spending*, https://www.ukpublicspending.co.uk/spending_chart_1980_2021UKm_17c1li011lcn_56t51t55t.

Chesshyre, Robert. 'Thatcher's "boot boys": When the unholy trinity of police, press and government took root.' *The Independent*, 15 September 2012. https://www.independent.co.uk/voices/comment/thatcher-s-boot-boys-when-the-unholy-trinity-of-police-press-and-government-took-root-8139816.html.

Coroner's Society of England and Wales. 'Recommendations on Procedure 1975.' HO 299/135, The National Archives, London.

Elliot-Cooper, Adam. *Black Resistance to British Policing. Racism, Resistance and Social Change.* Manchester: Manchester University Press, 2021.

Fisher, Henry. 'Report of an inquiry into the death of Maxwell Confait.' (London: Home Office, 1977), https://www.gov.uk/government/publications/report-of-an-inquiry-into-the-death-of-maxwell-confait.

Lahiri, Dee. '"I don't think I can die before I find out what happened to my son".' *The Guardian*, 15 May 2001, https://www.theguardian.com/world/2001/may/15/race.london.

Rickford, Frankie. '"I made errors"--fire coroner.' *The Star,* HO 299/135, The National Archives, London.

Unknown. 'No new inquest into Deptford fire deaths.' HO 299/135, The National Archives, London.

Analysis of forensic evidence presented, undated, NCM, NCM 2/3/1/4, New Cross Massacre Campaign 1980-1985, George Padmore Institute, London.

Analysis of forensic evidence presented, undated, NCM, NCM 4/1/1, New Cross Massacre Campaign 1980-1985, George Padmore Institute, London.

'Deptford: back to the beginning.' *The Guardian*, 14 May 1981, https://www.theguardian.com/uk/1981/may/14/race.world.

# AIR PRESSURE

Fawwaz Traboulsi, the Lebanese Marxist historian and former member of Socialist Lebanon and fighter with the Organisation for Communist Action, between the late 1960s and early 1980s, still introduces himself as a militant intellectual and historian, a left militant. There are no liberal militants. In the case of socialism-communism, the word militant has been liquidated out of use, even criminalised in the name of counter-terror, or extremism, putting out of use its leftist, liberatory practices of resistance. In 2023, this is as good a time to observe this as any. Constructed out of historical antagonism and contradiction, militancy is defined by struggle, and defines the preparedness of resistance, including by taking up arms. Certainly not a taboo in Traboulsi's era, a time of revolution and counterrevolution, now at a remove from us only in terms of the former.

Left militancy was never reformist. A word for militancy in Arabic—tahrik; taabi'a—also infers the mobilisation of the masses. On the left, it has another term connected to it: commitment—commitment to a perpetual struggle for freedom and life against undignified subjugation. Commitment to diagnosis, to critique, and to the struggle against capitalism, the vestiges of imperialism, racism, fascism, including in its literary and artistic forms. So, what is militant media today when thinking about art and commitment, when paranoia around militancy has turned into a flat denunciation of leftist politics, and an excuse for resignation, or mere gesturing under a liberal consensus. Can aesthetic forms, as well as visual and spatial research methods, still be called militant? What is the role today of militant art as it once existed within broader cultural and political struggle, today, especially under the mass commodification of art and culture and the counter-revolution against resistance?

Is the struggle, if any, for developing militant mediatic forms still an accompaniment to leftists and grounded political forms of struggle? Is there aesthetic debate and constraint around this under the aegis of contemporary art, or do we have to write one inherited from modernity, and into the future? Or, are these criteria now about evidence, and weaponising image and spatial technology for counter discourse?

Lawrence and I sat down in autumn 2022 for a conversation to discuss the implications of some of these questions. We discussed a new research and art project he embarked on some years ago, tracking the 50-year acts of war and spatial colonisation by the state of Israel: its jet incursions into Lebanese air space. In the context of the ensuing conversation, this struggle in part deals with the Israeli apartheid state's continued colonization, militarisation, and commodification of air and land and life, across Palestine, Lebanon, and Syria, but specifically within Lebanese air-space.

Diligently tracking these daily violations over several years, through witnesses on the ground and other open source forms of research, there turned out to be hundreds of thousands of them, by different manned and unmanned vehicles. These accrued within a broader political economy that affects air, and that uses air as its medium, within the context of long-term, geopolitical warfare and economic collapse. We talked about some of these things, interrogating these Israeli Defense Force (Israel Offence Forces, as they are now commonly referred to) flights in terms not couched only in legal violation and questions of sovereignty, but also in terms of the occupier and the more advanced army's impotence and lack of total power. We addressed the ways in which Lawrence's relationship to art-making could address these questions, both formally and socially.

**A CONVERSATION BETWEEN LAWRENCE ABU HAMDAN AND GHALYA SAADAWI**

**Ghalya Saadawi** My questions and thoughts about the work, Lawrence, can be roughly divided into three parts. First, and very broadly, what do you think are the ways one formally, as an artist, begins to address the aggressions and mistruths associated with the state; second, what light can be shed on the violence of the law itself within the context of Israel's aerial incursions, and what are the limits of the term *violation* in the context of your work; and finally, as it relates to the first point, what reconfigurations of witnessing are involved in the kind of work this art proposes, which do not rely only on first-person testimony?

*Air Pressure (A diary of the sky)* enumerates a portion of the 22,111 Israeli aerial incursions or violations above Lebanon over the last fifteen years. What began as a lecture performance became a video. You have structured the video and its voice-over as a recurring refrain of data and narrative diary entries, interspersed with historical context on the aural, political, and psychological impact of fighter jets and reconnaissance planes flying overhead. The voice-over is heard against upward-looking shots, mostly taken with mobile phones, of military aircrafts across the Lebanese skies. You present, typed on-screen, a chorus of data, gathering, counting, and documenting of airspace violations by date, aircraft type, and duration. In addition to the raw data, the effects of these incursions are told in the narrative weave of the script, which includes both informal autobiography and a sort of social history. It is as though you attempt to pin and name the violence of aerial threats in a language that captures it and yet cannot fully do so. The words and numbers cannot amount to what they are enumerating; they fall short of the experience perception, whilst insisting on documenting it. This approach is different to a strictly forensic one, which say may be more interested in timelines, evidence, different toolkits. Here, it wants to narrate the effects and tensions of the incursions themselves—they count, but no one really "counts" them, legally, militarily, or psychically.

You begin with August 2020, the month of missing data (the same month of the Beirut port explosion) which mysteriously reemerges online after you make a public demand for it. Presumably the Lebanese government had hidden it? You've noted in an earlier version of the script that "the absence of clarity is the bedrock upon which Lebanese autonomy is founded". Of course, misinformation, mistruths, and half-truths in the name of truth are constitutive of all states and their apparatuses. In the context of repeated and shape-shifting destruction in Lebanon at the hands of the state of Israel, I wonder if the task of the critic here is still to re-present the repetition and, through those changing forms, unveil the truth of the state's obfuscations, including the Lebanese state's total silence on this issue. In addition, I find the terror that the Israeli military poses in its routine repetitions across these skies compelling as a reverse shot of their desire to maintain an image of themselves as victims of terror. The work can be said to put up a mirror whereby shots of sky and warplanes taken by people on the ground act as both a concrete and an ideological reflection. Can you say something about your choice of visual method here?

## Lawrence Abu Hamdan

The project arose from a very simple desire: to make the first publicly accessible database of every Israeli military and combat aircraft that has circled Lebanon since 2007.[1] In doing this, I found that for more than half of the last fifteen years, there has been a vehicle in the sky over Lebanon, a combined flight time of eight and a half years. This block of time establishes the sky as a solid terrain that can be occupied just like land. In many ways, this work is trying to flip the earth on its head, to see the sky as a solid terrain while the land beneath it collapses. The enumeration makes an event of something that happens every day. It foregrounds the background noise we had stopped paying attention to.

Martin Chulov, the journalist who covered AirPressure.info in the *Guardian*, told me, "Well, the violations are not news, but fifteen years of them are". So the accumulation makes it news, makes it notable, even if, as he sees it, the daily occurrence has lost its discursive value. But it would be a misrepresentation to call such routine acts of violence, which are seamlessly integrated into life in Lebanon, "new". How do you speak about these flyovers in their own terms? How do you deal with this violence as an exceptional issue while not overlooking the fact that it has become unexceptional, something people have learned to live with? If we miss its mundanity, we miss what over time has really come to make these incursions violent. Brian Eno's description of ambient music is a useful reference. In the liner notes for '*Ambient I*' from 1978, he wrote, "Ambient music must be able to accommodate many levels of listening attention without enforcing one in particular; it must be as ignorable as it is interesting". I found that these incursions were as ignorable as they were lethal, and with this work, I set out to accommodate the many levels of "listening attention" that perceive these rumblings from above.

In the film, I am performing not only the data but also the act of its accumulation. You listen to that act of enumerating as you might listen to a continual drone. You hear the numbers, but you can't really imagine 229 combat jets in one week. It stops being data and crosses a threshold of comprehension into noise. This reflects my position in the project, a point of tension, as someone who is attempting to search for the truth, to reveal the numbers and what is going on, to find out what is happening. And the more I think I'm providing clarity, the more I get sucked into a political ecology of noise; I become an integral particle in an atmosphere of violence and control.

This is actually how the work began—it was born out of the noise of online discourse. After the August 4 explosion happened in Beirut, many were saying they had heard planes just before the blast. I listened to the audio and, based on my work the year before analysing Russian airstrikes in Syria, I concluded that this was not the sequence of sounds that happens during an airstrike. You would never have the noise of a plane in such close proximity to that of a blast. When I stated this publicly, I found myself in a culture war. I was positioned as the voice of authority, or expertise, contra that of personal experience, and in the middle of this argument, I began thinking, Why are we arguing about these planes at 6:07 p.m. on August 4? Why is this now the

1   See https://airpressure.info.

## A CONVERSATION BETWEEN
## LAWRENCE ABU HAMDAN AND GHALYA SAADAWI

time we talk about a plane, when there were 440 aerial violations the month before? We're not talking about them as a constant presence. We only seem to speak about them when there's an event. We're not thinking about the protracted nature of this noise and why it's going on every day. Yet, at the moment of peak anxiety, the moment when people's homes and lives were ruined, when the third largest non-nuclear explosion in the history of the world happened, the Israeli jets emerged as a kind of explainer. This noise from the background reappeared at the forefront of the discourse. This made me realise that even if they weren't physically present that evening, the jets are always with us. They live in the back of our minds, ready to emerge the minute the air is sounded. And I recognised that the work I needed to do was not to prove whether or not there was a plane at that particular moment, but to work to understand this constant noise as a protracted attack, a long bomb.

That's why I chose the format of the diary for the film. I wanted to explore the ways in which these violations are integrated and routine. This diary is not a personal diary, although it gets personal at points; it's more an enthusiast's diary, similar to a trainspotter's diary. A diary is a mode of literature that puts side by side the most significant and insignificant aspects of human life.

**Ghalya Saadawi**

Yes, the Israeli jets emerged as one of the theories for the potential perpetrator of the Beirut port explosion, for the generation that had lived through Israeli wars and for one that had not, as well as for those who saw the explosion and for those who only heard it. So this aerial imprint, socially speaking, emerges from Israel's own repetitive actions, which as you stated, stay with us. Who has historically inflicted such destruction on Lebanon from the air? No one. The diaristic methodology feels partly apt in this instance.

Yet, the idea of rendering data as noise could be compelling. The quantifying also speaks to both the abstract and concrete aspects of these endemic geopolitical and psychological aggressions. When you're repeating and documenting in this way, a pattern seems to emerge. The sky becomes an overhead screen onto which we can see an unfolding. The majority of the video as part of the wider project is, after all, composed of shot after shot of Israeli military aircraft in patch of sky after patch of sky. The air becomes materialised, or it is as if a newly visible sky is sutured above our heads. It is terrifying in light of the genocide they are committing in Gaza right now as we write, and given that this repetitive aerial warfare is what they trained for there and elsewhere, such as in the Lebanese skies. More obliquely, it reminded me of the presence of war planes in Lebanese cinema, most recently in Ghassan Salhab's 2021 feature film 'The River', in which innumerable fighter planes zoom overhead throughout the film, and even if the protagonists can't see them, they can hear their terrifying drone. They surround and undergird the allegorical love story that constitutes the film.

Yet, in the repetition of Israeli incursions of various kinds and scales, of—as you refer to it—atmospheric violence, I find the term *violation* to be limited and to lose some of its meaning. Of course, these incursions *are* violations (of airspace, of territory, of sovereignty, international law), but to be more incisive the term must acknowledge something beyond the legal question of sovereignty. There is a serious limit to the claim of legality, or rights like these. Sure, nation-states are like property bearers over the land, and they are defined contractually by their sovereignty, one that right-wing Lebanese nationalism has been going on about for over 60 years. Thus in a mere demand for it, it prevents us from the critique we are after, and after all acknowledges that which is said to proffer this said sovereignty, especially rendered redundant in states of war.

We also know that alongside surveillance and espionage, sonic terror and the *threat* of bombardment are Israel's tried and tested forms of warfare. The F-35 has a huge sonic range, as we've learned, and there is an entire history of adverse health effects resulting from jet noise in effects-based military operations such as these. Militaries test planes and gather information through surveillance, but the repeated flights may also be designed to affect morale, or even physiology (although, ironically, many inhabitants of Lebanon no longer hear them due to the constant hum of diesel generators). This reinforces the possibility that these aerial aggressions are not over literal land grabs (which persist in the South and all over Palestine), nor over alleged security as the state of Israel claims, but over seeking to know, occupy, and enclose Lebanon's air as part of Israel's strategy to eliminate Hezbollah. Thus, they can be seen as a way to force its disarmament (thus, dismantling). This in a move towards the eventual normalisation of relations with Israel, especially when Western soft and hard foreign policy is fully geared toward this (for example most recently, with Bahrain, the UAE and the recently thwarted Saudi normalization talks), and to violate Lebanese sovereignty in order to claim that Lebanon is *not* sovereign (from Hezbollah). So, these violations occur in the arena of international law, but should not be caged in the language of rights since it is also the very ideology of equal (property) rights and treaties that undergirds the international

A CONVERSATION BETWEEN
LAWRENCE ABU HAMDAN AND GHALYA SAADAWI

legal system in the first place, which cannot even adjudicate. Of note here is that Hezbollah and Lebanon recently negotiated and signed an unprecedented maritime border agreement with Israel, which led many on the Israeli state side to claim that Hezbollah now acknowledges Israel's existence. We can traverse the legalistic language of violation and of sovereignty, or at least invert its nationalism—as if merely demanding that the incursions stop would return everything to a state of so-called normalcy—to consider what Israel's military fantasy might be. What is needed in order to go further than the claim of "violation" by an already warring and settler nation structured on in-built "effects" operations? This is because claiming a violation assumes that law is capable of redress, when the law itself can permit legal, or illegal incursions. Law and state *are* endemic forms of violence and accumulation. So, the said violations are, following years of what Lebanon and Palestine have witnessed, foundational, operational to the violence of the law itself. Instead of *violation* we need another term, and I wonder if reintroducing the coordinates of enmity can serve us better—seeing these as acts of war and therein of land/air grab and of genocidally-based accumulation, makes clearer forms resistance to stop that.

### Lawrence Abu Hamdan

I made the decision early on that air is a very different kind of territory, and if we render the air in conventionally cartographic terms of sovereign violation alone, we lose some specificity about what's actually happening. I am trying not to depict this as a violation of airspace that belongs to someone in particular but rather to create an understanding of the ways in which air is turned violent.

It is true, though, that on AirPressure.info the trajectory of each flight is mapped in the form of a line. A line through the air is not a faithful representation of how these flights are felt on the ground. The fighter jets have an audible radius of almost five hundred square kilometres, so their sound is not a nice, neat, placeable line but a mass of noise with often obscure origins. As the animation unfolds on the website, however, the lines start to overlap and interlace, and they form a nexus of noise that engulfs the entirety of the country. I did not draw the boundaries of Lebanon, but the shape of the country becomes articulated through the interlocking vapour trails. So Lebanon as a kind of legal condition is not there; as a set of boundaries, it does not exist. Its shape is only constituted by the lines the planes have made in the sky, which happen to pretty much cover the entire area we know on a map as Lebanon.

In the accumulation of these lines, we see the ways in which noise produces its own territoriality. When you first see a line on the website, you see it as a simple depiction of a legal or sovereign violation; when the lines start to interlock and create these big webs, you start to realise that maybe this is not about the breach of a sovereign code or a UN agreement but something more visceral. It reads as a pressure that is being exerted. It starts with the basic, legal definition of invasion, a line moving across a territory, and then it builds and moves to a more complex rendering of a set of effects that far exceeds illegal sovereign violation. It was important to start with a legal question, as that's the framework by which this can even begin to enter mainstream discourse, but it became important to show just how much more this is than a violation of territory. Strategically, 22,111 violations of airspace are a headline, an entry point into the work for a broad audience, but once the audience was in the work, I needed to show them that there was more happening here. I wanted to speak about this issue in a way that was distinct from the completely facile way in which the Lebanese state had been addressing it. The Ministries of Defence and Interior only care about these planes in as much as they're a violation of their sovereignty, and I also deeply question the Lebanese government's sovereignty and right to rule. The air does not belong to them either.

**A CONVERSATION BETWEEN
LAWRENCE ABU HAMDAN AND GHALYA SAADAWI**

**Ghalya Saadawi**

We can agree that these actions constitute an aerial form of occupation—air grabbing—or at least a desire to remind us that this is possible. In the script for 'Air Pressure', you state that during World War I, British colonial strategy was to use aircraft presence and noise to threaten bombardment as much as to actually attack. The strategy here is less about who is sovereign and more about who has sovereignty, who can exercise the right *to* sovereignty, and in that regard it is an acquisitive nationalism on the part of the Israeli state, underlining all fundamental nation-state violence.

The counting of these incursions materializes not only the air but also time. Yet, it's a null rehearsal for something that has already happened innumerable times, where the repetition seems to cancel itself out. As the line from Marx goes, history repeats, first as history then as farce—at least in the case of Lebanon before October 2023. You need to take the incursions seriously. But also how can you take them seriously? Even if these flights are surveillance operations, they don't necessarily further Israel's military or political knowledge about their enemy. Following the 2006 war, does Israel know that much more about Hezbollah's operations and infrastructure from these flights? I doubt it. The flights may have gathered some information on hideouts, or what have you, but this military strategy has neither accrued any substantial knowledge, nor deterred anything. And there's thousands upon thousands, over the years, of these demonstrations of military might.

I am therefore compelled by the idea that these manoeuvres are not exclusively a threat of what is to come but also primarily a reminder of what has already happened (in spite of the F-35's novelty, obscene budget, and required test-drives). We know and have seen what Israeli occupation forces are capable of. Of course, a war can and will happen again, but not in this way, by invading airspace over the span of decades. They don't add up,

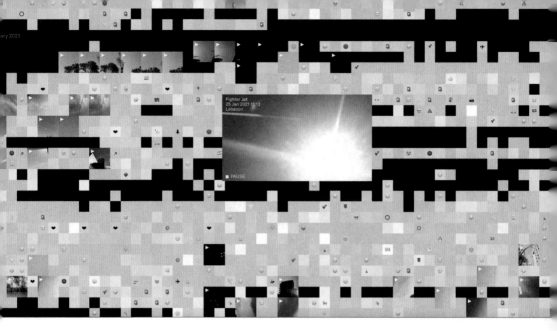

these particular enumerations, these repetitions of flight time. Even more undeniable is that these repetitions present Israel's force as not a total one, albeit a totalizing one, further demonstrated by the present moment. So, while jockeying for the place of master, Israel is weak. It does not possess total force as hard as it may try, or as far-ranging as the sonic effects on the population below may be; it is also impotent and parodical. It reminds me of what Mladen Dolar wrote in another context about both the loss of authority and the threat of authority—how the threat of force is also an index, or symptom of a loss of authority.[2] Its actualisation hangs over us, but not as omnipotently as it would have us believe. The repetition undoes the very conditions that it itself sets up in order to be a threat.

### Lawrence Abu Hamdan

In some ways, that is true, that becoming impotent sits in contrast to what we may assume Israel is trying to achieve strategically. Yet, the enemy is increasingly defined with every act of enmity. It would be hard to argue that all 22,111 of these flights were targeting only Hezbollah. This level of sur-veillance is in excess of what is needed to monitor Hezbollah alone and is, moreover, an unprecedented act by one foreign nation on its neighbour. Every person in this country, regardless of their political affiliation, has at one point or another been photographed by these planes and drones. Every text message and phone call bounces off the cell towers and straight into these aircraft. These are highly technical planes; they're not just making noise, they're also harvesting noise from the ground. They employ a technique called "pinging the system". They make a noise in the atmosphere to see what that noise does on the ground— that is, who starts to talk about the planes above them, who starts to move in response to being watched, etc.

2    Mladen Dolar,'The Future of Authority', *The Philosopher* 109, no. 2, accessed 29 October 2023, https://www.thephilosopher1923.org/post/the-future-of-authority.

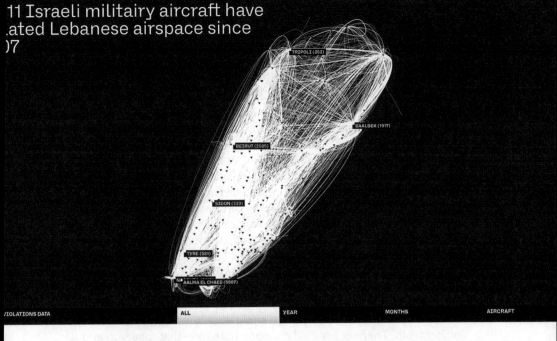

TRIPOLI (353)

BAALBEK (1917)

BEIRUT (2085)

SIDON (339)

TYRE (581)

AALMA EL CHAEB (5007)

VIOLATIONS DATA     ALL     YEAR     MONTHS     AIRCRAFT

It's a feedback loop. And the loop doesn't only include Lebanon and Israel; it includes all the countries that have invested in the F-35. The Lebanese atmosphere is a high-pressured nexus in a global weather system.

**Ghalya Saadawi**

Yes, that feedback loop is illuminating and disturbing. Yet, even the desire for, or illusion of "total" surveillance can be construed as limited. In any case, what is happening in the work as it tries to make the air *material*, is a demonstration of the unfolding of what Rob Nixon calls *slow violence*, via an image of aerial geography, flight sound and its effects, through filmed footage by people on the ground, as well as through the political econo-my behind these operations.[3] *Atmospheric violence* (your term) is thus an appellation for forms of possibly imperceptible, yet structural capitalist and state violence that need the media of time and air to unravel. I suppose the metaphor of "air pressure" is then the attempt to make the air active through looking at air and sky and what goes on in them via jittery human footage, the soundscape, the narrative told via voice-over, the archival research, and finally the website archive.

**Lawrence Abu Hamdan**

We feel the air as a material; it's materialised through the noise of aircraft. I wanted to close the conceptual gap between noise pollution and air pollu-tion because I think something is lost when we separate these conditions. What this work is trying to do is really take sound seriously as an activation of air. When we smell old diesel smoke emerging from some water supply truck, we are suddenly made aware of what's going into our lungs, whereas we may not have been before. This is what's happening with these F-35s

3    Rob Nixon, *Slow Violence and the Environmentalism of the Poor,*
(Cambridge, MA: Harvard University Press, 2011).

and our ears. Through the sounding of the air, the vibration of its particles, the air becomes a volatile compound—of noise, carbon dioxide, monoxide, nitrogen oxide, sulphur dioxide, and all the other toxic emissions of international militarism.

## Ghalya Saadawi

The medium of air also foregrounds another material conditon: not only the economy of the military infrastructures involved, but also the circumstances of the political economy of Lebanon. We have economic and banking collapse, catastrophic inflation, and state bankruptcy; we have hundreds of thousands of private diesel generators across the country powering electricity due to national grid and power plant breakdowns grid breakdowns and to fuel shortages—what we can hear and smell, and the related long-term health effects also occur on the level of sound, and of air particles and their penetrating toxicity. These can all be considered contiguous with a Lebanese post–civil war economic order that we can comprehend (and hear) when light is shed on what we *cannot* see.

The forensic eye, or ear, is usually keen on scales, as we know, and so we can talk about not only large-scale structures but also molecules, decibels, etc. There is a formal question here, one that research and forensic architecture, certain documentary filmmaking traditions, and Marxist critics have been trying to answer, about how to fathom, present, and critique less-perceptible capitalist violence—the structures, flows, and veils it produces. Whether the method is enough to account politically for all that takes place in the violence of warfare and extraction is another matter. Although the images in your piece are all found footage, and you did not employ computer-generated reconstructions, models, or any particular sensing or photographic technologies, you still seem to pursue an approach of quantification, enumeration, and contextualisation that thickens the air, *thickens the plot*, as it were. The voice-over and the text together seem to reconstruct a crime from decades of flight time, a detective story that can become a counter-claim, a counter-discourse to that of the Israeli state's. You are not aestheticizing violence, as many artists do, and in this context we know that there are forms of technical, spatial witnessing that help materialise atmospheric violence differently than first-person testimony and human witnessing, and can work in a more, say, cartographic way to chart the prolonged destruction enacted by state and capital apparatuses. How do you configure your usual practice with this approach in the video?

## Lawrence Abu Hamdan

The aesthetic demand of this work is to establish a new category of witnessing for these events. You might hear the plane, you might not; it might fly over you, it might not. With the website and with the installation 'Air Conditioning', I sought to disaggregate the position of the single witness—to render these small ephemeral invasions into the ears of individuals a collective experience; to see them as one long crime. I have made these numbers public for the first time; were the incursions to remain anecdotal personal experience, we would not have known how many planes entered Lebanese airspace, and the number way exceeds expectations. We would still think, as many did before, that these planes are flying into Lebanon to bomb Syria, when this has happened only three out of 22,111 times. We can now understand this as a specific military operation purposely targeting the atmosphere over Lebanon–the planes don't just circle the South or specifically target areas where Hezbollah is strong, but rather they broadcast violence across all of Lebanon, in spite of regional political affiliations.

The aesthetics make this disaggregation possible, make this crime sensible under new terms. In *Air Conditioning*, you don't hear military aircraft, as someone on the ground would, but for the first time you can perceive fifteen years of continued and accumulative violence. So it's not about the way we experience this with our ears and eyes in Lebanon but about using techniques and technologies to make the events sensible in ways they have not been previously. So that we can comprehend these acts strategically, structurally, collectively, and cumulatively.

'Air Pressure' does this too but in a different way. By bringing together mobile phone footage from hundreds of sources, each taken from an individual perspective, the video records the ways in which these planes intrude on the many lives beneath them. The people taking these videos are often trying to capture a background noise; they search the sky to locate the source of this blanket of noise above their heads. It takes careful work to document this rumbling in the background while it is obscured by dogs barking, people talking, and kids laughing and screaming. These voices piercing through the noise of the jets are as important as the sounds of the jets themselves, because they demonstrate how the jets are being heard and not heard. We hear both someone trying to document a sound and others ignoring it. We are listening to the often-competing kinds of attention these jets command of the populace beneath them as the exceptional and the quotidian natures of this violence are overlaid. We witness how others hear and live with these sounds.

**Ghalya Saadawi**

To go back for a moment to a point made earlier–who does the air belong to, what's in it, who owns it (the air as property)? In a basic sense, of course, there is intense air and noise pollution in the Lebanese atmosphere. In tracing these, we find a series of noxious activities that can help us read so-called pollution as the materialisation of particular political-economic activities–the special, accelerated breed of Lebanese capitalism–that highlight what else is in the air. The air becomes a ground against which we read a variety of other state policies, social actors, agreements, the accumulation and the drive to profit, and so on. In this way it becomes, as we keep saying, *material*. This is not specific to Lebanon alone, of course. But we were discussing, for example, the state's lack of electricity and the decades of shortages we've suffered as traceable back to, on the one hand (and this is keeping it brief) purposeful fiscal mismanagement and corrupt deals around the state-run Électricité du Liban, and on the other, direct thievery, since the private companies of some government and party officials, Nabih Berri and Walid Jumblatt, specifically, sold the good fuel Lebanon had received, back into the market and purposefully bought the wrong (dirty) fuel for local power plants, irrevocably damaging them.

**Lawrence Abu Hamdan**

I think a work is only political when it is a battle on multiple fronts. If we are only attacking one thing, that's antagonism, which can be useful too, but it's not what makes things political. Politics also means a war with yourself; not to be totally Maoist, but the self-critique of my own efforts to fight noise with truth is in the work for that reason. The work also emerges out of the 2019 uprisings in Lebanon from which the expression *kilon yaani kilon*—or "all of them means all of them"—was popularised. This movement demanded that sectarianism be seen as a theatre that occludes an interconnected system of corruption that was stealing the future from the people. The expression became a clear demand to pay attention not to divisions but rather to the interrelations between the supposedly warring factions within the government. Similarly, we could say that the Israeli industrial military complex needs Hezbollah, and Hezbollah needs the Israeli industrial military complex. We need neither. *Kilon yaani kilon* was a way to demonstrate the connections between us, the subjects of corrupt rule, no matter our inherited sect. This is at the foundation of my interest in atmospherics: to identify all the agents that inseparably join together to create a toxic or violent atmosphere. Atmospherics determines both the kind of violence we endure and the kind of resistance that must prevail. Atmospheric resistance stands in opposition to sectarianism and a politics of identity; it is a call to coalesce.

### Works Cited

Abu Hamdan, Lawrence. 'Air Pressure'. https://airpressure.info.

——— 'Air Conditioning', 2022, installation.

Dolar, Mladen. 'The Future of Authority'. *The Philosopher* 109, no. 2, accessed 29 October 2023, https://www.thephilosopher1923.org/post/the-future-of-authority.

Nixon, Rob. *Slow Violence and the Environmentalism of the Poor*. Cambridge, Massachusetts: Harvard University Press, 2011.

A CONVERSATION BETWEEN
LAWRENCE ABU HAMDAN AND GHALYA SAADAWI

# BIOGRAPHIES

**Huriana Kopeke-Te Aho** (Tūhoe, Ngāti Porou, Rongowhaata, Te āti Haunui-a-Pāpārangi, Ngāti Kahungunu, Fale'ula) is a self-taught artist and illustrator. Their work is primarily influenced by their Māori whakapapa, takatāpui identity, and political beliefs.

**Riccardo Badano** is an architect, researcher, and editor working at the intersection of migration circulations and critical ecologies. He is currently a Tutor on the MA City Design programme at the Royal College of Art. Badano completed his MA at the Centre for Research Architecture, where he is currently undertaking his PhD.

**Simon Barber** (Kāi Tahu) is a Lecturer in the Department of Social, Gender Studies and Criminology at the University of Otago. He completed his PhD at the Centre for Research Architecture. As part of his doctoral research, he undertook a postgraduate diploma in Ahunga Tikanga (Māori Laws and Philosophy) at Te Wānanga o Raukawa in Ōtaki. His thesis, developing a conceptual orientation that combined his learning from the university and the wānanga, traced the clash and entanglement of Māori and Pākehā worlds in Te Waipounamu through ongoing processes of colonisation.

**Ariel Caine** is a Jerusalem-born artist and researcher. His practice centres on the intersection of spatial (three-dimensional) photography, modelling and survey technologies, and their operation within the production of cultural memories and national narratives. Ariel received his PhD from the Centre for Research Architecture, where from 2016–21, he was a project coordinator and researcher at Forensic Architecture.

**Becky Clarke** is a Senior Lecturer in the Department of Sociology at Manchester Metropolitan University. Through her teaching, research, and wider work, she seeks to collectively examine and challenge inequalities and injustice. Clarke's current research interests include the gendered and racialised experiences of penal and welfare policies, processes of 'othering' and criminalisation, and the construction of knowledge (and ignorance).

**Sophie "Soph" Dyer** is a transdisciplinary designer and researcher combining visual, aural, and spatial storytelling with investigatory and participatory methods. Their interest in open-source research comes from working with nongovernmental groups, including Amnesty International and Airwars. Sophie completed a MA at the Centre for Research Architecture in 2017. Together with geographer Sasha Engelmann, they co-lead the feminist collective, Open-weather.

**Anna Engelhardt** is an alias of a video artist and writer. Her investigative practice follows the traces of material violence, focusing on what could be seen as the 'ghost' of information. The toxic information environments Engelhardt deals with stem from structures of occupation and dispossession. She has shown her work internationally. Engelhardt is a core faculty at the Design Academy Eindhoven and co-editor of *Chimeras: Inventory of Synthetic Cognition* (2022). She completed her MA at the Centre for Research Architecture.

**Kodwo Eshun** is a filmmaker, theorist, and artist based in London. His research interests include contemporary art, critical theory, post-war liberation movements, modern and contemporary musicality, cybernetic theory, the cinematic soundtrack, and archaeologies of futurity. In 2002, he founded The Otolith Group together with Anjalika Sagar. Their essayistic approach reflects on the perception and nature of documentary practice through films, texts and activities related to media archives. Kodwo is a Lecturer in Research Architecture.

**Katrina Ffrench** is the Founding Director of Unjust UK. Formerly the Chief Executive of a national charity, Katrina has overseen the publication of several evidence-based reports and has led a range of advocacy initiatives influencing policing policy and practice. Katrina is a Black British Voices Project Steering Group member and a trustee of Transform Drug Policy Foundation. In 2022, Katrina was elected as a Labour Councillor for Furzedown, Wandsworth.

**Júlia Nueno Guitart** is a visual researcher and engineer focused on the intersection between technology, data, and communities. Her research investigates algorithmic management and the repurposing of data as a medium for workers' organising. She was formerly the visual lead at Airwars, where she investigated and developed open-source tools for assessing and geolocating civilian harm in conflict-affected countries. She is currently a Forensic Architecture PhD fellow at Goldsmiths.

**Lawrence Abu Hamdan** is a *private ear,* listening to, with and on behalf of people affected by corporate, state, and environmental violence. Abu Hamdan's work has been presented in the form of reports, lectures, performances, films, publications, and exhibitions internationally. Abu Hamdan's audio investigations have been used as evidence at the UK Asylum and Immigration Tribunal and have been a key part of advocacy campaigns for organisations such as Amnesty International, Defence for Children International, and Forensic Architecture. He has held fellowships and professorships at the University of Chicago, the New School, and the Johannes Gutenberg University Mainz. He completed his MA and PhD at the Centre for Research Architecture.

**Charles Heller** is a filmmaker and researcher whose work has a long-standing focus on the politics of migration and aesthetic practice within and at the borders of Europe. He completed a PhD at the Centre for Research Architecture. He is affiliated with the Geneva Graduate Institute and the University of Bristol as a Research Associate. He is the director of Border Forensics, an agency mobilising spatial and visual analysis to investigate border violence.

**Allan Hogarth** is Head of Policy and Government Affairs at Amnesty International UK, where he is responsible for developing political analysis and strategy for the organisation. His work covers a wide range of human rights issues.

**Gabriela Ivens** is an open-source investigator who focuses largely on visual data to expose human rights violations. She works as the Head of Open Source Research in the Digital Investigations Lab at Human Rights Watch. Previously, Gabriela was a fellow at WITNESS researching synthetic media, worked for the Syrian Archive, and led the investigative portal Exposing the Invisible.

**Helene Kazan** is an artist, writer, and educator. Her work investigates 'risk' as a lived condition produced through the conjoined violent effects of capitalism and conflict. This is observed in the colonial roots of international law and their material formation of lived-built environment. In response, Helene engages in decolonial and feminist, critical legal and artistic theory and methods in order to dismantle the disproportionate human and non-human effects of risk. Her work has been exhibited and published internationally. Helene was a Research Fellow in Forensic Architecture and completed her MA and PhD at the Centre for Research Architecture.

**Tomas Percival** is an artist, researcher, and writer. His work critically investigates the intersections of space and security, with a particular interest in structures of assessment, risk governance, carceral geographies, data infrastructures, and border administration. He was previously a Lecturer at the Centre for Research Architecture, where he is completing his PhD. He is currently a fellow at Humboldt-Universität zu Berlin.

**Lorenzo Pezzani** is an architect and researcher whose work explores the spatial politics, visual cultures and political ecologies of migration and borders. He is co-director of Border Forensics, an agency mobilising spatial and visual analysis to investigate border violence. Between 2016-22, he was a Lecturer in Forensic Architecture at the Centre for Research Architecture. In 2022, he joined the Department of the Arts at the University of Bologna as Associate Professor.

**Waireti Roestenburg** (Ngāti Kahungunu ki Te Wairoa, Ngāti Pāhauwera, Rongomai Wahine, Ngāpuhi nui tōnu) leads the Social Health and Wellbeing degree for the Open Polytechnic/Te Pūkenga, where she specialises in the revitalisation of Māori/Indigenous wellbeing, and Kaupapa Māori approaches to Māori mental wellness and illness. She is the director of 'Te Wānanga o Te Mana Mauri', where she offers healing/teaching wānanga experiences to people, groups, and whānau. Her PhD reveals the ongoing existence and relevance of an unconquerable 'spirit' of Indigenous Vitalities. This 'spirit' has refused to allow us to disappear and is associated with Māori and Indigenous continuity, healing, and wellbeing. Her approach is informed by over 40 years of lived experience and practice as a wairua-centric healer, lecturer, academic, and Indigenous vitalities researcher.

**Arama Rata** (Ngāruahine, Taranaki iwi, Ngāti Maniapoto, Ngāti Apakura) completed her PhD in Psychology at Victoria University of Wellington in 2012, which focused on Māori cultural engagement, identity, and psychological well-being in State secondary schools. Arama is currently involved with research relating to Māori health experiences, Māori in rural communities, as well as iwi consultancy.

**Faiz Abu Rmeleh** was born in the Old City of Jerusalem. He studied photography at the Bezalel Academy of Arts and Design and works as a photojournalist for several local and global newspapers. In 2013, he joined Activestills, an international photographer collective covering political events in the Palestinian territories, considering photography a vehicle for social and political change.

**Ghalya Saadawi** is a theorist and writer whose research explores psychoanalysis and law, contemporary art and political economy, theories of witnessing and testimony, post-civil war Lebanese art and documentary. She is a member of the Beirut Institute for Critical Analysis and Research. In 2023, she won the Fitzcarraldo Editions/Mahler & LeWitt Studios Essay Prize for her forthcoming non-fiction book *Between October and November*. Saadawi teaches theory at the Dutch Art Institute and is a Senior Lecturer at the Centre for Research Architecture.

**MA Research Architecture 2022-23** collectively embarked on the *Burning an Illusion* research investigation. The team comprised: Siufan Adey, Moza Almazrouei, Merve Anil, Adeeba Arastu, Claire August, Fine Bieler, Rowena De Silva, Olivia Gresham, Jade Guinard, Faye Harvey, Oliver Goldman, Dafni Karavola, Katarzyna Łukasik, Bethan Mckinnie, Emmanuel Onapa, Leonie Rousham, and Veronika Varga. The contribution was compiled by Rowena De Silva and Claire August.

**Stafford Scott** is a community activist and race equality specialist with over

40 years of experience in anti-racist advocacy work. He has worked amongst different agencies, including Waltham Forest Housing Association, the Department of Health and The Kings Fund, providing grassroots solutions to issues of institutional racism affecting the Black community, whilst continuing to support local communities with issues around over-policing, miscarriages of justice and deaths in custody. He is the Director of Tottenham Rights and 2022-23 Guest Professor in Forensic Architecture at Goldsmiths.

**Susan Schuppli** is an artist-researcher whose work examines material evidence from war and conflict to environmental disasters and climate change. Her current work is focused on *Learning from Ice* and is the subject of numerous documentary films. Schuppli is the author of *Material Witness* (2020) and is the Director and Professor at the Centre for Research Architecture, as well as the Board Chair of Forensic Architecture.

**Ariadna Serrahima** is a publisher, researcher, and designer. Her research explores struggles in relation to autonomous spaces, the circulation of critical knowledge, and the production of collective insurgent learning. Serrahima co-founded the graphic design studio Oficina de Disseny, L'Automàtica cooperative printshop in Barcelona and I.F Publications. She completed her MA in Research Architecture and is a PhD candidate in Visual Cultures at Goldsmiths.

**Leila Sibai** is a legal investigator and doctoral researcher at the Centre for Research for Architecture. She co-founded Huquqyat, with whom she supported the development of case files pertaining to war crimes and crimes against humanity committed in Syria. Her research looks into performative aspects of the expression of political subjectivities in public space in regime-held Syria. She completed her MA in the Centre for Research Architecture, where she is undertaking her doctorate.

**Sanjana Varghese** is an investigative journalist, visual researcher, writer, and reporter. She currently works as an investigator at Airwars, where she utilises mixed methodologies to undertake multi-media investigations into conflict. She has also written for the *Economist*, *WIRED*, the *Baffler*, Al Jazeera, the *New Statesman*, the *British Journal of Photography*, and more. She received her MA in Research Architecture in 2021.

**Gwendolyn Wallace** is a researcher and children's literature author from Connecticut. Her work for children and adults centres Afrodiasporic voices to explore the unfolding relationship between the spatial logics of colonialism and our body-minds. An alumna of Phillips Exeter Academy, Gwendolyn studied the history of science and medicine at Yale University before completing a master's degree in public history at University College London in 2023.

**Eyal Weizman** is the Director of Forensic Architecture and Professor of Spatial and Visual Cultures at Goldsmiths, University of London, where, in 2005, he founded the Centre for Research Architecture. He is the author of many books, including *Hollow Land, The Least of All Possible Evils, Investigative Aesthetics, The Conflict Shoreline, and Forensic Architecture*. He is a member of the Technology Advisory Board of the International Criminal Court and of the Centre for Investigative Journalism. In 2019, he was elected life fellow of the British Academy. In 2020, he received an MBE for 'services to architecture'.

**Patrick Williams** is a Senior Lecturer in the Department of Sociology at Manchester Metropolitan University. He undertakes research in the area of 'race' and ethnicity, with a particular focus on racial disparity, disproportionality, and differential treatment within the Criminal Justice System.

A Centre for Research Architecture series exploring pedagogy, politics, and practices

Series Editors:
Riccardo Badano, Tomas Percival, Susan Schuppli, Ariadna Serrahima

Militant Media

Editors: Riccardo Badano, Tomas Percival, Susan Schuppli

Graphic Design: Oficina de disseny (Ariadna Serrahima)
Copyediting: Sanjana Varghese
Image correction: Xavier Tulleuda
Printed in Barcelona

Published by:
Spector Books
Harkortstrasse 10
04107 Leipzig
www.spectorbooks.com

The publication has been made possible through the generous support of the Graham Foundation for Advanced Studies in the Fine Arts, the Leverhulme Trust, and the Department of Visual Cultures at Goldsmiths, University of London.

Distribution:
– Germany, Austria:
GVA, Gemeinsame Verlagsauslieferung Gottingen GmbH & Co. KG,
www.gva-verlage.de
– Switzerland:
AVA Verlagsauslieferung AG,
www.ava.ch
– France, Belgium:
Interart Paris,
www.interart.fr
– UK:
Central Books Ltd,
www.centralbooks.com
– USA, Canada, Central and South America, Africa:
ARTBOOK / D.A.P.,
www.artbook.com
– South Korea:
The Book Society,
www.thebooksociety.org
– Japan:
twelvebooks, www.twelve-books.com
– Australia, New Zealand:
Perimeter Distribution,
www.perimeterdistribution.com

**Graham Foundation**